SWEET SURVIVAL

TALES OF COOKING & COPING

SWEET SURVIVAL

TALES OF COOKING & COPING

Laura Zinn Fromm

GREENPOINT PRESS
NEW YORK, NY

SWEET SURVIVAL: Tales of Cooking & Coping by Laura Zinn Fromm
Laurazinnfromm.com

ISBN 978-0-9906194-9-9

Library of Congress Cataloging-in-Publication Data

Book Designed by Robert L. Lascaro, LascaroDesign.com
Book text set in Georgia

Cover art by Bette Blank
Book illustrations by Sophie Friedman-Pappas

Greenpoint Press,
a division of New York Writers Resources
greenpointpress.org
PO Box 2062
Lenox Hill Station
New York, NY 10021

New York Writers Resources:
- newyorkwritersresources.com
- newyorkwritersworkshop.com
- greenpointpress.org
- ducts.org

Printed in the United States
on acid-free paper

Some names have been changed in order to protect the privacy and/or anonymity of the various individuals involved. There are no composite characters or events in this book.

For Steve Fromm

— and our sons, Matthew and David

Someone I loved once gave me
a box full of darkness.

It took me years to understand
that this, too, was a gift.

— Mary Oliver, *The Uses of Sorrow*

Table of Contents

INTRODUCTION

WHEN I WAS A LITTLE GIRL, I stood in our blue-and-white kitchen and watched my mother cook. She always seemed so happy as she puttered around the island, six burners going and both ovens on. We had one large sink where we would wash our hands and rinse dishes off to load in the dishwasher and then one prep sink, which had an arched silver faucet and was nestled deep into the island, near the burners. No one I knew had two ovens and two sinks, never mind six burners, two drawers stuffed with spatulas and mixing spoons, cabinets packed with soup pots and sauté pans of every size, as well as a fan over the burners, but we did. The kitchen was where my mother worked her magic. From her graceful hands, peppers were sautéed, veal chops were broiled, eggs were brought to room temperature and separated into whites and yolks, Dijon mustard was whisked into olive oil and vinegar, Yorkshire pudding was made from roast beef drippings, quails, hens and ducks were placed on racks in the top oven, lamb chops and pork chops were dabbed with salt and rosemary, meatloaf was molded into pans, and chocolate soufflés were baked, stuffed with chocolate mousse and decorated with home-made whip cream. Apple pies and cheesecakes wrapped in graham cracker crusts were baked from scratch. No turkey or chicken carcass was discarded; there was always soup to be made. Put the bones in a pot in the fridge, add some water and chicken broth, slice up celery leaves and bring that soup to a boil on Saturday morning. Asparagus was steamed, water chestnuts were sliced, onions and red peppers were bubbling in soy sauce in the wok, and salmon and shrimp were placed on the grill and seared during spring and summer.

Every weekday afternoon, my brother and I would tumble off the school bus, my father would drive home from the hospital, and just as the sky darkened, there in front of us would appear a multi-course dinner. Dinner was served in the dining room, where we used gleaming sterling silverware and my mother tapped a foot buzzer to summon the housekeeper to clear the table and bring in the next course. My parents sat at opposite ends of the dark oak table, and there, on top of a thick Persian rug and floor-to-ceiling white lace curtains that billowed across the window sills, we tucked into a salad of romaine lettuce and home-made Dijon mustard dressing, followed by china serving dishes piled high with meat, vegetables and potatoes, kasha and pasta. On lucky days, we ended the meal with a treat, something sugary, delicious and, of course, homemade.

If this all sounds a bit too idyllic and sweet, fear not: There's a reason I became a writer. My parents were not happy, my father's mood swings erratic. Two years after I was born, he climbed to the roof of New York Hospital and threatened to jump. He then spent several weeks in the psych ward at Payne Whitney. My childhood was fraught with my parents' fighting. Their 20-year marriage (the second of three for my mother, the first of two for my father) ultimately ended in divorce the fall of my brother's senior year of high school. Towards the end of their marriage, they were living together, dating other people and talking about their dates in the kitchen while my mother made dinner. Despite the bizarre nature of these conversations, dinner was always superb and the one thing I took away was that cooking shields you from chaos. You could always say, "Well, at least those Chinese vegetables were delicious."

My mother was an excellent cook. She cooked to keep the peace and to express herself at a time when her friends were getting their nails done and playing tennis. My father was a radiologist in Manhattan and came home from work hungry and irritable. My mother's mother, grandma Miriam, had worked full time as a teacher in Brooklyn, and wasn't much of a cook. Grandpa Sam taught math at Stuyvesant so dinner was a simple meal prepared after they'd gotten home from school and marked papers for the next day. Grandma warmed up soup and broiled chicken, while Grandpa made matzo-brei and cleaned up. They were careful, frugal people. My mother, on the other hand, had married my father while he was in medical school. He came from Brooklyn and had gone to Stuyvesant, where he had been a student of my grandfather's; he was clearly a catch. By the time she met my father, my mother had already left one marriage to another Brooklyn-born doctor so my grandparents were eager for this one to work out. Grandma encouraged Mom to stay home once she had kids, so at 23, Mom retired from her brief career teaching kindergarten and set up shop in her tiny kitchen on East 70th Street across from New York Hospital where my father was doing his residency. It was 1964 and Julia Child was a couple of years into her television career of teaching American housewives how to cook with pleasure and confidence.

My mother watched Julia Child's show every day at noon while she fed me lunch in my highchair. Out went the frozen vegetables and canned fruit, margarine tubs and tins of stale Waldbaum's chocolate chip cookies that Grandma had relied on. In came fresh strawberries and blueberries, bags of carrots, bottles of olive oil, jars of Dijon mustard and bars of sweet butter. An electronic mixer was purchased. So were rolling pins, spatulas, cookie sheets, pie tins, and an expensive set of pots and pans, so hardy that I still use them in my kitchen fifty years later.

Despite his mood swings, my father's career flourished, my mother had my brother, and we left Manhattan for the green backyards and finished basements of New Jersey. Their relationship degenerated but my mother coped with the vagaries of their marriage by throwing herself into cooking. For a few minutes every night, she placated her husband and her hungry children with a meal that left everybody sighing with gratitude and pleasure.

I watched her closely but didn't cook until decades later. In college, the food in the dining halls was filling and often divine. Mozzarella and broiled tomato slices melting on pita pockets, salad bars piled high with tofu, lettuce leaves and chickpeas, platters of donuts and bagels, huge buckets of yogurt and granola, plates of warm chocolate chip cookies, soft and huge. I was thrilled with what the Wellesley dining service prepared and felt no need to cook anything ever. But then there was this: I worked for the college newspaper, the *Wellesley News*. We were a small staff and we all did a little of this and a little of that. At the beginning of sophomore year, I became the features editor. That meant, I assigned and wrote stories on everything from tenured economics professors to the best local ice cream parlors in Cambridge. One afternoon, as I was opening the mail, looking for story ideas, I came upon a padded envelope. Inside was MFK Fisher's memoir, *The Gastronomical Me*. I took it back to my dorm room and devoured it. In class, I was reading Virginia Woolf, Emily Dickinson and Elizabeth Gaskell, but MFK Fisher, who wrote so beautifully about food and love, of botched dinners and ruinous love affairs, of fresh eggs and red wine, of dealing with husbands and boyfriends simultaneously, of delicious meals served in restaurants and boarding houses, as well as the deep and abiding pleasures of staying home and eating in, of the south of France and the north of California, became the woman I most wanted to be.

Still, I didn't cook. For most of my twenties and early thirties, I worked as a reporter at *Business Week*. While I wrote about retail, food, soft drinks, tobacco and liquor, I rarely made a meal. I didn't have much time and even less incentive: My husband was a banker and he worked all the time too. We shared a one-bedroom New York City apartment on West 68th Street and in our narrow, galley kitchen, I occasionally sautéed chicken breasts in honey mustard and baked batches of chocolate chip cookies, but I didn't view cooking as an expression or labor of love. We were content to order in from the local Chinese and Indian restaurants that lined our block, and go out for Japanese and Italian after work. And the truth is that most week nights, I made a beeline for the vending machines on the 39th floor of the McGraw Hill building, where a can of diet Coke, a pack of peppermint Lifesavers and a bag of Peanut M&M's (protein!) helped propel me to deadline. But you can only live on caffeine and sugar for so long once you're pregnant.

When we had our first son, I decided that I should start to cook, in earnest and for real, like my mother did for me. I took cooking classes at Food Emporium and in the Village, and then when we moved out to New Jersey and had our second son, I took classes at Kings supermarket and friends' houses. I became addicted to reading cookbooks by Julia Child, Craig Claiborne, Mark Bittman and the ladies who owned Silver Palette, as well as books that were not only about making delicious food but also about cooking your way through life's challenges: Nora Ephron's *Heartburn*, Bill Buford's *Heat*, Gabrielle Hamilton's *Blood, Bones & Butter*, Anthony Bourdain's *Kitchen Confidential*, Nigella Lawson's *How to Eat*, Darina Allen's *Lost Skills of Cooking*, Lisa Fain's *The Homesick Texan Cookbook*, Simon Hopkinson's *Roast Chicken and Other Stories*, Laurie Colwin's *Home Cooking* and *More Home Cooking*, and pretty much everything that MFK Fisher ever wrote. I loved to read about cooking so much that finally, I started to write about it, often calling my mother for advice. She had gone back to work full-time and didn't cook much anymore but she remembered the details of virtually everything she had ever made. She had been such a successful and knowledgeable cook that, in the mid-seventies, she had summoned Craig Claiborne, the noted restaurant critic and food writer for *The New York Times*, to our house in New Jersey for lunch. Claiborne had no idea who she was, but Mom wanted to generate some business for her friend John Cristaldi, a local kitchen designer and amateur cook. So she took out her typewriter and wrote Claiborne a letter, inviting him to eat a meal that Cristaldi would prepare with her recipes in our kitchen (which he had designed and built). And would you believe it? Claiborne came! Mom gave him a meal, Claiborne gave her the story

After we'd moved to New Jersey, my grandparents died, my father had another nervous breakdown, divorced his second wife, and then died of cancer. My brother-in-law got married, had a baby, and was diagnosed with lymphoma. Various friends and family members moved in and out of rehab. Several let their marriages dissolve. One died of breast cancer. A neighbor threw herself in front of a train one cold February night. One friend's father took cyanide in her childhood basement, another's mother overdosed on painkillers. Two more friends' fathers attempted suicide by train and car. Another friend's brother ended his life by setting himself on fire. My head spun. Through it all, I cooked and baked and wrote to keep myself sane and feed the people I loved. All of my friends who had weathered these upsets were busy cooking too. After every trauma, back into the kitchen we went. I started to wonder: What was it that brought all these people into my life?

There are certain women I have gravitated towards (and they to me, I suppose) because we have mental illness at the base of our families, and we are trying to keep it at bay. When we are in our kitchens together, our hearts are connected. Our families of origin become distant memories, and we attend to the families we have made, hoping they are healthy and safe. Amidst all those pots and pans and glasses of wine, the shared recipes, the extra folding chairs crammed around the crowded dining room table, the email invitations, the requests for gluten-free beer, the plans to eat and talk and celebrate, we end up in the kitchen, our arms around each other, laughing.

Years ago, my brother and I bought Mom a wooden plaque for her birthday. I'm not sure where we found it. All I remember is that one grey Saturday afternoon in March, my father drove us to the Livingston Mall to buy Mom a birthday present. At Herman's sporting goods, we found her a navy-blue and white V-neck tennis sweater that had tennis balls dancing across the front, and at a store a couple of doors down, we found a small wooden plaque that read: "Cooking is like love, it should be entered into with abandon or not at all." The woman on the plaque is busty and blonde – she's wearing a V-necked sweater and she looks nothing like Mom. But her smile is wide and her eyes sparkle as she swings her spatula in the air. The tennis sweater is long gone but the plaque still hangs in Mom's kitchen, right next to the oven.

Laura Zinn Fromm

▸ Some of these essays first appeared in *Huffington Post*, *Patch* and *NJ Life & Leisure*.

1

Cooking & Coping

A Moving Meditation

SOME DAYS we are seriously discombobulated and there's no accounting for it. Lack of sleep? Too much salt? Hung over? Who knows? One morning, I went to the supermarket with the express purpose of buying saffron, became distracted by the Fruit Jellies Kettle Cooked Candy with Real Fruit Extracts and walked out of the store with a plastic box of candy and no saffron. I'd already torn into the candies while waiting on line to pay for them. I went home, intent on getting high on sugar. I felt like a wreck.

FEATURING

- Kale & Brussels Sprouts Salad

My friend Angie, a fellow writer and mother who occasionally had herself been a wreck, urged me to read Julia Cameron's *The Artist's Way: A Spiritual Path to Higher Creativity*.

I had been employed on and off as a writer since the second Reagan Administration, but I had pretty much stopped writing for hire after I had my second son. An old friend from college who had moved to Northern California had given me *The Artist's Way* but I had barely bothered to look at it. My brilliant friend Angie, who also found herself underemployed and hyper-nesting in Northern California, told me to start reading it.

Angie and I were lucky enough to work together at *Business Week* in the 1990s, when we were young twentysomethings – freshly minted English majors who had written for our college newspapers.

Angie was blonde, freckled, beautiful and outgoing and had gone to a big mid-western Division I football school. I was dark, caustic and had gone to a small New England women's college. I was the eldest, with divorced parents and a small army of half and step brothers and sisters. Angie was a middle child, with two brothers and parents in the middle of a long and happy marriage. We seemed to have nothing in common. Still, we fell all over each other like flies on honey.

We had no idea how lucky we were to land jobs at a major business magazine and were oblivious to the fact that the glory days of journalism were fast coming to an end. We did not realize that the jobs we had—jobs that required we work long hours for low pay and take orders from cranky, flirtatious, middle-aged men —were actually munificent gifts from the publishing gods. We had regular weekly bylines and when we pitched our stories, we knew our editors would publish them. We were given "columns," (inches to fill) in the magazine, and had summer interns to make copies and do reporting for us. Complicated charts, four-color photos and beautiful illustrations accompanied our stories. Sometimes, the headlines we wrote actually ran on top of them. We took all of this for granted; this had been our life in college: stay up late, crank stories out, rewrite them, put the publication to bed, wake up, drink coffee, eat candy, drink more coffee, write some more. But writing for *Business Week* was even better than college because money changed hands! Plus, there was an art department mocking up layouts for us, a photo department sending out photographers to make our photo requests realities, copy editors to double-check our work, and a bunch of senior and managing editors nagging us with questions at 10 p.m. to make us feel busy and important. It was glorious. The fact that neither one of us was particularly interested in business was irrelevant. We made it seem as though we were and we were getting published all the time. As for the male editors looking down our shirts and checking out our butts, who cared about them when we had each other and our bylines?

Then Angie and I fell in love with men who weren't writers. We got married, had babies, quit our jobs. We wanted to raise our kids without stress.

We had no idea what we were giving up when we gave up our bylines.

There is no shame in driving off the highway of full-time work onto the quieter road of mothering and marriage but that doesn't mean there won't be deep potholes and major tolls to pay along the way. Angie and I each became depressed. We tangled with those incessant, am-I-doing-it-right questions: Should I go back to work full-time? Should I hire a full-time nanny who will, in all likelihood, take home more than I do? Is it really so important to publish what you write? Does thinking about writing almost count as writing?

Angie built a fire pit in her backyard and occasionally ran into Anne Lamott. I bought cords of wood at the supermarket and occasionally saw Wendy Wasserstein at the New York Society Library.

Neither of us had figured out that you could have *anything* you wanted as an adult, you just couldn't have *everything*. We thought we *should* have everything even though we didn't know anyone who did. Most of the successful female journalists I knew were divorced or never married. A few of them were widows. One of the most successful women I knew was married and then had a baby with another married editor. I didn't think I could be a full-time journalist and have anything close to a happy family life. My mother had started a successful public relations firm while I was in middle school and my parents' marriage had disintegrated in the process.

In fact, I didn't know anyone who had been intensely focused on her work and also able to raise kids and stay married, except one woman who did become a prize-winning newspaper editor. But her husband was an independently wealthy artist who threw pots on a potter's wheel while he looked after the kids. My husband was not independently wealthy and he didn't have a potter's wheel. If I went back to writing full time, I could end up divorced and alone. Better to move out of the city, play tennis, drive my kids around, and spend serious money talking to my therapist about why I wasn't working.

Meanwhile, Angie kept urging me to dive into Cameron's book.

In her chapter on Recovering a Sense of Compassion, Cameron says you have to admit: "*Yes, I do need help...The ego always wants to claim self-sufficiency. It would rather pose as a creative loner than ask for help. Ask anyway.*"

Angie had been spending her time cooking, writing and reading Cameron's book. "Just try the morning pages," Angie said to me, talking about the hurried, almost unconscious pages Cameron suggests we write just after we wake up.

Cameron's voice is firm but loving; she writes as if she is speaking to you directly, and understands your fears and fantasies. You end up *wanting* to take her advice. She says that sometimes when you can't do what you want to do, or what you think you should be doing, you should do something physical. In her chapter, Recovering a Sense of Autonomy, she writes: "*What we are after here is a moving meditation...one where the act of motion puts us into the now and helps us to stop spinning.*"

I followed Angie's example and started to cook. Cooking was an act of motion. I had seen my mother do it and knew I could. Standing around chopping, stirring, mashing and melting–food prep stills the mind like nothing else. The lovely smells of sautéing garlic, the sounds of pots and pans banging, the warmth coming from the stove, all make everyone in the house love you just a little bit more (or at least make you believe they do). And I noticed that if I stood in the kitchen and chopped, my children would sit in the kitchen and talk. And my friends, if they had a glass of wine or a large cup of coffee in hand, seemed to feel more comfortable staying longer standing in the kitchen than sitting in the family room or dining room.

But sometimes cooking backfires and becomes work, not play (Cameron says you're supposed to let the artist in you play). Occasionally, I went into overdrive and cooked too much. Did we really need chocolate mousse on a Tuesday afternoon? A cauliflower frittata and a pan of roasted Brussels sprouts? So, when I started cooking too much and the cooking felt like work, I told my family to order Dominos and went upstairs to do my "morning pages," even if it was night.

It turned out that Angie and I had more in common than we had originally thought. Shortly after she got married, her brother committed suicide. Angie was stunned but looked after her babies and stayed in her marriage. She dug in. I look at her as the essence of resilience and resourcefulness. Every night she cooks dinner with the beautiful vegetables that grow in the hills that surround her home. She roasts parsnips and beets and squash. At the beginning of the week, she broils Brussels sprouts and cauliflower, drizzles them with oil and stores them in neatly labeled glass containers. She grills fish and makes a fantastic sweet and sharp kale salad. Just like one of my oldest friends from high school, whose father went down to the train tracks near our house to try and end his life, Angie soldiers on. I have been lucky to find women who have cooked their way through the toughest moments of their lives, and who have showed me the treasure of following suit.

When Angie and I were at *Business Week*, we were young and carefree. Needless to say, neither one of us cooked much then at all.

Angie's Kale and Brussels Sprouts Salad

(Serves 8-10)

INGREDIENTS:

- 1/4 cup lemon juice
- 2 tablespoons Dijon mustard
- 1 tablespoon minced shallot
- 1 small garlic clove, minced
- 1/4 teaspoon kosher salt
- Pepper to taste
- 2 large bunches Tuscan kale, 1 1/2 pounds total, stems discarded, leaves sliced thin
- 12 ounces Brussels sprouts, finely grated *(you can buy bags of grated Brussels sprouts at Trader Joe's, grate them in a food processor or slice them thin with a sharp knife, though this will take a long time)*

- ½ cup extra virgin olive oil, divided
- ⅓ cup almonds, coarsely chopped
- 1 cup grated Pecorino cheese

PREPARATION:

1. **Combine lemon juice**, Dijon mustard, shallot, garlic, salt, and a pinch of pepper in a small bowl. Stir to blend.
2. **Mix kale** and shredded Brussels sprouts in a large bowl.
3. **Measure ½ cup oil** into a cup. Spoon 1 tablespoon oil from cup into a small skillet and heat over medium-high heat. Add almonds to skillet and stir frequently until golden brown, about 2 minutes. Transfer almonds to a paper towel-lined plate. Sprinkle almonds lightly with salt.
4. **Slowly whisk** remaining olive oil into lemon-juice mixture. Add salt and pepper to taste.
5. **Add oil-and-mustard dressing and cheese** to kale mixture. Toss to coat, and sprinkle with almonds.

▸ *This dish is bitter, satisfying and delicious.*

2

WHEN VEGETABLES TASTE LIKE CANDY

My Foray Into Roasted Vegetables

For hundreds of thousands of years the evolving human race had eaten its food raw, but at some time between the first deliberate use of fire... and the appearance of the Neanderthals on the prehistoric scene, cooking was discovered. Whether or not it came as a gastronomic revelation can only be guessed at, but since heat helps to release protein and carbohydrate as well as break down fiber, cooking increases the nutritive value of many foods and makes edible some that would otherwise be inedible. Improved health must certainly have been one result of the discovery of cooking [and] by all the laws of probability, roasting must have been the first method used, its discovery accidental.

— *Food in History*, Reay Tannahill

FEATURING

- Broiled Brussels Sprouts
- R&B (Roasted and Broiled) Cauliflower
- Roasted Haricot Verts (String Beans) with Almonds
- Baked Stuffed Potatoes

All hail the mighty Brussels sprout and its big-headed friend, the divine Miss Cauliflower. Broiled, roasted, coated with olive oil and kosher salt, I could eat pans of these every night, and share them only because I have to.

But I'm not going to lie. I didn't always love cauliflower and Brussels sprouts. I grew up pushing them around my plate, wrapping them in paper napkins and throwing them away before my mother could see what I'd done. The cauliflower was white so if you pressed on it hard enough, you could make it disappear into the plate. But with Brussels sprouts, the situation was more complicated. I let Mom put five on my plate, six if I felt compliant. Mom was an ambitious cook but when it came to vegetables, she played it very plain. There were always platters of steamed asparagus and string beans at dinner and I could tolerate them because of their crunch. But they were tasteless. I'm pretty sure Mom didn't add salt, and I would be shocked if she used butter or olive oil to make them flavorful, because they weren't. Not even remotely.

Occasionally, though, she redeemed herself through potatoes. She would make this wonderful dish called "stuffed potatoes." I yearned for it but it only showed up a few times a year. Mom would stuff potato skins with scooped-out potato, hot milk, sour cream, butter, grated Parmesan and salt. Occasionally, I would be given the task of scooping out the potato innards very carefully with a tablespoon. But usually, the potatoes were stuffed and waiting to go into the oven by the time we got home from school. They were better than fabulous. They were soft, dreamy pillows of lusciousness. My mother made them as a special treat on our birthdays and when Grandma and Grandpa came to visit, probably because they were fattening. I was always thrilled to see them emerge from the oven, and recognized them by their telltale red tops, which I learned decades later was paprika.

But the Brussels sprouts arrived on our plates like green, tasteless, shrunken balls, their leafy heads soft and springy to the touch. The cauliflower was bland and watery, resembling the small brain of an animal, a frog or a fetal pig perhaps, shrunken and heated up.

Would you like some more, darling?

Hell no.

There's a time and place for steamed vegetables and that place is in an omelet. Or perhaps a wok in a Chinese restaurant, where the vegetables will be rescued by peanut oil and soy sauce.

When I grew up and had my own family, I decided to abandon the way Mom had done things veggie-wise (except for those yummy stuffed potatoes). I steamed vegetables but added salt and oil. Call me a rebel— moving back to my hometown, two miles away from Mom and adding flavor to steamed vegetables! Needless to say, these steamed veggies were only okay. My kids ignored them, and ate raw red peppers, cucumbers and carrots instead. That was fine, but at the time, my kids were still little, so I had to chop the vegetables into tiny little pieces all day long so they wouldn't choke. Cooked vegetables are softer; they feel safer. I wanted my kids eating warm, safe vegetables. They refused. Then I receive an email from my friend Angie.

In the middle of one long winter, Angie went on a cooking and writing tear. Instead of starting a blog, like most former journalists who have decided to let their writing muscles wither while they stopped working and raised *les enfants*, Angie started sending around inspiring cooking stories to everyone she loved. There were always cheery little notes attached. I had seen her the summer before, when she had just built a tiny beautiful new house (she lives in California, that's what people there do) and lost a bunch of weight (ditto). She looked fabulous and I knew she and her husband were fantastic cooks because I had happily tucked into their food one warm, glorious August night. Angie's husband Josh had made platters of quinoa and vegetable salad, grilled salmon and a corn and cilantro salad that was out of this world. We had just eaten at Chez Panisse in Berkeley with my husband's brother and his wife. Angie had warned me that we would be disappointed by the food at Chez Panisse and promised that the food her husband would cook for us the next night would be much, much better. She was right on both counts. After that, I always paid close attention to her emails, which were bossy and commanding, but in a loving way.

Here is what the first note said (*italics*, **bold** and CAPS are hers):

> **HERE IS MY LATEST UNSOLICITED ADVICE:**
>
> **ROAST AT LEAST ONE VEGETABLE WITH ANY DINNER YOU MAKE.** *People often think of "Roasted Vegetables" as a specific yet generic dish served in nasty cafeterias or fancy restaurants. Or they think that if you*

> *do cook them yourself, it means you are making mushy vegetables that are tedious to prep, take forever to cook (at some low temperature and a duration you're never sure of) and end up as a heap of hot, ambiguously tasting brown matter.* ***WRONG! Reorient your thinking to instead choose one vegetable, take three minutes to prep/throw on a cookie sheet, then roast it at high heat for a short amount of time. Main idea is: MINIMAL time, effort and clean up but lots of hot, crispy tasty veggies, which you should fill ONE HALF OF YOUR PLATE with at dinner.***

Real friends don't let friends eat badly. So Angie did what friends do: She shared her recipes.

> *1) Brussels Sprouts: I roast them either whole, sliced in half or shredded in my Cuisinart for crispy shreds. At end you can add some currants and lemon zest too.*
>
> *2) Carrots: Slice down the middle and add a little honey and curry powder into the olive oil so they'll caramelize.*
>
> *3) Kale: Better to chop, dry well, and roast at 300 degrees. Watch carefully so they don't burn–they taste insanely like potato chips and my kids LOVE them!*
>
> *4) Cauliflower: You can chop into big chunks but also fun to roast a giant head whole, just pour olive oil all over the top, serve on table with a big knife and let everyone hack off their own piece. (Sometimes, right after I take it out of the oven, I add a sprinkle of Parmesan cheese and/or a squeeze of fresh lemon.)*
>
> *5) Potatoes: Roast your potatoes whole! Just drizzle with smallest amount of olive oil, rub each potato with your hands until there's a thin coat of oil, then salt. With the high heat and olive oil, they will turn slightly crispy and the sweet potatoes will often sort of caramelize. I often cook up to five or six sweet potatoes on Sunday, when I cook a bunch of stuff for the week, then keep them in a container and eat for lunch/snacks.*
>
> *In each case, I follow these steps:*
>
> *a) Rinse, dry, chop*
>
> *b) Throw on cookie sheet lined with foil (that I can toss and so I don't even have to clean my cookie sheet)*

c) Toss with a TEENY bit of olive oil and salt (start with one tablespoon and go from there, just need a thin coat)

d) Roast at 400 degrees until brown–usually 15-30 minutes

e) Whatever veggie you roast, it should come out of the oven and be eaten immediately–hot and crispy.

Angie's email was a revelation to me. Did you see how many times she mentioned the word "roast?" Roast veggies with oil and salt? Wasn't that fattening! Yeah, a smidge. But delicious and so much more satisfying than vegetables that are merely steamed. Do you think our ancestors sat around steaming vegetables because they were limiting their salt and fat content and wanted to look like Gwyneth Paltrow's ancestors? No, they did not. They wanted great, fast taste. Early humans thought about making things as flavorful as they could, as quickly as they could, because you never knew when you would have to gather your fruits, nuts and veggies, stuff them in your sack and run. A roasted vegetable that's been sitting in a sack tastes a lot better the next day than a steamed vegetable does. And what good is making a bunch of vegetables that you're not going to want to eat the next day, anyway? You're not Gwyneth Paltrow. You can add salt and fat to your veggies. You don't have to look skinny and deflated all the time.

And so my roasting and broiling journey began. I started roasting sweet potatoes, then moved on to Brussels sprouts. Just nine minutes under the broiler, with a little olive oil and kosher salt. Trust me, this stuff is good. Can you drown your sorrows in Brussels sprouts? Yes, you can. My husband became addicted to them. "Do we have any more Brussels sprouts from last night?" he'd say in his sweetest tone, as he called from the train. Even if he'd had a slice of pizza at Penn Station, he'd want some Brussels sprouts when he got home. They were wonderful fresh, hot and crispy out of the oven, where their leaves had just been caramelized and they arrived in your mouth crunchy and sweet. But the beautiful part comes the next day when you can eat them by yourself with your fingers, standing at your counter, alone in the kitchen, wondering where these gorgeous vegetables have been all your life, because these babies are even better cold.

You will be a hit if you bring them to a party too. One New Year's, my sister-in-law asked me to bring vegetables and I offered to bring Brussels sprouts. "How are you going to make them?" my sister-in-law asked. She sounded suspicious. Knowing that I was addicted to sugar and a secret lover of cream, she was probably wondering if I was going to stealthily bathe them in both.

"I'm going to slices off their tiny heads and cut them into little pieces," I said.

"You are cruel," she said.

Perhaps, but the best way to make Brussels sprouts is to decapitate them and slice them thin, almost as thin as potato chips. Because that's the point–the more pieces, the more surface area and the more likely they will taste like potato chips. And that's the goal, ultimately: You want all these vegetables to taste like potato chips, but with less grease and no packaging.

So off I went on New Year's Eve, with my huge platter of Brussels sprouts. The leaves were crispy and brown, crunchy and buttery on your tongue. I was proud of that platter. Still, I was nervous too. I mean, not everyone loves Brussels sprouts as much as we do.

When we sat down at the table, my friend Isabel nudged me. "Did you bring the Brussels sprouts?" she asked.

"Yes." I said, not sure how they would go over.

"Everyone seems so excited to see them!"

I started to relax. "I think Brussels sprouts are enjoying a renaissance," I said, my confidence rising.

"Cauliflower is enjoying a renaissance too," Isabel said, as she speared a sprout and said nothing more.

But her off-the-cuff remark stayed with me. Cauliflower? Or as the French say, *le chou-fleur*? Oh, the possibilities! I thought back to Angie's email, the one that mentioned roasting a whole head of cauliflower. She'd certainly been right about the Brussels sprouts. The trouble was I didn't want to roast a whole head. A head of cauliflower looks too much like a human brain–large, white, bumpy. But then my friend Denise invited us over for dinner on a Saturday night. This was a treat, not only because we hadn't been to a dinner party in 20 years, but because we didn't have to bring anything. Can you imagine? Going to someone's house empty-handed? Okay, maybe we brought wine. But Denise had decided to hire a chef who was willing to make us whatever we wanted and share the recipes with us afterwards. He made a roast lamb (delicious, but I never made it because my older son is allergic) and a small platter of cauliflower that didn't look like anything special: It was crunchy, slightly blackened, and there wasn't much of it. I took a bite to be polite and my brain was like, "Back-up, buddy! Was he kidding? What was that stuff?"

This cauliflower was fantastic. It had a flavor that I couldn't place. There were six of us around the table and we all wanted more. *Tant pis*. There wasn't enough for seconds. But because the chef was a man of his word, the next day he emailed the recipe to Denise.

My friend Julia was also there and she too had fallen in love with the cauliflower. We both started playing with the recipe until it became so delicious that we started talking about it whenever we saw each other. "I made the cauliflower again," she'd say in spin class. "Me too!" I'd say. We were both experimenting with cooking times. She roasted the cauliflower for 25 minutes, I roasted it for 20 minutes, then broiled it for 5 minutes, because I liked that extra brown crunch that broiling adds. We were giddy like schools girls, bragging about our beautiful cauliflower. But this is awesome stuff. My husband and older son grab at it. I make it almost every Monday afternoon, and try not to eat it all before everyone else comes home. I usually make it again on Wednesday or Thursday. My younger son isn't wild about it and calls it, "the albino version of broccoli." Ah well, more for us. And you will love it. Come on over some Monday and try some.

As for my mother's stuffed potatoes, they are still a special treat. I'm looking at the recipe now, written out in my mother's neat, round, schoolteacher script. Look at that. Those potatoes are baked at 425 degrees. I still remember the taste of that buttery, milky, soft potato on my tongue, the best stuff of childhood. Mother love. Proust would be proud.

R&B (Roasted and Broiled) Cauliflower

This cauliflower is even better *cold the next day and the next day after that. It stays delicious for several days after you first make it, assuming you don't eat it all the minute it comes out of the oven.*

INGREDIENTS:

- 1 large cauliflower
- 1/4 cup extra virgin olive oil
- Zest and juice from one medium lemon
- 1 teaspoon kosher salt
- 1 teaspoon ground pepper

PREPARATION:

1. **Preheat oven to 450 degrees.**

2. **Slice cauliflower very thin.** Spread on cookie sheet (*one cauliflower, cut up, should cover one cookie sheet*). Sprinkle olive oil on cauliflower, and then follow with salt and pepper. Grate lemon right onto cauliflower, then slice lemon in half and squeeze both halves onto cauliflower. Cook the lemon along with the cauliflower.

3. **Roast cauliflower for 20 minutes.** Then take it out of the oven and turn the broiler on. Take the lemons off cookie sheet (they will burn under broiler, but save them to throw in with cauliflower later) and squeeze their remaining juice onto the cauliflower. Put cauliflower under broiler for 5 minutes. Eat immediately.

Broiled Brussels Sprouts

INGREDIENTS:

- Bag of Brussels sprouts (one pound)
- 2 tablespoons olive oil
- 1 teaspoon salt
- 1 teaspoon pepper

PREPARATION:

1. **Turn broiler on.**
2. **Wash and dry Brussels sprouts.** Slice Brussels sprouts into halves or thirds. Remove any brown leaves.
3. **Lay Brussels sprouts out flat on a cookie sheet.** Sprinkle olive oil all over them, and then follow with salt and pepper.
4. **Broil for 8 minutes** until brown and crunchy. Devour.

Roasted Haricot Verts with Almonds

INGREDIENTS:

- ½ cup slivered almonds
- 2-3 pounds of green beans, trimmed (*if you are feeling fancy, splurge on haricots verts*)
- 2 tablespoons extra virgin olive oil
- 1 teaspoon kosher salt

PREPARATION:

1. **Preheat oven to 425 degrees.**
2. **Place almonds in dry skillet over medium heat.** Cook the almonds, shaking and stirring often, until they start to smell (*good*). When they are golden around the edges, put them on a plate and let them cool. You can do this several days in advance.
3. **Mix the string beans with the olive oil**, salt and a little pepper. Spread them out flat onto 2 cookie sheets. Roast 12-13 minutes, until they are slightly brown. Mix with almonds.

BAKED STUFFED POTATOES

INGREDIENTS:

- 12 baked Idaho potatoes
- ½ cup hot milk
- ½ pint sour cream
- 4 tablespoons butter
- Grated Parmesan
- Paprika, to taste
- Salt to taste

PREPARATION:

1. **Bake potatoes in 425 degree oven** for 45 to 60 minutes.
2. **Remove potatoes from oven** and turn oven down to 350 degrees.
3. **Cut potatoes in half** and scoop out insides.
4. **Smash insides and mix** with butter, salt and milk.
5. **Beat well** and add sour cream.
6. **Return potato mixture to shells** and sprinkle with Parmesan and paprika. Put stuffed potatoes back in 350 degree oven for about ½ hour.

3

With Love, From Lolly

Karma Is a Boomerang; If You Catch It, Throw It Back

MY HUSBAND AND I met on a blind date. Once it was clear that we planned to be together for a while, he took that next serious step: taking me out to meet his best friend and his best friend's girlfriend.

FEATURING

- Meatloaf From the Mother You Always Wanted
- Surprisingly Delicious Hot Dogs with Mustard and Black Currant Jam
- Five-Minute Cake in a Cup
- Chocolate Cake with Peach Preserves
- Pretzel Kisses

Best Friend had graduated from Midwood High School in Brooklyn, the same high school my mother graduated from and not too far from where my father had also grown up. It turns out Best Friend had grown up ten blocks from where my grandparents had lived for more than 60 years, so his accent and mannerisms were instantly familiar to me. In fact, he reminded me a lot of my father, both of them brusque, direct, funny, and risqué – first born males with a fondness for smoking cigars and grilling steaks.

Best Friend and his girlfriend were living together in a white brick apartment on the Upper West Side. When my husband and I decided to move in together, we moved into their building. (Think: Jewish *I Love Lucy*.) We spent a lot of time drinking wine, eating humus and flatbread, and making plans to eat and drink together some more. We were engaged within a few months of each other and had our first babies nine months apart. (My husband took one look at their new daughter and said, "I want one.") I felt very lucky and promised the Universe that one day I would try to set up another couple on a blind date that yielded a marriage.

But this is not only a story about young or romantic love. In fact, I wouldn't be telling you this story at all if it weren't for Best Friend's mother, Lolly, an astute and cheerful woman who was not only smart as a whip, but also an excellent cook. Once her kids went to college, Lolly and her husband Al packed up the house in Brooklyn and decamped for Greenwich.

On summer weekends, my husband and I would pile into Best Friend's car and drive up to see them. Compared to our one-bedroom apartment, their house was Shangri-La. Lolly and Al owned a ranch with a big white kitchen and a pool surrounded by flowers. The family room had a white vinyl couch to accommodate kids coming in wet from the pool. Al was a gruff obstetrician with a dry sense of humor. By the time I met him, he had retired and was content watering his flowers with a garden hose, pulling leaves out of the pool and wandering into the kitchen to see what was for lunch. He was happy enough to see us but didn't dote on us the way Lolly did; he seemed to regard my husband and me as the freeloaders we were.

Lolly, on the other hand, stood in her kitchen and greeted us with platters of fruit and vegetables. "Come in, come in," she'd say as we pulled up in the driveway, as if she had been waiting all week for us to arrive. She is one of those women who has taken care of people her whole life and doesn't seem to have resented a minute of it.

Lolly grew up in Michigan, and when she gave birth to her fourth son, her mother, Billy, came to live with her and help raise the kids. The kids grew up and moved out, but Billy never left.

Lolly and Billy's love for each other was palpable, and their love for their sons and grandsons, well, don't get them started on that. It always amazed me how mother and daughter could live together so happily for so many years. I'd watch them move quickly around the kitchen, laughing and talking. "You hungry?" they'd ask. We'd nod and they'd hand us plates of cheese and cut-up veggies. "Here, dear, take this outside."

The kitchen looked out onto the pool and as we sat on our butts in the sun, Lolly and Billy whipped up the kind of comfort food that children crave and grown-ups try to grow out of but can't: meat loaf with chili sauce, hot dogs swimming in mustard and black currant jelly, spinach dip in a "bowl" of bread, and chocolate layer cake made from Hershey's chocolate syrup and peach preserves. Sometimes, I would go into the kitchen to see what they were doing and ask for the recipes. "Oh, honey, you don't need a recipe for this," they'd say. "It's so easy." Then one of them would recite it from memory. Though my mother and grandmother got along well, my parents did not; as for my mother and me, we could just about manage lunch. To watch these three adults move peaceably around the same house in a love triangle that worked, to me, bordered on bliss.

As the years passed, things changed. Billy passed away. Then so did Al. At his funeral, I wondered what Lolly was going to do with herself without her husband of 41 years, but other than exchanging holiday cards and the occasional email, we didn't talk much.

Then, one Christmas, my husband and I took our kids on vacation. On the plane we met another couple traveling with their two kids and the grandfather. We were all headed to the same resort so we ended up spending a lot of time together, sitting on the docks and circling the mediocre buffet in the restaurant. The grandfather, Walter, was a radiologist whose wife had just died. He liked to talk about books and sailing but it was clear he was at loose ends, grieving for his wife. At the end of the vacation, his daughter-in-law and I exchanged email addresses. I meant to keep in touch but as with Lolly, it was sporadic.

When next we got together with Best Friend and his family, I was happy to learn that Lolly was dating, although she hadn't found "the one." I mentioned Walter; he lived near Lolly, maybe they should meet? My husband was skeptical; he didn't remember our promise to the Universe. I went ahead and emailed Walter's daughter-in-law.

"I have someone for Walter," I typed. We made a date to get Walter and Lolly together, with us "kids" as chaperones.

One sunny August afternoon, we all went sailing on Walter's son's boat. As the sun was setting, I pulled Lolly aside and asked what she thought. She shrugged. "Maybe."

After we docked, I asked Walter if he wanted to see Lolly again.

"Maybe," he said.

Too slow. "I have Lolly's email address and phone number right here," I said.

"Okay, I'll take it."

Six years later, Walter and Lolly are going strong. She watches what he eats and makes him go on walks; he takes her sailing. They go to the opera, the ballet, the Philharmonic, medical conferences and out for dinner. They've been kayaking, white water rafting and to the Galapagos. Lolly just turned 81; Walter is 84.

When I called Lolly to tell her I was writing about her, she offered to send me some recipes. "I have lots of great tips to share," she said.

It was raining and miserable the night I made Lolly's meatloaf. It only took a few minutes to mix up. While it was cooking, the kitchen smelled wonderful. But the result wasn't pretty. My older son poked at it and said, "This looks strange." Then, he took a bite. "This is actually really delicious," he said, and asked for seconds and thirds.

The next night, I decided to make Lolly's "Cup of Cake." This cake takes five minutes to make. Yes, you read that right. In five minutes, your microwave will give birth to an awesome piece of chocolate cake, sitting in a coffee cup. I shared our cup of cake with our housekeeper Maria and my younger son. We were shocked by its lusciousness and the ridiculously short time it took to make.

As I write this, I am looking at Lolly's meat loaf recipe, which I scribbled in green magic marker on a piece of notebook paper a few weeks after my husband and I met in 1991. I had no idea then our lives would continue to intersect or that I would be lucky enough to help her find new love. I just knew that her food was delicious and I wanted to be able to create the kind of life she had made for herself, where grown children hang around the pool, the table is forever full and there is always someone nearby, angling to eat your meatloaf.

Meatloaf From the Mother You Always Wanted

(Serves 4-6)

Modest and unassuming? Yes. Fantastic? You betcha. This meatloaf is so plain and humble, it's almost self-effacing, but it is great, heart-warming stuff. Delicious right out of the oven, it is even better the next day, when you stand at the kitchen counter and eat it cold.

INGREDIENTS :

- 2 pounds chopped meat, 15% fat
- 1 Portuguese roll
- 1 onion
- 3/4 cup Heinz chili sauce
- A little garlic, fresh or powder
- Salt and pepper to taste

PREPARATION:

1. **Preheat oven** to 350 degrees.
2. **Soak Portuguese roll** in water until it's mushy (*about a minute*). Squeeze out water. Mix the roll with the meat. Add salt, pepper and a little garlic (*fresh or powder*).
3. **Press mixture** into an 8x8 square pan.
4. **Pour chili sauce on loaf.** Slice a small onion and lay slices on top of sauce. Bake for 45-50 minutes. If using a meat thermometer, until meat gets to 165 degrees.

SURPRISINGLY DELICIOUS HOT DOGS WITH MUSTARD AND BLACK CURRANT JAM

(Serves 8-10)

Kids love this. Adults may not admit to loving it, but will lunge for it anyway.

INGREDIENTS:

- 2 packages Hebrew National Hot Dogs
- 2 ounces Gulden's Spicy Brown Mustard
- 24 ounces (2 jars) black currant jam

PREPARATION:

1. **Put jam and mustard** into a pot.
2. **Slice up each hot dog** into 4 or 5 pieces.
3. **Put hot dog pieces into the pot** and cook until they "pop."
4. **Serve with toothpicks.**

FIVE-MINUTE CAKE IN A CUP

(Serves 1)

When you're craving a single piece of chocolate cake, make this.

INGREDIENTS:

- 4 tablespoons flour
- 4 tablespoons sugar
- 2 tablespoons cocoa
- 1 egg, beaten
- 3 tablespoons milk
- 3 tablespoons vegetable oil
- 3 tablespoons chocolate chips
- A little vanilla

PREPARATION:

1. **Take one large, microwavable coffee cup** and add the flour, sugar and cocoa.
2. **Mix well. Then add** the egg, milk, vegetable oil, chocolate chips and vanilla.

3. **Put in microwave** for 3 minutes on high. It will rise over the top. Cool before tipping out onto a plate.

CHOCOLATE CAKE WITH PEACH PRESERVES

(Serves 6-8)

You probably have all the ingredients for this cake sitting in your cupboard. If not, run and get them.

INGREDIENTS:

- ¼ pound butter, softened
- 1 cup sugar
- 4 eggs
- 1 can Hershey's chocolate syrup
- 1 cup self-rising flour
- 1 teaspoon vanilla
- Jar of peach preserves

PREPARATION:

1. **Preheat oven** to 350 degrees.
2. **Grease and flour** a 3-quart Pyrex dish. Cream butter, gradually add sugar. Add eggs, one at a time, beating after each addition. Add chocolate syrup, flour and vanilla. Mix.
3. **Pour into Pyrex dish** and bake for 40 minutes. Serve with peach preserves on top.

PRETZEL KISSES

(Serves a crowd)

"These are fun for the kids to make. Love, Lolly"

INGREDIENTS:

- Large bag of small square pretzels *(the ones that look like waffles)*
- Bag of Hershey's chocolate kisses
- Bag of plain M&M's

PREPARATION:

1. **Preheat oven** to 225 degrees.
2. **Lay the pretzels flat** on a cookie sheet.
3. **Place a Hershey's kiss** on each one. Put in oven for a couple of minutes until the kisses are soft but still hold their shape.
4. **Press one M&M** onto each kiss to slightly flatten it.
5. **Cool and eat!**

4

Let Them Eat Cake

Some Nights, Cake Solves Everything

FEATURING
Grandma Becky's Chocolate Chip Pound Cake

THERE ARE NIGHTS when you just want to bury your head in the sand and ask for mercy. My older son came home on one of those nights, looking miserable.

"Today was nothing but bad news," he said. He hadn't done well on a test and had banged his head again in wrestling, getting another concussion and causing the school trainer to say he couldn't wrestle again until he saw a doctor. I had just gotten back from my own doctor with another prescription for antibiotics for an infection that would not go away. My birthday was in five days, and I was pretty sure no one had made any plans for it – except me, in my head. It was cold, grey and December. Not yet the holidays, but you could feel all the anxiety and pressure of having to get stuff for people hanging in the air. I hugged my older son and tried to make him feel better.

"Oh," he said. "I have to bring snack for advisory."

"What does that mean?"

"I have to bring in snack for advisory," he said slowly, as if English were not my first language.

"When is advisory?"

"Tomorrow morning at 9:20."

"You're telling me now?" It was 6:15 p.m.

"You can just get donuts or bagels or something."

When was I supposed to do that? My younger son had basketball practice that night and I had to read papers for a writing class I teach.

"Sit down and have dinner," I commanded.

As much as I enjoy cooking, the nights when I don't cook, or don't cook much, can be just as pleasant as the night when I do. That night, dinner was macaroni and cheese out of the box for my younger son and heated-up chicken soup from the night before for my older son. My husband was out with someone from work. We ate and tried to be cheerful.

When we finished, I felt oddly energetic. I could suddenly see why people didn't feel the compulsion to cook like maniacs all the time. I tried to figure out when I was going to run to the local Dunkin Donuts or bagel place, neither of which was open at night. I could get up early in the morning and run out but that seemed too cold and awful. Then I remembered a recipe I had found on my computer earlier that afternoon. The advisory kids would love it.

It was a recipe for chocolate chip pound cake. I couldn't remember who had sent it to me but I thought it might be my husband's aunt Elaine, who had made a chocolate chip pound cake the prior Saturday night when we went to her house to celebrate her son's birthday—although this pound cake had a cinnamon and sugar topping, which Elaine's cake didn't have. Plus, the recipe was typed in Courier, not a font Elaine normally used. I thought the recipe might have come from my friend Denise, who is super organized and sends recipes out as soon as you ask for them. But her son has celiac and she was unlikely to use a recipe that called for two cups of cake flour. Finally, I went through my emails and saw the recipe was from my friend Terri, who always sends out fantastic cooking ideas. But Courier wasn't a font she used either.

Determined to get to the bottom of it all, I emailed Terri. "Whose recipe is this?"

"Madeleine Weiner's friend's grandmother," she typed back.

"Do you want to call her?"

Yes, I wanted to call her. This was a night that called for talking to a grandma. My own grandma was dead so I called Madeleine, who said the recipe came from her friend Jodi. I called Jodi and she confirmed that the recipe had indeed come from her late Grandma Becky. "She made it for the brunch for my bat mitzvah," Jodi said. (Jodi's bat mitzvah was in May 1979.) "That was when everybody started to eat it and ever since then, everyone has been taking the recipe and making the cake." She also told me about a great apple cake her grandmother made—heavy and delicious.

No talking to any grandmas tonight, I guess, unless we held a séance. But, maybe she could send both recipes?

"Sure," she said. "And I'll tell you a little tip. I always freeze the pound cake, and cut it frozen. It's really good frozen."

This chocolate chip pound cake has very simple ingredients that you're likely to have on hand. There is no sifting of flour or waiting for the chocolate to melt or cool, no rolling out of pie dough, no separating of eggs. It took me five minutes to gather the ingredients. Then I asked my older son if he wanted to bake the cake with me. Normally, when I ask this, he says he's busy and it turns out he is doing something very important and meaningful on Facebook. But this night, he said sure.

This is one of the easiest cakes you'll ever make. For 25 minutes, we stood together in the kitchen and baked. He buttered the tube pan and mixed up the butter, cream cheese, and eggs while I measured out the dry ingredients. We started at 6:52 and finished at 7:17, then put the cake in the oven.

An hour later, out it came. It was old fashioned and wonderful! We could not wait for it to freeze, so I sliced it up, collected the crumbs, put them on a plate and called for my kids to come down. I thought about my own grandma, who had a massive sweet tooth that she had willed to me. She would have eyed the cake, smiled, taken a little nibble between her thumb and forefinger, put it in on her tongue and cooed, "Mmm, I shouldn't, this is delicious!" We all stood around the kitchen, cooing and licking the hot crumbs off our fingers. That cake pretty much solved all our problems that night. Or it seemed to, which is almost the same thing.

GRANDMA BECKY'S CHOCOLATE CHIP POUND CAKE

(Serves 6-8)

INGREDIENTS:

- 8-ounce package cream cheese
- 1 stick butter
- 1 ¼ cups sugar
- 2 eggs
- 1 teaspoon vanilla
- ¼ cup milk
- 2 cups cake flour
- ¼ teaspoon salt
- ¼ teaspoon baking soda
- ¼ teaspoon baking powder
- 1 package mini chocolate chips

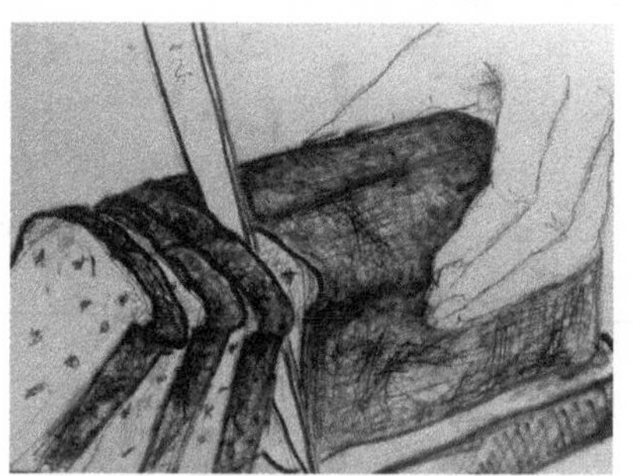

Topping:

- ¼ cup cinnamon
- ¼ sugar

PREPARATION:

1. **Preheat oven** to 350 degrees.
2. **Beat together cream cheese,** butter, sugar, eggs and vanilla.
3. **In another bowl, mix flour,** salt, baking soda and baking powder.
4. **Add dry ingredients** to creamy mixture. Add milk and mix all together.
5. **Add chocolate chips**. Mix well and pour into greased loaf pan.
6. **Mix together** ¼ cups cinnamon and sugar. Sprinkle mixture on loaf.
7. **Bake for 50-60 minutes** until an inserted toothpick comes out clean.

5

Ugly Apple Cake

Finding Love on New Year's Eve

FEATURING
- Grandma Becky's Apple Cake
- Magic Cookie Bars

I LOVE TO COOK, but I love to bake even more, and what I love the most is when someone shares a recipe she (or he) really loves and it turns out to be shockingly spectacular.

This happened one New Year's weekend. Every year since Y2K, we've been going to my brother's house for New Year's Eve. It's always a heady crowd. My sister-in-law is a psychologist. She has two sisters. One is a high-powered TV executive who is married to a psychoanalyst. The other sister, a law professor, used to be married to a psychiatrist and is now married to a physics professor. Their mother writes for *The New York Times*; their father is a retired judge. You can see where this is going. They're all really smart. Worse, they all know food – know it and love it.

My brother likes to make turducken – that's a turkey with a duck and a chicken cooked inside it. The psychoanalyst makes extraordinary combinations of roasted vegetables. The law professor makes a fabulous salad full of sunflower seeds and dried cranberries, topped with a wonderful dressing. The bottom line is I go to this New Year's Eve party every year and I'm often the dumbest person in the room. And not even the best cook.

Last year, I brought Key Lime Pie. That was a disaster, not

because it tasted bad (it didn't) but because all the other desserts were beautiful, and mine was ugly. This year, I planned to bring dessert again, but my sister-in-law warned there would be other desserts as well—a spectacular sorbet situation known as The Bomb, and a dramatic chocolate fountain to honor the birthday of a niece. My sister-in-law (remember, she's a psychologist) gently said that given the competition, maybe I should just bring appetizers.

Fine, I could pick up some cheese and crackers but I was intent on making dessert too. I had already bought the condensed milk for Magic Bars and damn if I wasn't going to use it. The thing about Magic Bars is they are a crowd pleaser. People don't realize how much they love sweetened condensed milk until they bite into one. Then they can't stop eating it.

But Magic Bars are nothing new. They take almost no effort to assemble and everyone knows it. With just five ingredients (six, if you add nuts), your five-year-old could make them. I felt a little sheepish bringing Magic Bars to this party of foodies, even though they were my favorite things to make (and eat). I wanted to bring something that showed real effort. That is to say, I wanted to show off.

I had this new recipe for apple cake, which came from a friend of a friend. "It's heavy," warned Jodi, the woman who sent me her Grandma Becky's recipe. "And it's great."

Heavy and great sounded perfect. Plus, we had all the ingredients. Or so I thought. I uncharacteristically neglected to check the pantry before I started to cook. The recipe called for vegetable oil instead of butter. Fortunately, I knew we had a big bottle in the pantry. See? There it is. Oh, look – it's empty! But we had corn oil. Corn was a vegetable, right?

I smelled the corn oil. It smelled way too strong to be mixed up with a bunch of apples and flour. I called my neighbor, who sent her kid over with a cup of vegetable oil. Well, not quite a cup. I had to top it off with a little corn oil. Then I went to work. The batter was thick, heavy and yummy.

The cake had apples on top. When I took it out of the oven, it too wasn't pretty. In fact, when I flipped it over, it fell apart. I put it right side up. Now it looked worse.

Steeling myself, I showed the cake to my mother. My mother is a beautiful woman. My grandmother was not as beautiful, but she was beautifully dressed and her house was precise and elegant. Everything glowed. Growing up, I knew that presentation mattered. The crystal chandelier sparkled. The linen napkins were ironed and neatly stacked. The silverware was polished, as were the silver bangles around your wrist. If you wore a diamond solitaire, you soaked it in solution and cleaned it every morning. The lace overlay that lay atop the flat, linen tablecloth was snowy white, and the tablecloth fell evenly around the dining room table. There were no piles of papers waiting to be sorted, no dust mites floating around the corners. Hems and seams were sewn tight, buttons weren't missing, faces were washed, fingernails were cut, and you did not leave the house with a hole in your jeans or your hair hanging in your face, young lady. In retrospect, presentation mattered more than it should have but to this day, I still can't shake the idea that everything and everyone must be beautifully aligned. My younger son says I am the most superficial person he has ever met.

"That cake is ugly," my mother said, but conceded it would probably taste good.

When I put it on the dessert table, people stared at it. Then they pounced on it. There was no serving utensil. People simply grabbed pieces of it with their hands. "Wow!" "Oh my God!" "What is this?"

"I think that's the best dessert I've ever had," my brother said.

"People seen to love your cake," my husband said reassuringly as he took another piece.

I made this cake again to bring to my brother's Super Bowl party a few weeks later. The crowd was almost identical to the New Year's Eve group. The cake was just as ugly as it had been before. The reaction was the same. The cake was gone in minutes. I don't know why this cake is so good. Maybe it's the combination of vegetable oil and orange juice. Maybe it's the four eggs. Or maybe it's Grandma Becky, who knew exactly what she was doing when she baked. What she didn't know was that several decades after she first started baking this cake, generations of people she didn't know would be pulling it apart and gobbling it up, ugly or not.

Apple Cake and Magic Bars are objects of desire. Make them for the foodies you love. Goodies don't have to be beautiful to be perfect.

GRANDMA BECKY'S (UGLY) APPLE CAKE

(Serves 6-8)

INGREDIENTS:

- 3 cups flour
- 1 cup vegetable oil
- 2½ cups sugar
- 4 unbeaten eggs
- ½ teaspoon salt
- ⅓ cup orange juice
- 2½ teaspoons vanilla
- 3 teaspoons baking powder
- 6 thinly sliced apples
- 2 teaspoons cinnamon
- 3 tablespoons sugar

PREPARATION:

1. **Preheat oven** to 350 degrees.
2. **Beat together** flour, oil, sugar, eggs, salt, orange juice, vanilla and baking powder until smooth. In another bowl mix together apples, cinnamon and sugar.
3. **Grease and dust tube pan**. Place one layer of batter and one of apples in the middle. Add another layer of batter and top with remaining apples.
4. **Bake for approximately 1½ hours** until top looks done and toothpick comes out clean.

MAGIC COOKIE BARS

(Yields 16 Bars)

INGREDIENTS:

- ½ cup (*1 stick*) butter or margarine
- 1½ cups graham cracker crumbs
- 1 can (*14 ounces*) sweetened condensed milk
- 1 package (*10-12 ounces*) semi-sweet chocolate chips
- 1 cup flaked coconut
- 1 cup chopped walnuts (*optional*)

PREPARATION:

1. **Preheat oven** to 350 degrees.
2. **Melt butter** in 13 x 9-inch baking pan in oven; remove from oven. Sprinkle graham cracker crumbs over butter. Stir well; press out onto bottom of pan, making a "bottom layer." Pour sweetened condensed milk evenly over crumbs. Sprinkle with morsels, coconut and nuts; press down firmly.
3. **Bake for 25-30 minutes** or until light golden brown. Cool completely in pan on wire rack. *(You can put them in the fridge for a few hours.)* Cut into bars.

6

Saying Goodbye to Gluten

Baby Steps Towards a Gluten-Free Diet

FOR THE PAST FEW YEARS, I have been waving goodbye to gluten. I haven't thrown it out of my life completely – I still love baking (and eating) cookies, cakes, brownies and pies, and that includes giving in to gluttony and licking spatulas covered with raw batter before pans go into the oven. But those activities have also made me sick – as in sick in bed sick, with sore joints, runny nose, fever, gas, etcetera. I decided that gluten was the culprit and scheduled an endoscopy with my gastroenterologist.

FEATURING

- Pretzel Chicken with Honey Mustard Dip
- Ants Climbing a Tree *(Bean-Thread Noodles and Ground Chicken)*
- Lynne's Curried Quinoa

An over-reaction, you say? Well, my grandmother died of colon cancer so paying attention to my colon wasn't totally crazy and I also just like going to see my gastroenterologist, a cool and petite New-York lady who, like me, has two teenage boys. In an attempt to head off colon cancer, she has been giving me colonoscopies every three years for the past nine.

"You don't have celiac," Dr. Gastroenterologist told me after I woke up from the endoscopy.

"So what *do* I have?" I asked, all innocence and hypochondria.

"A gluten sensitivity," she said slowly, as if she were trying to figure out what to give me for my birthday and this was the most generous gift she could find.

Celiac disease is an autoimmune disorder triggered by the ingestion of gluten, a protein found in rye, barley, and malt. It destroys the villi in your small intestine. You need those villi: They are small, finger-like protrusions that help the body absorb nutrients. Without them, the body has trouble absorbing food and left untreated, celiac can lead to depression, osteoporosis, lymphoma, infertility, and neurological disorders, among other things. If you have celiac or gluten intolerance you know some of the symptoms: bloating, joint pain and diarrhea. Celiac is often found in people who have thyroid disease, anemia and type 1 diabetes.

Approximately 18 million American have some kind of gluten intolerance and there are lots of new gluten-free products out there. You can get gluten-free beer, pancake mix, flour, cereal, tortilla chips, and buttercream frosting in addition to bagels, bread, cupcakes and muffins. Really, almost everything that is filling and fattening now comes in a gluten-free form.

Since an endoscopy is the gold standard for establishing a celiac diagnosis and my endoscopy confirmed I didn't have it, I probably could have gone back to eating challah French toast. But whenever I eat gluten—bread or pasta specifically—I wish I hadn't. So, without sending my kids into a pizza-and-pasta-starved panic, I slowly started to make meals that were gluten-free.

Of course, if you really want to make your gluten-free life as simple as possible, you will avoid prepared foods altogether and stick to grilled and broiled meats, fish, chicken, vegetables, nuts, rice, pudding, meringue cookies, and ice cream. That's what I've been doing. But we're all human and occasionally we want food that feels sinful and fun.

My friend Denise has been cooking without gluten for a while. Her older son has celiac and she has been diligent and creative about making foods that he can eat. For her birthday last summer, she threw herself a dinner party and hired Scott Savokinas, a former regional chef at Williams-Sonoma and now a personal chef, to make gluten-free dishes. (Savokinas's older daughter has celiac.) His recipes for that birthday party included Ants Climbing a Tree (noodles and chicken) and Pretzel Chicken with Honey Mustard Dip (exactly what it sounds like). We were out of town for the party so Denise sent me the recipes.

The Pretzel Chicken was a huge hit right away. It takes about forty minutes to make and that includes pounding the pretzels, which is therapy in and of itself. If you cut the chicken into small strips, this dish will happily remind you of McDonald's chicken nuggets (in the best possible way) but will taste much better and be infinitely healthier. I've made it several times and every time, there are raves. The dipping sauce is just a combination of honey and mustard but it is so good that you might think about doubling or tripling the recipe so you can use it for other dishes.

Ants Climbing a Tree combines bean thread noodles with ground chicken. A pound of ground chicken isn't all that much, but together with the various sauces and herbs, this dish generates some serious volume, enough to feed several people several meals. My kids loved it and the dish actually improved as it aged; my younger son had seconds on the second night I served it, and asked for it again on the third night.

Also, my friend Lynne shared her recipe for Curried Quinoa. It was delicious, easy and also better on the second and third days. I doubled the amount of frozen peas the recipe called for because I really like peas and you know how it goes with a half-bag of frozen peas: you put the bag back in the freezer and don't see it again until you clean out the refrigerator and sell the house. Plus, there is something magical about frozen peas. They are always sweet and in the dead of winter they remind you of spring.

If you're going to make one gluten-free dish, start with the Pretzel Chicken. Whether you're gluten-free or not, it is awesome. One afternoon, I was upstairs working while my younger son was watching TV. I came downstairs and there he was, on the family room couch, a bag of gluten-free pretzels in his lap.

"What are you doing?" I screeched.

"Eating pretzels," he said contentedly.

"Those are for dinner!" I yelled.

But inside, I was celebrating another baby step away from gluten, and thinking, "Throw that bag over here, son."

Pretzel Chicken with Honey Mustard Dip

(Serves 4-6)

INGREDIENTS:

- 2 pounds boneless, skinless chicken breast tenders, cut into strips
- 1 bag Snyder's or Glutino Gluten Free pretzels, crushed into small pieces
- 1 cup rice flour
- 2 eggs
- 1 tablespoon water
- Salt and pepper, to taste

PREPARATION:

1. **Place flour into shallow bowl.** Season with salt and pepper.

2. **In a second bowl, crack eggs, add water** and whisk until completely mixed.

3. **In a third bowl, place crushed pretzels.**

4. **Take chicken strips and dredge them in the bowl** of seasoned flour. One at a time, remove chicken from flour and dip it into the egg mixture, thoroughly coating the chicken pieces. Again, one at a time, coat each piece in pretzel crumbs, covering all sides.

5. **Preheat medium sauté pan** over medium high heat. Place enough oil in pan to cover bottom. *(You may need to add more oil as chicken cooks.)*

6. **Place chicken in sauté pan and cook** on both sides, until thoroughly cooked, about 4-5 minutes, possibly more.

HONEY MUSTARD DIP

(Serves 4-6— double this recipe if you want more)

In a medium bowl, stir the following ingredients together:

- 1/4 cup whole grain mustard
- 1/4 cup honey
- 1 tablespoon poppy seeds

ANTS CLIMBING A TREE

(Serves 4-6)

INGREDIENTS:

- 8 ounces bean thread noodles
- 3 tablespoons peanut oil
  (you can substitute grape seed or canola oil)
- 4 tablespoons minced garlic
- 4 tablespoons finely minced fresh ginger root
  (I shredded it in food processor)
- 2 bunches scallions, thinly sliced
- 1 pound ground chicken
- 2 carrots, julienned

SAUCE

In medium bowl, combine the following:

- 1½ cups chicken stock
- 1/4 cup oyster sauce or ground bean sauce
- 3 tablespoons soy sauce
- 2 teaspoons sugar
- 1 teaspoon sesame oil
- 2 teaspoons Chinese chili sauce

▸ *I added a tablespoon of hoisin sauce. If you add this, make sure it is gluten-free.*

PREPARATION:

1. **Place noodles** in a large bowl. Cover with hot water and let sit for 10 to 15 minutes. When noodles are soft, cut in half with kitchen shears or scissors.

2. **Heat large non-stick fry pan** or wok over high heat. Add peanut oil.

3. **Add garlic, ginger and scallions,** and stir continuously, until fragrant, about 20-30 seconds.

4. **Add chicken and cook** until it is evenly browned and cooked through, 3-5 minutes.

5. **Add carrots and the sauce.** Cook for 1 minute. Then, add noodles and continue to cook until they absorb the color from the sauce.

LYNNE'S CURRIED QUINOA

(Serves 4-6)

INGREDIENTS:

- 1 cup quinoa
- 1 ½ tablespoons vegetable oil
- ½ cup diced onions
- 1 teaspoon grated fresh ginger root
- ½ fresh green chili, minced, or ⅛ teaspoon cayenne *(I used cayenne)*
- ½ teaspoon turmeric
- ½ teaspoon coriander
- ¼ teaspoon ground cinnamon
- ½ teaspoon salt
- 1¾ cup water
- ½ cup fresh or frozen peas (*I used 1 cup*)
- 1-2 tablespoons chopped fresh cilantro (*optional*)

PREPARATION:

1. **Place the quinoa in a fine-mesh strainer** and rinse it with cold water. Drain well.
2. **In a heavy saucepan**, warm the oil and sauté the onions on medium-high heat for 4 or 5 minutes.
3. **Add the ginger, chili or cayenne, and the quinoa** and cook for a minute, stirring constantly. Stir in the turmeric, coriander, cinnamon, and salt and cook for another minute, stirring.
4. **Add the water and bring to a boil**. Cover, reduce the heat, and simmer for 15 minutes.
5. **Stir in peas, cover, and cook** for 4 or 5 more minutes, until peas are tender and the water has been absorbed.

▸ *Before serving, fluff with a fork and add the cilantro, if you wish.*

7

Happy Birthday to Me

If You Want Your Birthday Done Right, Make Yourself These Cookies

MY BIRTHDAY WAS COMING UP. You know how that goes. If your children are teenagers and you've been with your significant other a long time, you're probably not going to be the center of attention you might have been thirty years ago. Your family's attitude towards your birthday is probably—what's that French word?— oh right, lame. In order to make sure you're not curled up in a ball at the end of the day wondering why nobody remembered you, you have to plan ahead.

FEATURING

- Super Rich, Fiercely Fudgy Chocolate Meringue Cookies

I told the spinning instructor at Flywheel my birthday was coming up precisely so she would ask me what song she should play.

"The sexist one with the sexist video?" I said, my voice a combination of shame and yearning. "I can't remember the name."

The instructor was standing with two other women. One shouted, "Blurred Lines!"

"Yes, that's it!" Now that was settled.

Then I called in an order for my favorite cake from my favorite bakery (an 8-inch vanilla cake with buttercream frosting) and asked the baker to decorate it with the words, "Happy Birthday, Mom." I asked my sister-in-law to pick it up because she lives nearby.

"Don't you think it's pathetic that we have to do this?" she asked and handed the cake to me in a parking lot halfway between our homes.

"No," I said. "If you don't want to be disappointed, you have to plan everything."

Then I made sure that a friend who thought she might have to work could actually meet me for lunch (she could). After lunch, I knew that the rest of the day would be given over to motherhood and math tutors and I'd be lucky if my dog remembered to lick me. So I decided to prepare even further. I would call in the chocolate.

My friend Denise had given me a recipe for some awesome chocolate meringue cookies. The problem with Denise is she is very precise and scientific. She has an MBA from a fancy school and excels at spreadsheets and following directions so sometimes her recipes are really complicated. I had opened the email with her cookie recipe, worrying it might be three pages long. But it was simple – only one page and the list of ingredients was double-spaced. Plus it was gluten-free! I printed it out, tucked it into my recipe binder and decided to make it at a time when I needed to go to a happy place.

The night before my birthday, it was time for the happy place. It was snowing heavily. The roads were bad and my kids' bus was almost an hour late. While I moved around the kitchen, pulling ingredients for Denise's cookies off the shelves, I kept looking out the window. I called the kids to see if they were close. Finally, they arrived and ran upstairs. While they toiled on Facebook and YouTube, I went to work, melting chocolate, separating eggs yolks from egg whites, and measuring out sugar. I doubled the recipe and made the cookies too big but figured, what the hell, I was turning 49, I could handle some big cookies. As they baked, my 17-year-old, bless him, came downstairs and asked me how I felt about my birthday. "I'm just glad we're all safe and healthy," I said, slurping chocolate off a spoon.

Thirteen minutes later, the cookies were done. Five minutes later, they were cool enough to eat. I called my kids down for a dinner of day-old squash risotto and two-day old brisket. My 13-year-old came downstairs first and grabbed a cookie.

"Eat your dinner first!" I yelled.

"It's leftovers," he said. "I can have a cookie first." Then he took a bite. "Oh my God, these are the best things you've ever made!"

"If you're going to eat cookies, at least tell your brother to come downstairs and have one too."

He called upstairs. "Matt, don't come eat these cookies, they're terrible, they have raisins!" (They don't.)

My older son came running down, grabbed a cookie and, usually more eloquent, said simply, "Oh, Jesus. Oh my God."

The actual day of my birthday, I directed my sons to write me a card. They looked at me blankly, then produced an acrostic and a poem that included the words *Arctic, cathartic, heart* and *fart.*

The next morning, I went downstairs. The cookies were gone, all 30 of them. A large white plate covered with a dusting of cookie crumbs was all that was left. Had mice gotten them? Then I saw, hanging from the doorknob of the front door, a paper bag. The cookies were neatly packed up inside. I forgot: Both my kids had to bring snacks for their school holiday parties. Needless to say, my 17-year-old had packed up *all* the cookies for himself. My 13-year-old still needed some for his party. I guess I would have to make more, which meant another chocolate-filled day for me. And you too, when you make them.

SUPER RICH, FIERCELY FUDGY CHOCOLATE MERINGUE COOKIES

(Yield: 30-40 cookies)

INGREDIENTS:

- 2 cups bittersweet chocolate chips, divided in half
- ⅔ cup unsweetened cocoa powder
- 3 cups powdered sugar, divided in half
- 4 teaspoons cornstarch
- 4 large egg whites, bring to room temperature
- 1 teaspoon vanilla extract
- ¼ teaspoon cream of tartar
- ¼ teaspoon salt
- Nonstick vegetable oil spray

PREPARATION:

1. **Preheat oven** to 350 degrees.
2. **Coat 3-4 large baking sheets** with non-stick spray. Melt one cup chocolate chips in saucepan over double boiler so it doesn't burn. Cool chocolate for 10 minutes. While chocolate is cooling, whisk together 1 ½ cups sugar, all the cocoa and all the cornstarch in a bowl.
3. **Beat together egg whites,** vanilla, salt and cream of tartar until peaks form (about 5 minutes). Slowly add remaining 1 ½ cups sugar and beat until mixture is stiff and glossy. Add in cocoa mixture, melted chocolate and the remaining cup of chocolate chips.
4. **Drop batter by teaspoons** onto cookie trays. Bake cookies for 6 to 7 minutes. Then remove trays from oven, turn them around, and cook for 6 more minutes. Let cookies cool for 5 minutes. Transfer cookies to racks to cool.

▸ *Try not to eat them all.*

8

Under Debbie's Wing

My First Suburban Sister

FEATURING
- Chicken with Balsamic Vinegar

WHEN WE MOVED from the city to New Jersey in 1999, I knew almost no one. You'd think that I would have known everyone because we were moving back to my hometown, but in fact, the only person I knew well was my mother. All the other people I grew up with had fled—or shall we say, relocated—to other towns or states. The house we bought came with toile wallpaper, wall-to-wall mint green carpeting and brass chandeliers. Our street was dark and winding. I used to sit in my driveway and think, "What the hell have I done?" When I told one of my professors that we had moved to New Jersey, she winced and said, "I'm sorry." She refused to meet me for coffee after that.

I scrambled to find a few familiar faces in the nursery school parking lot, waited for new friendships to hatch. They didn't. One of our neighbors brought over a plant, invited us for brunch and sold me some maternity clothes. A different neighbor brought over another plant and invited me to a UJA/Federation event. That was it.

It was my husband who held the ace in the hole: his roommate from college had already been living in town for a few years. And the roommate had a wife.

Her name was Debbie and I'm not sure she actually liked me all that much in the beginning. I was always kvetching about leaving bright, beautiful Manhattan behind. I'm pretty sure Debbie thought I was acting like a spoiled brat. *Boo-hoo, you grew up here and now you have to move back. Most people would kill to grow up in this town. Let me get out the world's tiniest violin.* Still, she had us over for dinner, scheduled play dates for our toddlers, invited me to Hadassah functions and tried to reassure me that suburban life was really not so bad. I wanted to believe her, but I didn't. I continued to run into New York for grad school and therapy.

Suburbia was lonely. Everyone seemed to have settled here years before we had. Many women had moved there pregnant with their first kids. By the time we got there, our son was already three. Most of the moms had law degrees or MBAs or had pursued careers in public relations and event planning. You couldn't find many writers or artists. Everyone was talking about renovating their kitchens; nobody wanted to hash through feelings and old memories.

Three years before we moved back to New Jersey, my father had jammed a knife through his heart in an old quarry twenty miles from our new house. Because he'd done this the day after Christmas, a slow news day, the local and state newspapers had run the story on their front pages. I carried that knowledge like a brick on my back.

Then there was my mother. She had married a handsome politician who was famous within the state, a charming, intelligent man who had been married when they'd started dating. That had made the newspapers too. When people talked about my family, they usually knew what they were talking about.

I didn't pop anti-depressants, gulp vodka from a water bottle or have affairs with other people's spouses, as many people I was meeting did, but I was aware of my shortcomings and my family's dark and public history. It was easy to shirk that in New York, where I could write about it and wonder about it, but never actually bump into anyone who knew about it firsthand.

We found a house two miles away from the one I'd grown up in. It was near the highway and the train station; the local elementary school was good. The backyard was lovely, filled with tiger lilies, daffodils, azalea bushes and towering silver maple trees; the house was old and made of stone. Ivy crept up the stone and made the house look vaguely like a chicken farm in Sillé-le-Guillaume, a little town in the Loire Valley where I had lived one summer in high school. Though the exterminator had warned that ivy was a "highway for mice," we let it climb. The house itself was delightful. It was the consequences of setting down roots in a town where people knew all about me that wasn't.

When people smiled and asked how things were going, I realized very quickly that I had been crazy to move back here. At least in Manhattan my shrink was only a few blocks away. Adding insult to injury, I'd gone to a women's college and most of the women I was meeting had gone to school down South or to Big Ten schools. I felt like a lesbian separatist in a town filled with sorority girls.

In other words: a freak.

Weeks went by without any invitations except to random kids' birthday parties. So imagine my glee when a month after moving in, Debbie invited me to her 35th birthday party. And not just any party, a cooking class birthday party! The class was held in a cooking studio in another town, and the food was delicious and made me feel welcome.

Fifteen years later, Debbie is one of the people I love most in the world. We've had Seders and break-fasts together, gone to each other's kids' bar mitzvahs, walked our dogs, and talked about books. Every summer, we pile our husbands into our cars and go biking in Vermont. Debbie pedals faster than I do but sometimes she takes pity on me, slows down and agrees to describe the plot of the book she is reading. (One afternoon, she told me all about Lionel Shriver's *We Need to Talk About Kevin*, and she described it so well, I felt no need to read the book or see the movie.) When she lost her dad, she said, "Come sit shiva with me." When I lost my dad, she came and sat with me.

The recipe below is from Debbie's long ago birthday party. I made this dish last night. It works for large dinner parties, small family dinners and also just for you, alone in your kitchen, picking out the pieces that are sitting on the bottom, licking your fingers and loving it. The recipe is one of my favorites because it has only six ingredients and you probably don't have to shop for any of them. Not even fresh herbs – all you need is that old jar of oregano that's been sitting in your pantry. But the best things about this dish are that it's awesome, it only takes half an hour and it's even better the next day. I've never met one person who doesn't love it.

The main ingredients are cheap – balsamic vinegar, canned chicken broth, an onion and chicken parts. My four-pound package of chicken made at least two dinners. If I were a really good friend, I'd bring the leftovers to Debbie. But instead I usually just keep them for a couple of days, then throw them in a pot of water, add a can of chicken broth, bring it all to a boil, let it simmer a while with the lid on, and call it soup. Make a bowl of noodles to go with it and you could do worse on a weeknight.

This dish is sort of like living in New Jersey – ordinary ingredients adding up to something special and getting better over time. Thanks for saving me, Deb.

Chicken with Balsamic Vinegar

(Serves 4-6)

INGREDIENTS:

- 1 small chicken, 3-4 pounds, cut up into eighths *(Use frozen chicken and cut into pieces when it's just beginning to defrost–it's easier to cut this way.)*
- ½ cup olive oil
- ½ cup balsamic vinegar
- ¾ cup chicken broth

- 1 medium onion, cut into slices
- ½ teaspoon dry oregano
- salt and pepper

PREPARATION:

1. **Sprinkle salt and pepper** on chicken parts.
2. **Heat oil in large sauté pan** (*I use two pans*). Don't crowd chicken. Brown chicken on both sides for several minutes. When chicken is browned, remove from pan and add onions. Cook onions until tender but not browned. Remove onions to another plate, and pour oil out of pans. Leave the small pan in the sink; you only need the large pan now.
4. **Put pan back on stove** and deglaze the pan with balsamic vinegar. Reduce heat slightly and add chicken broth. Add back the onions and oregano and then the chicken. Turn chicken over several times until is nicely coated.
5. **Reduce heat to simmer,** cover pan and let simmer for 10 minutes or so.

9

Red Hot Chile Peppers

Handle These With Care

FEATURING
- Texas Chile Chowder
- Chicago Turkey Chili

MAYBE IT'S BECAUSE I'd been reading too much about Rick Perry and had just finished K.L. Cook's gorgeous novel about the Texas Panhandle, *The Girl From Charnelle*, but at one point I found myself wanting to go to Texas and see what all the fuss was about. Since that wasn't practical, I started to read *The Homesick Texan Cookbook* by Lisa Fain and decided to make one of her recipes on a Sunday afternoon.

New cookbooks make me dreamy, but Fain's cookbook took me to another place entirely. By the time you finish her book, you will be in Texas, eating Frito Pie, shucking corn and driving a tractor. A seventh generation Texan who moved to New York in her twenties, Fain set about making recipes to remind her of home while living in a small apartment with a tiny kitchen. In her book, she packs in stories of the pimento cheese served at her grandfather's funeral alongside recipes for fried green tomatoes in buttermilk dressing, short ribs made with Dr Pepper (Texans love to cook with soda), her grandma's Chocolate Pie, and her Dad's chicken fried steak with cream gravy (a dish she calls "dangerous" because of all the hot oil splattering and small chunks of meat flying).

Fain offers helpful hints, like: Run milk over your hands to get rid of the heat from chile peppers. Mixed in with fond memories of her grandmother, she offers up her grandma's recipe for piecrust, which calls for the odd combination of oil and milk but which Fain says makes the best crust you'll ever eat. There are also excellent-looking recipes for two kinds of Texas chili, crab cakes with chipotle chiles and corn, fancy pants chicken casserole, jalapeno mustard roast chicken, tomato cobbler and tomatillo cheese grits. But the recipe that caught my eye first was the green chili chowder.

Whenever I see a recipe that calls for cumin, cilantro, garlic and lime juice, I'm in. Fain's green chili chowder called for all of that, plus four poblano chiles, two jalapeno chiles, and two pounds of potatoes. Fain tells you to rub the skin off the poblano peppers and then chop them. At first, this seemed easy, like peeling a scab. Then it got harder. The poblano skin stuck to the pepper meat. I figured I could stand there for forty minutes and peel the skin off, or I could tug at the skins gently for one more minute, give up and hope no one was the wiser. I chose the latter.

If you're like me–lazy–you will look at those six peppers and think, *oh I don't need to chop all those, the food processor can do that*. The food processor *can* chop chile peppers up to a point, but then you must take your spatula, spoon the peppers out and start chopping them yourself. The good news is that after the stint with the peppers, the rest of the recipe is easy and the chowder is so good, it's shocking. At the end of the night, when I wasn't hungry at all, I was still licking the pot. My kids, my husband and my mother (who showed up unexpectedly) all devoured it. The only complaint I have is that Fain does not tell you how long a recipe takes. This chowder takes an hour. Your lips will be tingling pleasantly for hours.

With one recipe under my belt, I decided to make Fain's Seven-Chile Texas Chili the following Sunday. It called for twenty chile peppers! Though it sounds delicious, you don't learn until you turn the page that the Seven-Chile Chili takes all day. Hmm, I don't think so. I checked out the One-Hour Texas Chili, which looked less daunting, and saw that it called for two teaspoons of masa harina. I didn't have masa harina (dry corn flour) and didn't know where I could get some. (Fairway carries it.) I wanted to make chili but I wanted it to be easy, or at least, easier. Then, out of the blue, my friend from Chicago emailed me a recipe for turkey chili.

So that's what I made. It breaks the cardinal rule of Texas chili, in that you mix the chili in with beans, which no self-respecting Texan would do. But if you can get past that, this recipe is a winner. It only takes twenty minutes and is so easy that I was able to start making it, drop my older son off at the gym, go back to cooking, and then pick him back up. The chipotle peppers we had weren't in adobo sauce but the dish was terrific anyway. And because part of me can't leave well enough alone, and the other part loves to jam garlic through the garlic press, I added two cloves of mashed garlic.

TEXAS CHILE CHOWDER

(Serves 6-8)

INGREDIENTS:

- 4 poblano chile peppers
- 2 jalapeño chile peppers
- 1 tablespoon unsalted butter
- 1 medium yellow onion, diced
- 2 cloves garlic, minced
- 2 pounds Russet potatoes, peeled and diced
- 4 cups chicken or vegetable broth
- ½ cup cilantro
- ½ teaspoon ground cumin
- 1½ cups whole milk
- 1 cup half-and-half
- Salt and pepper, to taste
- 2 tablespoons lime juice
- Grated Monterey Jack cheese, tortilla chips and chopped cilantro, on the side

PREPARATION:

1. **Roast poblano chile peppers and jalapeños** under broiler until blackened, about 5 minutes each side. Place poblano chile peppers in paper sack or plastic food storage bag, close tightly and let steam. Meanwhile, remove stems and seeds from jalapeños and dice. After 20 minutes, take poblanos out of the bag and rub off the skin. Remove seeds and stems and then dice the poblanos.

2. **In large pot, melt butter over medium heat.** Add diced onions and cook for 10 minutes until they brown. Add garlic and cook for 30 more seconds. Add to the pot the diced poblano and jalapeño chile peppers, the potatoes, chicken broth, cilantro and cumin. Bring to boil, then simmer for 20 minutes or until potatoes are tender.

3. **Scoop out 2 cups of soup and set aside.** Puree the rest of the soup until smooth, and then mix the smooth with the chunky. Add milk and half-and-half to soup and cook until warm. Add salt and pepper to taste. Squeeze in lime juice and serve warm or cold, with grated cheese, tortilla chips and cilantro on the side.

Chicago Turkey Chili

(Serves 4)

INGREDIENTS:

- 2 tablespoons extra virgin olive oil
- 1 onion, diced
- 2 cloves garlic, mashed
- 1 green bell pepper, seeded and diced
- 2 chipotle peppers in adobo, minced, plus 2 teaspoons sauce
- 1 to 1½ pounds dark ground turkey meat
- 1 28-ounce can diced tomatoes
- 1 15-ounce can kidney beans, drained and rinsed *(pinto beans are okay too)*
- Kosher salt, to taste
- ½ cup grated cheddar cheese, for topping

Garnish *(which can and should be turned into guacamole)*

- 1 avocado, peeled, sliced, mashed
- 1 lime, juiced
- 1 small red onion, diced

PREPARATION:

1. **Heat oil in medium pot** over medium heat. Sauté onion, garlic and bell pepper until tender, 6-8 minutes.
2. **Add chipotle pepper** and adobo sauce and cook for 1 minute.
3. **Add turkey,** breaking it up with the back of a spoon, and cook until it is no longer pink, about 3-5 minutes.
4. **Add tomatoes with juices and beans.** Bring to a boil. Reduce heat and simmer, stirring occasionally, until slightly thickened, about 30 minutes *(add water if you want to thin it out)*. Season with salt.

10

Shamefully Delicious Chicken

Kid Tested, Texan Approved

FEATURING

- Jalapeño Chicken

I SPEND TOO MUCH MONEY on books, particularly cookbooks, which are usually hard-covered and filled with exquisite pictures of food. If I don't cook from them right away, I never cook from them and then they sit like expensive art books on the shelf. When I ordered Lisa Fain's *The Homesick Texan Cookbook*, I was determined to get my money's worth from it

After reading her poignant and vivid essays about growing up Texan, and because most of her recipes aren't all that complicated, I actually started cooking from the dang thing.

One day, I decided to make her jalapeño mustard chicken. I'll just admit right now, I'm a cilantro junkie. It makes me high and I look for reasons to smell, chop and eat it. Fain writes that she made this recipe, which calls for a half cup of cilantro, for her friend who was homesick for Texas. Her friend said it was the best roast chicken she ever ate.

The only problem is that Fain recommends that the chicken sit in its marinade for eight hours. That's a long shift. But the marinade isn't hard to make - you dump a bunch of ingredients in the food processor, cover the chicken with it and go about your day. The main ingredients are cheap and easy enough to buy and keep in your fridge until you're ready to use them, so you just have to make this recipe on a day when you'll have time in the morning to think about what you'll be eating that night.

The morning that I moved my roasting chicken out of the freezer and into the refrigerator to defrost, I hadn't bothered to look at how much it weighed. It was over seven pounds and the recipe called for a 3-4 pound roaster. Fortunately, I had enough ingredients to double the marinade. The chicken was $1.99/pound. If we had leftovers, so what? Two points to Mom for making two dinners at once.

Fain says the secret to success for this dish is to butterfly the chicken, remove its spine and lay it flat on a roasting pan, a process called spatchcocking. This, she writes, "is just a fancy way to say 'cut out the backbone and lay that bird flat."

If you're from Texas, and you know about hunting, removing the backbone of your dinner probably sounds easy enough to do. But I'm from New Jersey and had never hunted or deboned anything in my life. And the thing about a seven-pound roasting chicken is that it looks like it once had a life. It may be headless but it's the same weight as a new baby, and looks about as helpless.

I removed the roaster from its plastic wrap, put it on a cutting board breast side down, stared at it, and couldn't bring myself to make the incision. It seemed too cruel. So I prepared the marinade (took about ten minutes), spread it all over the chicken, covered it with plastic wrap, put it in the fridge and went for a walk with my neighbor. I told her about the chicken and my fear of hurting it.

"You should have asked the butcher to do it at the supermarket," she said. Oh yeah, the butcher. I'd forgotten about him. You shouldn't.

Eight hours later, I screwed up my courage, took out a poultry knife and a fork, and cut the bird's spine out. For once I felt like a hunter instead of a gatherer, and it felt pretty good. I put the chicken in the oven. The whole house immediately started to smell delicious. Two hours later, it was done. I let the chicken rest a bit, made some pasta, chopped up raw vegetables and called for my kids. It was 5:45 and I still had carpooling to do so we had to eat quickly. I started to carve the chicken and told my younger son to call for my older son who either didn't hear him or ignored him. Finally, I started to yell.

My older son sauntered into the kitchen in his boxer shorts. "I'm not hungry," he said, yawning. "Civilized people don't eat before 6 p.m."

I glared at him while I carved. "When someone makes you dinner, you sit down and eat it."

Just as my kids started to bicker, I brought the chicken to the table and they dug in. I waited for their reaction.

"Oh my God, this is shamefully delicious," my older son said. "Can you perpetually have a bowl of this sitting in the kitchen? This is friggin' incredible."

"Yeah, can you make this every night?" my younger son said. He reached for the platter. "This sauce is amazing."

Yes, they really said all that. The combination of cilantro, lime juice, yellow mustard and honey delivers an extremely pleasant shock to your tongue, at which point your tongue tells your brain that happiness is on its way up. The chicken would have gone well with the frisée salad I meant to serve, but we were so busy gobbling up the chicken that I forgot about it. We finished the meal in great moods. While we were cleaning up, my older son kissed and hugged me. My younger son started to sing. "Laura Fromm, she is the bomb..." Before I sicken you any further, let me just say, this chicken is the bomb. Make it tonight.

JALAPEÑO CHICKEN

(Serves 4-6)

INGREDIENTS:

- ½ cup yellow mustard
- 1-2 jalapeño green chili peppers, steams and seeds removed, chopped
- ¼ cup lime juice
- 6 gloves garlic

- ½ cup cilantro
- ½ teaspoon ground ginger
- 1 teaspoon ground cumin
- 2 tablespoons honey
- Salt, to taste
- One 3-4 pound chicken

PREPARATION:

1. **In a food processor**, blend mustard, jalapeño, lime juice, garlic, cilantro, ginger, cumin and honey. Add salt if needed.
2. **Rinse chicken and remove giblets.** *(I cooked them along with the chicken and they were shamefully delicious as well.)*
3. **To butterfly the chicken for more even cooking**, remove the spine from the back of the chicken with poultry shears.
4. **Lightly salt chicken all over.** *(I used kosher salt, 1-2 teaspoons.)*
5. **Take mustard marinade and rub** all over chicken, gently lifting skin so you can spread some of it on the meat underneath. Place coated chicken in a plastic bag or put it on a plate and cover it with plastic wrap. Refrigerate for 8 hours.
6. **Preheat oven to 400 degrees** and line a cookie sheet with tinfoil.
7. **Take chicken out of fridge**, lay it flat on sheet, breast side up. Let sit for 20 minutes before putting it in the oven. Cook for 45 minutes to an hour for a 3-4 pound chicken, and about 2 hours for a 7-pound chicken. Let chicken rest for 10 minutes before serving.

11

Short Ribs Made With Soda

Texans Cook With Soda. You Can Do It Too

I DON'T USUALLY COOK WITH SODA, though God knows, I've drunk enough of it. I spent my high school years sneaking Tab at my friends' houses because my mother refused to keep it in our own. In college, I chugged diet Coke, always keeping a couple of six-packs in my refrigerator cube.

FEATURING
- Ribs with Dr Pepper (or Coke)

When I was a reporter at *Business Week*, I wrote about Pepsi, but the vending machine stocked Coke, so that's what I drank, relying on the sugar and caffeine to help me make deadline. As an adult trying to set a good example for my kids, I keep soda out of the house, except for my secret stash in the basement refrigerator. Somehow, I manage to sneak it by them, making sure to toss the can in the recycling container before they get home from school.

So when I saw Lisa Fain's recipe for Dr Pepper ribs in *The Homesick Texan Cookbook*, I settled in for a closer look. I wasn't a big fan of Dr Pepper but I'd been stalking Fain's blog and read on it that you can substitute Coke for Dr Pepper in this recipe. So I decided to make the ribs and soda the week I had jury duty.

I imagine jury duty is the same in Newark, NJ as it is in most places: a lot of sitting around, waiting for your name to be called, with ample time to think. Here, at the Veterans Courthouse in the Superior Court, they've spruced the place up in recent years, so I spent two mostly pleasant days sitting at a bright yellow carrel in a modern computer lounge, enjoying free Wi-Fi and using a Kindle for the first time. In other rooms, potential jurors sat and watched flat-screen TVs that were set to CNN, ESPN and HGTV. I drank strong, free coffee that a nice government employee made just for me from one of those nifty Keurig single-cup coffee makers and waited for my name to be called. All around, people banged away at their laptops and checked their iPhones. It was like being in Starbucks except the parking was free and there were loudspeakers in the bathroom. But the courts stop serving coffee at 11:45 a.m. so in the afternoon, I wandered to the vending machine, looking for a jolt. One machine stocked diet Dr Pepper. This was a day of new beginnings: If I could read a book on a Kindle and enjoy jury service, I could try a new soda. That Dr Pepper was delicious. I immediately decided to use it with ribs. All I needed was another can.

But then I was assigned to a courtroom in another building. The judge told us we had to return there the next morning. One of the clerks mentioned that we should also leave ourselves a little extra travel time because a film crew was taking over City Hall to film the third installment of the Batman franchise. He cheerfully warned us there might be a lot of traffic. Then he handed us directions for alternate routes to the courthouse.

By the time I got to my car at the end of the day, I was in no mood to buy more Dr Pepper. But I had to make dinner. I knew we had ribs and a six-pack of Coke tucked away somewhere. I arrived home, mixed up the ingredients for the dry rub and got the ribs out of the fridge. Then I saw the words: *Coat the ribs with the rub, cover them with plastic wrap, and place in the refrigerator for at least 4 hours.* How had I missed those instructions? I blamed Batman and ordered a pizza.

The next day, I was released from jury duty. I got myself some Dr Pepper and set about making the ribs. Because I now had both Coke and Dr Pepper in the house, I decided to make two different sauces, using a different soda in each, and see if anyone could taste the difference. My kids, of course, were delighted I was cooking with soda and kept asking how much I planned to use so they could drink the rest.

While I was cooking, my mother came over. She went to college in the South and developed a taste for ribs. She declared both sauces delicious, but spicy. I tried to cut the spice by adding brown sugar but the ribs still kept their kick. The problem was the chipotle powder. Fain's recipe calls for 2-4 teaspoons. I used four. That was too much. I made pasta and put out red grapes and a challah, and those took the edge off. The Dr Pepper barbecue sauce was a bit mellower than the Coke sauce, but both were sweet and spicy.

At the end of the evening, under the cover of darkness, I tasted the ribs again. They were even better cold. If you plan to make these, try using one or, at most, two teaspoons of chipotle powder so you don't set your mouth on fire.

Also, a note on beef versus pork: Fain calls for St. Louis pork ribs, which are long and thin. My husband grew up kosher so I used three pounds of beef short ribs.

Real Texans eat ribs with their hands. Even if you are from Texas, I suggest setting your table with a fork, knife *and* spoon so you can scoop up that soda-filled sauce at the end.

RIBS WITH DR PEPPER (OR COKE)

(Serves 4-6)

NOTE: Ribs cook for a total of 2½ hours plus 8 minutes but you need to put the dry rub on them at least 4 hours beforehand.

INGREDIENTS *for the ribs*:

- ¼ cup kosher salt
- ¼ cup black pepper
- ¼ cup brown sugar
- 4 teaspoons mustard pepper

- ½ teaspoon cayenne
- 2 teaspoons chipotle powder
- ½ teaspoon ground allspice
- 2 racks of St. Louis ribs *(I used beef)*
- ¼ cup Dr Pepper or Coke *(don't use diet)*

INGREDIENTS *for the glaze:*

- 2 cups Dr Pepper or Coke *(don't use diet)*
- 1 cup ketchup
- ½ cup yellow prepared mustard
- ¼ cup apple cider vinegar
- 2 tablespoons molasses
- 2-4 teaspoons of chipotle powder
  (use 1-2 teaspoons if you don't want them too spicy)

PREPARATION:

1. ***Four Hours Ahead***
   Make the rub: Mix the salt, black pepper, brown sugar, mustard powder, cayenne, chipotle powder and ground allspice. Coat ribs with rub, cover with plastic wrap and place in refrigerator for at least 4 hours.

2. **Once you're ready to cook, preheat oven to 300 degrees** and bring ribs to room temperature. Line large baking pan with tin foil, arrange ribs meat-side up, pour in ¼ cup Dr Pepper or Coke, cover pan tightly with foil and place in oven for 90 minutes.

3. **While ribs are cooking, make the glaze.** In a saucepan, pour 2 cups Dr Pepper or Coke, ketchup, mustard, apple cider vinegar, molasses and chipotle powder. Bring to boil, then turn down heat to low and simmer for 20 minutes until thick and syrupy. Set aside.

4. **After 90 minutes, take ribs out of oven.** Spread some glaze on both sides of ribs. Place back in oven, meat side up and cook uncovered for 30 minutes. After 30 minutes, take out ribs and spread more glaze over them, then cook for 30 more minutes. Take ribs out of oven and turn broiler on. Spread remaining glaze on ribs and cook ribs on each side under the broiler for 4 minutes *(8 minutes total).*

▸ *Serve warm and eat the leftovers later, cold.*

12

Under Pressure

Pressure Cooking Gives New Meaning to the Term PC

MY FRIEND TERRI is a generous and terrific cook. When she asks if you want to have lunch, she means, "Do you want to come over so I can make mushroom soup with three different kinds of mushrooms and the most delicious salad you've ever tasted with homemade lemon dressing?" Terri is the kind and resourceful sister you always wanted. She always knows where to get an organic chicken, a kosher turkey, a frozen challah and a mind-blowingly good homemade granola bar. So one cold March, when she asked me if I wanted to take a pressure cooking class at her house, I knew at a minimum I'd be well fed and drive home with a sheaf of new recipes.

FEATURING

- Beef Bourguignon (Beef Stew with Red Wine)
- Risotto with Cheese and Rosemary

The class was taught by Arlene Ward, a lovely woman with a fierce attention to detail and a delightful sense of humor. Ward is co-author with Rick Rogers of *Pressure Cooking for Everyone* and an expert on using the pressure cooker in unexpected ways. For more than 20 years, Ward ran a cooking school and store called Adventures in Cooking until a huge flood forced her to close the business. Since then, she has taught cooking classes in supermarkets and privately in people's homes.

Along with a large group of Terri's friends, I sat in Ward's class at Terri's house for three hours, took notes, ate some fabulous food, then went home and ordered a Kuhn Rikon 5-quart pressure cooker. When the pressure cooker arrived, I put it on top of the stove.

There is something energizing about a new appliance. Oh, the things that you'll make! But that energy can work against you if you don't actually use the thing. The pressure cooker was big. As I read the owner's manual, I became nervous. The physics of it scared me. When the pressure builds up, a little black button on top (aka the safety valve) pops up and if there is too much pressure, the pot will hiss, signaling you need to lower the flame or push down the valve so it can let off some steam. Who needs an appliance that hisses? As Terri and my other PC-loving friends got busy making risotto, stews, soups, meatballs, brisket, turkey breast, chicken, butternut squash gratin, bread pudding, Bolognese sauce, applesauce and cheesecake in their pressure cookers, I made nothing. I didn't even wash the contraption to get it ready. I did, however, buy Ward's book and read through the recipes. They all looked delicious and none looked hard. Still, I was intimidated. What if I opened the pot too soon and instead of getting a mini facial, was burned by the steam? I had also heard stories from years ago of pressure cookers blowing up. After a few weeks of staring at my new menacing appliance on the stovetop, I opened our oven, put the pressure cooker inside and closed the door.

Time went by. Every so often, Terri would ask, "Have you used the pressure cooker?" I'd shake my head no. "It's so easy!" she'd say and then describe the great ropa vieja (shredded flank steak or brisket) she'd just made. My neighbor, who had also taken the class, would rave about how much her kids liked the turkey breast and pea soup she'd cooked in the PC. "I'm going to come over and help you," each offered. I was too embarrassed to say, "Really? When?"

So a few weeks ago, when Terri said that Arlene was coming back to teach another class in her kitchen, I signed up for a second time.

The class was terrific and inspiring, Arlene made barbecue chicken, corn pudding and a cauliflower and mushroom gratin in the pressure cooker. Outside the pressure cooker, she whipped up a *farfalle* (bow tie pasta) in creamy vodka sauce, a super easy, gluten-free, chocolate pot of cream and a salad made with vanilla vinaigrette. She made a plain roast chicken in the oven and showed us how to carve it properly.

The next morning, I followed Ward's suggestion: I took a practice run. I washed out the pot, poured in two cups of hot water, locked the lid in place and brought it to a boil over high heat. After 10 minutes, I turned off the burner and pressed down the valve to release the steam through the vent, tilted the lid of the pot away from me, and dumped the water down the sink. I'd used the pressure cooker to heat up some water. Whoopee! At least now I was confident enough to make risotto and barbecue chicken for dinner.

There is nothing more delicious and satisfying than a rich, creamy risotto, especially on a cold night after daylight savings time kicks in and the days get dark so early. But risotto requires a lot of standing and stirring. If you've had a long day, you'll probably skip it. The great news is the pressure cooker makes the risotto beautifully without any standing and stirring, and in half the time. I followed Ward's recipe for risotto and was doing a little mental victory lap in my kitchen when I saw how easy and fast it was to make it. (Note: You do have to stay in the kitchen when the pressure cooker is on.)

My only mistake was adding one teaspoon of *dried* rosemary. Ward's recipe called for two teaspoons of *fresh* rosemary. That's the usual rule of thumb when using dried versus fresh herbs. But as Ward points out in her book, "Pressure cooking intensifies flavors, so about half the amount of dried herbs, spices and salt are needed than in traditional cooking methods." I had read those words and then promptly forgotten them. But you shouldn't. Use your dried herbs sparingly when using a pressure cooker.

Emboldened, I decided to make *boeuf bourguignon* (beef

stew in red wine with onions and mushrooms) the next night. Beef bourguignon is one of those classic French dishes that tastes delicious and takes forever. Recipes from Julia Child's *Mastering the Art of French Cooking* and Craig Claiborne's *The New York Times Cookbook* are easy enough to follow, but they'll have you cooking for three to four hours. Not tonight, love. The beef bourguignon recipe in Ward's cookbook promised that it only needed twenty minutes at high pressure. That was nothing! I'd already started making a list of ingredients when my neighbor called.

"The risotto and barbecue chicken turned out great!" I crowed. "I'm going to make beef bourguignon tonight and it's only going to take twenty minutes!"

My neighbor chortled. "It's not going to take twenty minutes," she said. "Whenever you cook big hunks of meat, it takes the pressure cooker a long time to get up to pressure." Oh.

At 4:50 p.m., I started making dinner. My kids were hungry; I was determined to be done quickly. Ward's recipe called for one cup of hearty red wine, such as a Zinfandel. Craig Claiborne recommended a Burgundy. Julia Child recommended every wine but the one we had, which was Cabernet Sauvignon. At 5:20, that's what I opened.

At 5:21, my neighbor popped over with her dog. "You're opening wine?"

"It's for the beef!" (Really, it was.) Although, knowing she's a sophisticated red wine drinker, I decided to do the neighborly thing and offer her a glass.

"It's kind of early," she said. I shrugged, took out two wine glasses and poured. We toasted and drank. What fun!

She peered at the three pounds of meat cut into 1.5-inch chunks. "You're going to have to do those in batches," she said. She was right. I browned three batches in the pressure cooker, then added the mushrooms, shallots and garlic. Our dogs wandered around the kitchen hoping something tasty would drop. When she and her dog left, I poured myself another glass of wine, slid the lid on the pot and turned up the pressure.

The pot took a few minutes to reach high pressure and start to hiss. This time I wasn't afraid; I pressed down on the valve with a long wooden spoon, as Ward had advised, and let out some steam. By 6:10, the beef bourguignon was done.

I tasted the sauce. It was flat. Something was missing. The wine! We had been so busy drinking it, I had forgotten to add it. Oops. I added it to the sauce, put the heat back on, whisked it for five minutes and poured it back on the meat. Julia Child might have noticed the difference but no else one would. In the end, it took 90 minutes to make beef bourguignon in the pressure cooker. That's not 20 minutes, but it's less than half the time it would have taken to make it the classic French way. *C'est bonne.*

RISOTTO WITH CHEESE AND ROSEMARY

(Serves 4 as a side dish, 2 as an entrée)

INGREDIENTS:

- 4 tablespoons unsalted butter
- ½ cup chopped red onion
- 1 tablespoon chopped garlic
- 2 teaspoons fresh rosemary, chopped
- ¾ cup carnaroli or Arborio rice
- ¼ cup white wine
- 1¾ cup chicken stock
- salt and pepper to taste
- ⅓ cup grated Parmesan cheese
- 1 tablespoon butter

PREPARATION:

1. **Heat 4 tablespoons butter and sauté onion and garlic** until softened. Add rosemary and rice and thoroughly coat it with butter. Add wine and cook until absorbed. Add stock, salt and pepper to taste.

2. **Turn heat to high and lock lid** in place. Bring to high pressure and adjust heat to maintain pressure. Cook for 6 minutes. Reduce with quick release and remove lid, tilting it away from you to allow any excess steam to escape. Add Parmesan cheese and butter.

BEEF BOURGUIGNON

(Serves 6-8)

INGREDIENTS:

- 1 tablespoon olive oil
- 3 bacon strips, coarsely chopped
- 3 pounds beef bottom round, cut into 1 ½-inch pieces
- ½ teaspoon salt, plus more to taste
- ¼ teaspoon freshly ground black pepper, plus more to taste
- 10 ounces fresh white mushrooms, quartered
- 4 medium carrots, cut into 1-inch lengths
- ½ cup chopped shallots
- 2 garlic cloves
- 1 cup red wine *(I used Cabernet Sauvignon)*
- 2 cups beef stock
- 1 tablespoon tomato paste
- 4 tablespoons *(1/2 stick)* unsalted butter, at room temperature
- ¼ cup all purpose flour

PREPARATION:

1. **In a 5- to 7-quart pressure cooker**, heat the oil over medium heat. Add bacon and cook, stirring occasionally until crisp. Drain bacon on paper towels. Pour bacon fat into small bowl. Return 1 tablespoon of fat to cooker, reserving the remaining fat.
2. **Heat fat over medium-high heat.** In batches, adding more fat as needed, add beef and cook, turning occasionally, until browned, about 4 minutes. Transfer beef to a plate and season with ½ teaspoon salt and ¼ teaspoon pepper. Set aside.
3. **Pour 1 tablespoon of the reserved fat** (use olive oil if the fat has been depleted) into the cooker. Reduce heat to medium. Add mushrooms, carrots, shallots and garlic. Cook, stirring

occasionally until mushrooms soften, about 5 minutes. Add wine. Bring to a boil, scraping up any browned bits from the bottom of the pan. Stir in broth and tomato paste. Return beef and any juices on the plate to cooker.

3. **Lock lid in place.** Bring to high pressure over high heat. Adjust the heat to maintain the pressure. Cook for 20 minutes. Remove from the heat and quick-release the pressure. Open lid, tilting it away from you to block any escaping steam. Stir in reserved bacon. Using a large skimmer or slotted spoon, transfer the meat and vegetables to a deep serving bowl. Cover with aluminum foil to keep warm. Let liquid stand for 5 minutes.

4. **Skim any fat from the surface of cooking liquid.** Bring to a boil, uncovered, over medium-high heat. In a medium bowl, using a rubber spatula, work the butter and flour together until smooth. Gradually whisk about 1 cup of the cooking liquid into the flour mixture to make a thin paste. Briskly whisk paste into the boiling liquid. Cook, stirring occasionally, until sauce is thickened and no trace of raw flour taste remains, about 5 minutes. Season with additional salt and pepper. Pour the sauce over the meat and vegetables, stir gently and serve.

13

To Maria, With Love

Salvaging Stew, Stirring Up Soup

I USED TO TEACH news and business reporting at a local state university and every week we read different sections of *The New York Times*. The *Times* was still free online then (unlike the more financially savvy *Wall Street Journal*), and the student center gave out free copies. I was grateful for the wide range of riveting stories it ran—and the ease with which it allowed me to teach journalism. I tried to teach the students, most of whom were journalism minors, how to follow, interpret, cover, research and write about the news. We made our way through the front section, the Editorials, the Op-Eds, the Weekend section as well as Business, Sports, Science, and the Arts. I did periodically assign the students stories from *The Star Ledger*, *New York* magazine, *The New Yorker*, and various news websites, all of which offered free stories online, but my go-to publication was the paper of record.

FEATURING

- Pumpkin Soup with Turkey Sausage & Turkey Bacon

Now that I've gotten that out of the way, I'll confess that the part of the paper that really made my heart race was the Dining section. But I never had the nerve to assign that particular section of the paper to my students.

I spent years writing about business, and a few years writing and studying fiction in grad school, but the topic I like to read, write and think about the most is food, especially the preparation of it. When Wednesday rolls around, I grab the Dining section. Generally, the recipes are reliable. Occasionally, they're extraordinary. There's always some quirky approach to making or contemplating food. Once there was a story about the discovery of Marilyn Monroe's stuffing recipe. The writers were trying to figure out what had prompted Monroe to incorporate raisins, chicken livers, oregano, grated Parmesan, chopped eggs, sourdough bread and three different kinds of nuts into the recipe, but to leave out garlic. (Apparently, Joe DiMaggio, Monroe's husband at the time, didn't like garlic.)

This may not sound like big news but it turned out to be one of the *Times*' ten most popular stories for the day, so I was not the only fool reading it with rapture. One Wednesday, I decided to make the *Times*' version of Herbed White Bean and Sausage Stew. We had a bag of Great Northern beans in the pantry and sausage in the fridge. The writer of the story bragged that unlike most recipes, this one didn't require that you soak the beans first. I dumped a bag of dry beans in the pot, added some water, threw some carrots and celery into the food processor, took out the various herbs that were required, and started cooking sausage.

Our housekeeper, Maria, a lovely Portuguese grandmother who is the definition of old-world courtesy and decency, stopped and watched me. Usually, when I cook, she doesn't say much except, "Smells good," or, "Looks nice." I always give her a container to take home. This time, she looked at the pot of beans with concern.

"I usually soak my beans overnight," Maria said.

"I know," I said. "But the recipe says you don't have to."

"I soak mine overnight," she shrugged, and went upstairs.

My older son heard this exchange and said out loud what I'd been thinking: "Maria never criticizes us unless we're doing something really stupid."

The white bean and sausage stew took forever to make. Even after cooking it for hours, the beans never properly softened. Despite the interesting mix of vegetables and herbs, and the lovely, salty sausage, the stew didn't taste very good. Plus, it was ugly. The only good part about that bean stew was all the nice bits of sausage I had cut up, fried and thrown in.

The next night, the stew was still sitting in the refrigerator. We had a *lot* left. I opened up the container and got ready to throw it out. But then I spotted those little sausage pieces. One of the wonderful things about sausage is all the salt and fat that goes into it to preserve it. The sausage pieces looked lonely and lost in that container of undercooked and poorly seasoned beans. "Save us," they begged. "Look how tantalizing we are!" What else could I do? I picked them out, ate a few, put the rest in a container and dumped the stew into the garbage.

The next morning, I woke up with sausage on my mind so I made some for my younger son for breakfast. He had complained *in front of the pediatrician* that I wasn't feeding him enough for breakfast and he was hungry at school. The pediatrician suggested he start eating more protein so I started making him boiled eggs and turkey sausage, on top of his regular bowl of cereal, cheese stick and banana. This morning, he ate the eggs but skipped the sausage. I put it in the refrigerator and figured I would use it for something, eventually.

Then I saw the enormous pumpkin sitting on the counter.

A couple of weeks earlier, in a fit of family fun (or forced togetherness, as our older son referred to it), my husband suggested an outing for Saturday afternoon. We took our dog and drove west for a half an hour to a pumpkin farm. (Lest you think that we are all *Leave It to Beaver* and punch-drunk with family harmony in our house, the last time we went pumpkin picking was when my younger son was in nursery school–five years prior.)

Since it was pretty late in the season, most of the pumpkins were gone, but my kids managed to find six big ones. They carved one for Halloween, and put all but one on the front porch, where squirrels nibbled on them. They put the last one on the kitchen counter and asked me to cook it.

I let it sit there a good two and a half weeks. Then I couldn't stand it anymore. Thanksgiving was coming. I needed to clear out the debris of one holiday before we started on another. I decided to make pumpkin soup. The only problem was that the pumpkin was enormous. I knew we had smaller pumpkins but they were outside. What if the squirrels had peed on them? I found a recipe for pumpkin soup, which sounded great. The author called it "meager," in that it was mostly made from basic ingredients like water and bread. I love the idea of making something out of nothing, but opted for another recipe, which required cream, minced fresh parsley leaves and snipped chives for garnish. We didn't have any of that but I figured we could improvise. The recipe also called for a pound of crisp, tart apples. My older son is allergic to apples. What could I put in the soup that would make it crispy and crunchy, with a hint of fat? Those meager meats, sausage and bacon.

My younger son wandered in and asked what I was doing. "Making pumpkin soup," I said.

"But I wanted pumpkin pie," he said.

I ignored him and soldiered on. The soup was really good. Even my pie-loving son gulped down a big bowl, then yelled for more. The rest was for Maria.

Pumpkin Soup, with Turkey Sausage & Turkey Bacon

(Serves 4-6)

INGREDIENTS:

- 3 tablespoons butter
- 1 pound pumpkin, cut into 1-2 inch cubes *(about 4 cups)*
- 2 onions, chopped
- 4 cups chicken stock
- ¼ teaspoon dry tarragon
- 1 cup heavy cream *(I use skim milk)*
- ½ cup dry white wine
- 1 sausage link, cooked and cut up
- 5-6 strips of turkey bacon— cooked and chopped up
- Salt and pepper, to taste

PREPARATION:

1. **Place butter in large, deep saucepan.** Cut pumpkin into cubes. Put onion, cooked sausage, and chopped turkey bacon in a food processor for 30 seconds or so.

2. **After butter melts**, add the pumpkin, sausage, bacon and onion to the saucepan and cook for about 10 minutes, until onion softens. Add salt and pepper.

3. **Add the chicken stock, wine and tarragon** and turn heat to medium high. Bring to a boil. Turn heat down to low, partially cover and cook for about half an hour.

4. **Cool for a few minutes, then put soup into food processor** and purée. Return soup to saucepan and cook for a minute or two over medium-low heat and stir. Add milk and stir for another minute or so.

14

Oh, Duck!

A Recipe (or Two) For Happiness

NEW YEAR'S EVE is full of resolutions. You'll be thinner, kinder, and happier. You'll eat better and healthier. You'll load up on raw vegetables and fresh salmon. You'll play fewer games of Words With Friends online and—gasp!—maybe even play Scrabble with people in person.

You will, you will, you will and then, of course, you won't. January is a cruel month. You get back from whatever holiday you've taken, start out with the best of intentions, try to be good for a few days, amend your New Year's resolutions and then what do you have? The rest of winter to muddle through. If you live in the Northeast, January is the harshest month because it's cold and when you finally get to the end, all you get is a nose-dive into freezing February.

FEATURING
- Duck Salad with Almonds, String Beans & Watercress
- Canard à l'Orange

To stay sane post New Year's Day, I try to do something new every January. Often that turns out only to mean buying a new cookbook to cook from, but I always start out planning to take up some new game or sport. One year, my neighbor and I talked about taking an EMT course, doing competitive rock-climbing and buying snowshoes. Oh, the fun we would have! As always, our conversation soon turned to food. My neighbor's goal was to make hundreds of meatballs to sell at a wrestling tournament her son was competing in. I planned to make duck while my kids watched the Giants game.

Yes, duck is expensive and fattening. So what? In winter, we have to find our pleasures where we can. Plus, the duck dish I was thinking about was worth saving for. It had been almost two years since I had made it and I could still remember how happy we all were sitting down to a scrumptious platter of duck in the center of the table.

The beauty of duck is it lasts a while. Make this recipe on Sunday and you will still be joyfully nibbling on it Wednesday. And this particular dish is so rich, delicious and nutritious you won't need dessert or a side dish to go with it (though you may need a cup of coffee later to keep you awake).

I learned to make duck from my mother; when I was growing up she made *Canard à l'Orange*. There are plenty of things about my childhood that I'd rather forget but my mother's food is not one of them. She made elaborate meals almost every night and her bible was Craig Claiborne's *The New York Times Cookbook*.

My parents eventually divorced but for years my mother bent over backwards to make the dishes that my father loved – Yorkshire pudding and roast beef, filet mignon, veal scaloppini, lamb chops, spare ribs, spaghetti with meatballs, lasagna, tongue, stuffed potatoes, fried chicken, matzo ball soup, garlic bread, chocolate mousse surrounded by lady fingers, chocolate and Grand Marnier soufflés, and apple pie. From my parents, I learned that to cook is to please.

A few years ago, I found a version of this duck recipe in *The New York Times* Dining section. I love the Dining section. When I was growing up, it was called the Food section, and my mother was once featured in it in a story that ran on December 10, 1975: "He Designs Meals–And Kitchens as Well." My mom and her friend John Cristaldi, a carpenter turned kitchen designer, cooked a meal for Craig Claiborne, then the food critic for the *Times*. "Uncle John" had just renovated our kitchen and Mom was trying to help him expand his business. He often came for dinner, and I loved it when he did. He was a gentle, funny man and his presence seemed to calm my temperamental father.

Every time John came over, he and Mom cooked up a storm. My mother typed up a letter to Craig Claiborne and somehow persuaded him to drive out to Short Hills, NJ and sit down in her kitchen so Uncle John could cook an old-fashioned Italian meal for him. A few weeks later, Claiborne and his driver arrived at the house. While Mom poured him a glass of wine, John made sesame steak, broccoli raab, zucchini with tomato sauce and sautéed chicken with Italian sausages.

John discussed his cooking philosophy, sharing that he grew his own basil and oregano, and learned to cook from his father, a stonemason. I'm looking at the story now. There are the blue tiles from my parents' kitchen, there is Uncle John, there are the dark brown cabinets with the shiny white knobs, there is the island where my father used to stash the Famous Amos chocolate chip cookies he brought back from Zabar's. John used to be a frequent guest at our house for dinner on weeknights. On those nights, my father wouldn't call my mother "sleazily charming" or me "a fat tub of lard." John knew how to take the tension out of tense situations, and my father respected his easy manner as well as his culinary and carpentry skills. Eventually, my mother left my father, and John married, started a family of his own, and bought a house a mile down the road from us. For years after he stopped being part of our lives, I used to run or drive by his house, blissful in the knowledge that he was alive and well and cooking in the beautiful kitchen he had built there.

John and Dad are both gone now, and my mother doesn't cook much anymore. But she still lives in that house and the stovetop and brown cabinets are still there.

And every Wednesday morning, I still turn to the Dining section before I read the more pressing news of the front page. Some days, I'll cut or print out some recipes, put them in my recipe binder and forget about them. But other days, I cook whatever the *Times* tells me to. This duck recipe is adapted from one of those days.

One Sunday, I took out the duck recipe and while my kids watched the Giants play the Falcons, I made duck.

All I can say is, *Oh, Mama*. This dish will make your heart race. I doubled the amount of string beans the recipe calls for so I could pretend this was a watercress and string bean salad with a little duck thrown in, and not the other way around.

You start by melting honey in a pot. Nothing beats the smell of warm honey. Once you add the raw sugar, salt and nuts to it, your party has started. If you do nothing else with your life, make these nuts.

The first time I made this recipe, the wax paper stuck to the nuts. This time, I let the nuts cool and put the tray into the refrigerator for half an hour. When they were really cold, the wax paper came off easily.

The duck itself takes little time to make—12-15 minutes to cook two thick duck breasts. The original recipe said it would only take eight minutes, yet after eight minutes, the duck was gorgeous and grilled dark on top, but raw inside. I sliced the duck breasts in half lengthwise, so there were four thin duck breasts on the platter, and cooked them a few more minutes.

My mother showed up just as I was arranging the duck on a platter with the greens. "Oh, duck!" she said. Her eyes lit up. I like to think that I've lived my life in opposition to my mother but the reality is I've chosen to return to my hometown and, like her, I cook all the time. I made her a plate to taste. As my mother bit into the duck, she looked happier than I've ever seen her in my life. "I think this is the best thing you've ever made," she said. Thanks, Mom.

DUCK SALAD WITH ALMONDS, STRING BEANS AND WATERCRESS

(Serves 2-4)

INGREDIENTS:

- 2 duck breasts, trimmed (1½ pounds total)
- 1 tablespoon honey
- 1 cup slivered almonds

- 2 tablespoons raw sugar
- 1 teaspoon kosher salt
- 1 teaspoon chipotle or other chili powder
- ½ teaspoon freshly ground black pepper
- ½ teaspoon cumin
- ¼ teaspoon ground cinnamon
- ¼ cup, plus 1 teaspoon extra virgin olive oil
- 1 garlic clove, minced
- 2 tablespoons lime juice
- 1 bunch watercress
- 1-2 pounds string beans or *haricots verts*
- Pinch salt

PREPARATION:

1. **Preheat oven to 350 degrees.**
2. **In a small saucepan over medium heat**, cook honey and salt until thin and runny, and then mix in almonds until coated. Add sugar and toss to coat. Spread nuts on baking sheet *(lined with parchment paper)* and bake, stirring once, until deeply golden brown, 10-12 minutes. Let nuts cool *(put them in the refrigerator for half an hour or so)*, then peel off the wax paper and break up clumps with your fingers.
3. **In a medium pot on medium-high heat**, bring 6 cups salted water to boil. Fill a medium bowl with ice water. Cook green beans until bright green and tender, 2-4 minutes depending on thickness of beans. Drain, and then plunge into ice water to stop cooking. Drain and pat dry.
4. **Raise oven heat to 400 degrees.** Using a sharp knife, score duck fat into a crosshatch pattern, with cuts a half-inch apart. You want to cut through fat but not into flesh of duck.
5. **In a small bowl, mix salt,** chili, pepper, cumin and cinnamon. Rub mix all over duck, working it into the fat.
6. **Set an ovenproof pan on the stove** over medium-low heat. Add 1 teaspoon of oil, heat for a few seconds, and then add duck, fat side down. Sear without moving until dark brown, about 10 minutes *(if it starts to burn, lower the heat)*. Flip duck and cook for 1 minute, then transfer pan to oven and roast until meat is

done to taste, 4-8 minutes longer for medium rare *(an internal temperature of 130 degrees)*. Let duck rest on a cutting board. Reserve 2 tablespoons of fat from pan. Mash up garlic and make a paste from garlic and a pinch of salt. In a small bowl, mix it with lime juice and a half-teaspoon salt, then drizzle in remaining olive oil, whisking well.

7. **In a large bowl, toss green beans and watercress** with reserved pan drippings and just enough of dressing to coat. Taste and add salt if desired.
8. **Slice duck breasts and toss with salad.** Garnish with almonds and serve.

MOM'S *CANARD À L'ORANGE*
(ROAST DUCK WITH ORANGES)

(Serves 4)

INGREDIENTS:

- 1 whole seedless orange
- 1 4-5 pound bone-in duckling
- ¾ cup chicken broth
- ¼ cup sugar
- ¼ cup red wine vinegar
- 1 tablespoon water
- 2 tablespoons Grand Marnier (orange flavored cognac)
- 1 teaspoon cornstarch
- Salt and pepper

PREPARATION:

1. **Preheat oven to 375 degrees.**
2. **Use a vegetable peeler** to peel off and reserve the extreme outer orange surface of the orange. Get rid of the white pulp that clings to it. Cut the orange zest into fine shreds. Boil some water, drop zest into water and let simmer for 30 seconds. Drain and set aside.
3. **Take the remaining sections** of the orange and cut them into thin slices. Set aside.
4. **Truss the duck** with string and sprinkle it with salt and pepper.

Chop neck into 1- to 2-inch lengths and cut away the gizzard. Sprinkle salt and pepper on neck and gizzard. Place duck on its back in roasting pan. Put neck and gizzard next to it. Bake in oven for 30 minutes.

5. **Remove pan from oven and spoon off** accumulated fat. Set fat aside. Turn duck onto its side and return to oven for 30 minutes. Remove duck from pan again, spoon off fat and again set aside, put duck on its stomach (breast side down) and bake for 30 more minutes.

6. **Remove pan from oven.** Throw away trussing string. Transfer duck to another roasting pan and cook for 10 more minutes. Set original roasting pan aside and while duck is cooking, put first roasting pan on top of two burners, add chicken broth and stir, scraping in the brown duck pieces that are clinging to the pan. Bring to boil, then carefully strain sauce into a bowl and set aside.

7. **Blend the sugar and vinegar in a saucepan and cook** until large bubbles form on surface. Continue cooking until syrup thickens and caramelizes slightly. Add the strained sauce from the original roasting pan. Bring the sauce to a boil. Blend teaspoon of cornstarch and water into a small bowl, and then add to the sauce.

8. **Just before serving, add orange zest and Grand Marnier** to sauce. Add in orange sections. Cook, stirring gently, until sections are hot. Do not break orange sections or overcook. You don't want the orange sections mushy.

9. **Carve duck.** Pour a little sauce over each duck serving and serve the rest of the sauce separately.

▸ *C'est magnifique*!

15

SWEET SURVIVAL

Chocolate Mousse on a Silver Spoon

I GREW UP EATING CHOCOLATE MOUSSE with a silver teaspoon. I know this is sort of like saying, *I grew up spooning caviar into my mouth, darling, and when we ran out of that, we sipped Dom Perignon out of crystal champagne flutes and nibbled on truffles and skied in Gstaad and sailed around Virgin Gorda and one summer when I was too old for sleep-away camp, my parents sent me to live on a chicken farm in France because I already knew how to play tennis and they thought I would benefit from speaking fluent French and it was all so marvelous!* And it was. Except when it wasn't. Some of it was pretty dreadful, but some of it truly was marvelous, as in you could marvel at it. One of those marvels was my mother's chocolate mousse.

FEATURING

- CHOCOLATE SOUFFLÉ MOUSSE PIE

By the time I started paying attention to them, my parents had become glamorous people. During the day, my mother wore pearls and A-line dresses, silk scarves and Ferragamo pumps, and at night, she slipped into long, form-fitting silver lame and navy blue jersey dresses. She had a fabulous body and she knew it. Looks were very important to her and fortunately for her, she looked like Jackie O (if Jackie O were Jewish and lived in New Jersey). My father wore aviator sunglasses, carried a monogrammed leather brief case and had his suits custom made in Hong Kong. He wore tennis whites on the weekends, picked up groceries from Zabar's and, to me, looked like a movie star. They were a handsome couple with a shared goal: They wanted a more lush and exotic life than either of them had growing up in Brooklyn.

Both my parents were raised in two-family houses in quiet neighborhoods on tree-lined streets. Mom was from Midwood (her sister Bernadette was in the same high school class as Woody Allen). Dad grew up in Borough Park (blocks away from Alan Dershowitz and Sandy Kofax) and graduated from Stuyvesant. My mother's parents were schoolteachers and my father's father sold fur coats. Both their parents scrimped and saved to get what they wanted. Both my parents had mothers who knew what it was like to sacrifice and yearn. My mother's mother went to what was called "normal school" and trained to be a grade school teacher. Her father taught math at Stuyvesant for thirty years. Grandpa then became treasurer of the New York City teacher's union, eventually retired and began a long and successful career as a stockbroker on Wall Street. But for much of my mother's childhood, my grandparents lived modestly on schoolteachers' salaries, summering in the Catskills with their friends and playing bridge on each other's screened-in porches. My mother's maternal grandparents were divorced, and my great grandmother raised nine children alone until her two older sons left Brooklyn to live with her ex-husband in Michigan. My grandmother learned, from an early age, how to deal with poverty and the unpleasant truth of an absent father: When people asked her where her father was, she told them he was dead. Both my parents watched their mothers aspire to the finer things in life — food, travel, beautiful furniture, closets full of clothes, and household help. Once my parents arrived in New Jersey, they were able to satisfy all their cravings and one of those cravings was for chocolate mousse.

We moved to a posh New Jersey suburb when I was six, a town Philip Roth made famous in his novella *Goodbye, Columbus*. Most people who moved to Short Hills had money. That sounds crass but it's the truth. The schools were excellent, the downtown was safe, the commute to New York was easy, and you paid for all that ease and access. There were several fancy department stores (Bloomingdale's, B. Altman and Bonwit Teller) that would later be enclosed and turned into a fabled mall. There was a small regional theater company and a decent movie theater, some high-end women's clothing stores, a couple of upscale shoe stores, a few hair salons and bridal shops, and a handful of jewelry and furniture stores. If you lived in Short Hills, things were going well. Still, it wasn't perfect. For one thing, it was pretty much lily white. When we moved in, there were no African Americans, and only a few Indians and Asians. Also, the town was home to certain neighborhoods that did not allow Jews. We moved in anyway.

We settled in the newer part of town, which was informally known as the "Golden Ghetto." Here, the houses were new and made of brick, stucco and glass. Most had been built in the 1960s. The trees were small and low, and there were no sidewalks, but the roads were newly paved and there were always lots of kids riding their bikes. Most of the houses were split levels or modern-looking faux Frank Lloyd Wright structures with huge glass windows and elaborate rock gardens. Ours was unusual in that it was a traditional center hall colonial, red brick with black shutters. There was a maid's room off the garage, which made my grandmother ecstatic, thrilled that my mother could hire and house live-in help. We had a quarter-acre of woods in the back, which separated our house from the Berger's. Next door lived the Krishnas (he was also a doctor, like my father), and across the street were the Goldmans, the Steinbergs, the Baums and the Josephs. Most of the neighbors didn't seem to want to mix with us, except for Judy Baum who, like my mother, was a young, pretty woman with two kids and married to a doctor. While my mother had left her first husband while he was still in medical school, Dr. Baum had left his wife and kids for Judy, a nurse who worked in his office. Though the circumstances were different, both couples knew what it was like to leave one household and begin another.

One of the reasons the other families kept their distance was that my mother wore a mink coat over her tennis clothes to go grocery shopping. She had great legs and as much as she cooked, she never gained weight. The other mothers didn't seem to like that. Mrs. Baum had beautiful smooth skin and a tall, willowy frame. She was bosomy with long, slim legs and curly frosted blonde hair, but sometimes she drove around in her bathrobe and curlers in her hair, making her seem vulnerable and more likeable. My mother curled her hair with white, hot curlers in the privacy of her bathroom, rarely drove us to school in her bathrobe and never seemed vulnerable at all. Neither did my father; he drove a silver Cadillac, with bags of tennis rackets and cans of balls stashed in back. Driving home, with his sunglasses on and the sun in his eyes, he looked like he could conquer the suburban world.

Another thing that set us apart was that we had live-in help and no one else in the neighborhood did. Most of the other women on the street were traditional housewives who ran their homes on a tight budget. They had money in the bank but didn't spend it on expensive food or live-help. They made grilled cheese and hotdogs for dinner, had barbecues (without us) and periodically complained as I sat in the backs of their cars that my mother needed to drive the morning shift on rainy days, it just wasn't fair that she only picked up in the afternoon. I really had no idea what they were talking about. I just knew they didn't like my mother.

My parents bought their house in 1970. Before that, we had rented houses in other parts of New Jersey as my father jumped from job to job, bettering his prospects as he moved up the ladder in various radiology departments of local hospitals. This was their very first house, but my parents did not take out a mortgage. My grandfather was by then a successful stockbroker and gave my parents $100,000 to pay for the house. Two years later, my father, whose career was thriving and who did not want to be in any kind of debt to his father-in-law, financial or otherwise, paid Grandpa back in full.

You can say a lot of things about what my family was missing —sanity, sweetness, solicitude—but money wasn't one of them.

Every night, we ate with sterling silver in the dining room. My parents drank wine out of crystal glasses and my mother buzzed for the housekeeper to clear the table and bring in the next course. The silver was always polished and kept in the kitchen in a wide, neatly compartmentalized wooden drawer that was wired to the alarm system.

Peeking inside that drawer was like looking at pirate's treasure. The silver shone and there was so much of it! In addition to a range of silver serving pieces, my mother collected exquisite engraved and embossed antique spoons. Her main service was a beautiful French-looking pattern called International Silver Angelique Flatware. My parents had the starter set, which included service for 14. My grandmother had bought the service in 1959, for $350, and had it appraised in July 1960. The price of the sterling wasn't remarkable but the date of the appraisal was. The silver service had been purchased for my mother's first marriage to a man named Nathan, in 1959. Mom left Nathan some months after they married and married Dad in 1962. Her reasons were vague. In pictures, Nathan looks sweet and accommodating. My mother doesn't like sweet and accommodating. She likes charming and confident, even if the charm comes with a price. She had the marriage annulled and returned Nathan's engagement ring, but the silver service, by rights, belonged to my grandmother so my mother brought it along with her when she married my father.

The service was 79 pieces, consisting of teaspoons, hollow handled butter knives, meat knives, salad forks, dinner forks and five serving pieces. We also had ornate antique pieces from people we didn't know, which my mother had picked up at silver shops and antique stores. There were ornately carved scissors designed specifically for cutting grapes, heavy ladles for soup and gravy, a cold meat server, pickle forks, forks for fish and meat, tongs, cake knives, slotted spoons, deep, chased spoons meant for spooning out fruit, with pictures of berries melded into them. My grandmother had acquired her own set of silver during the Johnson Administration, Onslow hand-forged English silver, which she bought when my grandfather's business was taking off and she was finally able to retire from teaching. LBJ's initials are engraved on the back. Grandma's sterling was heavier and simpler than my mother's, and she had an even larger collection of beautiful pieces: In addition to groups of teaspoons, soup spoons, salad forks, shrimp forks, entree forks, butter knives and longer knives for cutting chicken and soft meat, Grandma had a set of long, skinny spoons for stirring iced tea, another bunch of smaller, sharp-edged spoons for cutting out grapefruit sections, a group of slender silver forks and matching filigreed knives with mother-of-pearl handles that were used to scoop out oysters, clams and lobster, and a set of glazed porcelain Sheffield silver knives that had pointy curved silver blades and were meant for a first fish course. She also had a Mexican sterling silver tea set and tray, which came with a coffee pot, covered sugar, creamer and "waste" bowl. She had dozens of white linen napkins, edged in gold trim, which she kept ironed and neatly stacked, and which she ultimately gave to my mother and me. Our china was white, trimmed in gold.

I loved using it all. Eating with antique silver every night was glamorous, elegant and civilized. I didn't know from Edith Wharton or Henry James, but I knew that sitting down to eat in the dining room, with a maid to summon and a homemade dessert to look forward to, meant that my parents were no longer in Brooklyn. And I took it all for granted because my parents sent my brother and me to private school and that's what all the other kids were doing too. Most of them had second homes and yachts to boot. When my husband and I met, I was a broke journalist living paycheck to paycheck, but he thought I was an heiress. Maybe not, but I did know the difference between silver and silver plate.

So in keeping with the rest of the things my family did—the vacations to St. Marten and Puerto Rico and Martha's Vineyard, the private school, the ski camps, the tennis camps, the summers in France, the tutors, the housekeepers, the insistence on good manners and writing thank you notes on heavy, monogrammed paper *immediately*—my mother mastered the art of French cooking and became an excellent and expert cook. She made the best food she could, as often as she could, and my father truly (and mostly) appreciated her efforts. Food was both an aphrodisiac and a sedative and my mother understood that. Plus, food brought people together. When my beautiful, charming mother and my handsome, funny father didn't go out for dinner on Saturday nights, they threw dinner parties for their friends. Mom would cook or have it catered; whatever was served was delicious. Even on weeknights, we ate well. Mom made duck, sautéed shrimp, grilled steak, and marinated fish. There was always homemade salad dressing, steamed asparagus or string beans, and fresh garlic bread, soft, buttery and warm, neatly tucked under a blanket in a warming basket. My mother cooked it all and the housekeeper cleaned up. For desserts, Mom baked coffee cake, cheesecake, apple pie, meringue cookies, brownies and chocolate chip cookies, and the most exquisite chocolate mousse.

For every birthday, holiday and return from camp, Mom made the most delicious and richest dessert imaginable, a chocolate soufflé mousse pie. It was like eating a bowl of rich, thick chocolate pudding that had been lovingly placed on top of warm chocolate cake. It dissolved slowly on your tongue. The chocolate was flavored with a hint of Grand Marnier and a spoonful of strong coffee and had so many nuances to it that every mouthful was dense and sweet, luxurious and complex, deeply satisfying and delightfully surprising. The mousse was surrounded by thin, sugary ladyfinger cakes and topped with dollops of thick, homemade whipped cream. You never knew when you'd be lucky enough to bite into a tiny shard of chocolate that hadn't totally melted.

First, Mom would make the chocolate soufflé. She'd let it fall and then fill it with mousse. Before she assembled the pie, she'd put the big, silver, mixing bowl of mousse into the refrigerator. She would disappear into the den to read the newspaper and as soon as I heard her sit down and crinkle the front page, I would sneak into the kitchen and dip finger after finger into that bowl of cold chocolate, luxuriating in the thrill of eating the creamy softness alone without being chastised or apprehended. Occasionally, my mother would open the fridge, look in the bowl and ask, "Who ate half the mousse?"

My mother made mousse on special occasions, and occasionally when we begged for it. Eating my mother's chocolate mousse is the single happiest memory of my childhood.

But once I graduated from high school, Mom stopped making mousse. My father moved out, my mother's slim, weight-conscious boyfriend moved in, and since I was away at college and my brother didn't think to make demands, the chocolate mousse pie went into hibernation for thirty years. I never thought to make it on my own.

But a few months ago, my brother asked my mother to come to his house and show his kids and mine how to make mousse. The grandchildren, five teenage boys, were eager to learn, so one grey Saturday afternoon in January, my mother assembled them in my brother's kitchen and showed them what to do. My children returned home, happy and excited; they said the mousse was delicious and brought me a sample. I'm eating it as I write this: Creamy, rich, complicated, intense, smooth, deliciously addictive — all my happy memories of childhood come rushing back. Why had I never made this? My children demanded that I recreate it so I asked my mother for the recipe.

Mon dieu. She handed me two copies, both typed with the font I remembered from our old electronic typewriter. The recipe wasn't hard but it wasn't easy either. Two weeks later, I set about making it.

I made mistakes. For one thing, I ended up making an enormous amount of mousse. When I poured it into the pie pan, it reached the top and then tumbled over the sides of the pie plate, making for a beautiful and delicious mess in the oven. I took a spoon and ladled the mousse off the oven floor into my mouth.

I took that chocolate soufflé out of the oven and it began dripping everywhere—the counter, the stool beneath the counter, the floor. I put it down and started scooping up chocolate with my index finger. It was a bonanza. All this spilled chocolate mousse, just for me!

"Your mother would have been shitting a brick by now," said my older son, walking in just in time to see me scramble to eat–I mean clean up–the chocolate dripping off the pie plate. It was true: The chocolate mousse wasn't pretty and Mom would have wanted pretty.

Once out of the oven for while, the souffle still hadn't fallen. Maybe I hadn't waited long enough. If I had let it fall, it wouldn't have overflowed like it did. But even after an hour, it was still high and cakelike. It was supposed to sink into the pan so I could pour more mousse into it and then decorate it with whipped cream. Eventually, I grew impatient and poured the mousse in anyway, hoping the weight of it would flatten the soufflé. It did, until it didn't, and then the mousse, and the soufflé, started to spill over the pie pan all over again.

The cake was a disaster. A beautiful, delicious disaster.

And yet, it generated multiple pleasures too. First, there was the initial pleasure of separating warm eggs with your hands. You have to bring a dozen eggs to room temperature and if you remember to do this, you feel like a genius. When I started separating the eggs, pouring yolk from hand to hand, pulling the white away from it, the way I had seen my teachers in cooking class do it, I remembered the precise and more hygienic way my mother had taught me: Tap the middle of the egg with a long knife, then split the eggshell into two even pieces. Carefully, shift the yolk and the white back and forth, until the yolk separates from the white and you can let the white slide into a bowl. Do not let any yolk get into the white. If it does, take it out immediately with the tip of a small teaspoon. Most important: Keep the whites and the yolks in separate bowls, and separate every egg first into two small bowls. The process calls for four bowls: Two bowls to separate each egg, one bowl to pour egg whites into and one bowl to pour the yolks in. You never separate a new egg directly into the big bowl of already separated whites. This is too dangerous. You could inadvertently get a little yolk in there and that would ruin the whole bowl of whites. My mother was very insistent about this. She was right. The yolks weigh down the whites and these egg whites have to be light as air.

This chocolate mousse is powerful as a drug. It hits your bloodstream all at once and then, bam, you have to eat more! A little goes a long way, but a lot is so electrifying, why stop at a little? You hide it from yourself, you try to stay away, but the moment always comes where you *need* it. You can't stop eating it, and I didn't.

By the time I was done, there was mousse everywhere – in the oven, on the stovetop, on the counters, in the fridge, in the freezer, all over my face. I used my finger to get it off the countertops, then I just started licking it off everything directly, slurping the fallen chocolate mousse right into my mouth. I—I mean *it*— was a mess. Still, it was heaven.

Five days after I made the chocolate mousse, my mother came over. "I made chocolate mousse," I said. "Want to try some?"

"Sure," my mother said, sitting down on a stool. "Did you use that coffee liquor?"

"Yep," I said. I spooned out some chocolate mousse and apologized. "I made it five days ago and it's been in the freezer."

My mother waved me away. "Doesn't matter," she said. "Chocolate mousse is a survivor."

As she was. And is. As we all hope to be.

CHOCOLATE SOUFFLÉ MOUSSE PIE

(Serves 8-10)

INGREDIENTS:

- 12 ounces semisweet chocolate
- 1½ tablespoons instant coffee *(or more to taste)*
- ½ cup hot water
- 12 eggs separated
- ⅔ cup sugar
- 2 teaspoons vanilla
- ⅛ teaspoon salt

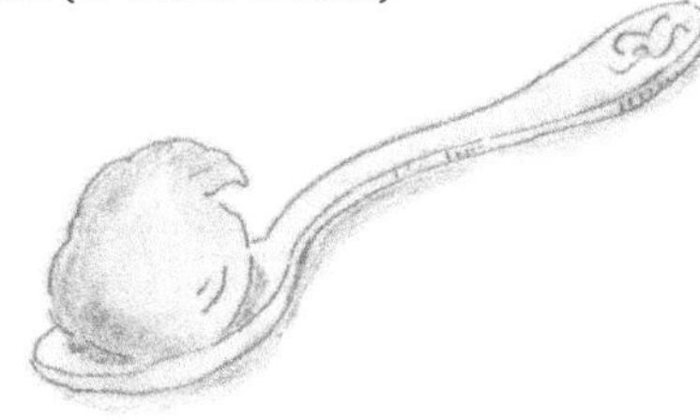

- Bread, cookie or cracker crumbs (optional)
- 2 cups heavy cream
- 1 tablespoon sugar
- 1 envelope plain gelatin
- 1 tablespoon coffee liqueur (or more, to taste)

▸ *Note: This recipe should be made in at least a 10-inch pie pan.*

PREPARATION:

1. **Preheat oven to 350 degrees.**
2. **Place chocolate in top of a double boiler** over hot, not boiling, water. Dissolve the instant coffee in the hot water and add to the chocolate. Cover and let stand over low heat. Stir occasionally. When the chocolate is almost melted, remove from heat and stir until smooth.
3. **Meanwhile, beat the yolks until thick.** Gradually beat in the sugar until the mixture is thick and lemon colored. Gradually beat chocolate into the yolk mixture. Add the vanilla.
4. **Beat the egg whites and salt until stiff.** Stir one quarter of the whites into the chocolate mixture. Fold in the remaining whites until blended.
5. **Dust a well-buttered 10-inch pie plate** with crumbs (or leave crumbs out). Fill plate with part of mousse mixture so that it just comes level with the edge. Bake for 15 minutes. Remove and cool. Refrigerate remainder of mousse.
6. **Dissolve gelatin in a very little bit of water** and heat gently until clear. Cool.
7. **Beat heavy cream until stiff**, adding gelatin at the point where it has just thickened. Refrigerate until ready to use.
8. **When mousse has cooled** and sunk, fold about half of whipped cream into remaining mousse and fill the sunken "shell" with it.
9. **To the rest of whipped cream**, add sugar and liqueur, and decorate with a flourish! Refrigerate for 2 hours.

▸ *This freezes beautifully, completely assembled.*

16

The Land of the Free

What Happens at the Spa, Stays at the Spa (Except for the Cookies)

FEATURING

- Gluten-Free Chocolate Chip Cookies

IT WAS A COLD SUNDAY evening in winter. February, to boot. But I had nothing to complain about because I had just spent a weekend sleeping, eating, watching the first season of "Girls," and reading Ann Patchett's *Truth and Beauty* and *This Is the Story of a Happy Marriage*. I had gone away with a group of women, two of whom are like sisters to me. The trip was a gift from my mother. This has become her annual birthday present. She does not insist that we travel together; because I moved back to my hometown, we already see enough of each other and we both know that being alone together would not be relaxing for either one of us. But seeing each other in small doses works fairly well.

While I slept late and missed their bracing early morning walks in the snow, my women friends did not pass judgment on me. The spa we went to is in the Berkshires, a few blocks from the all-girls sleep-away camp I spent five summers at and two hours from the women's college I attended. Women need women, and after more than twenty years of being married to a man with two brothers, raising two boys of my own and being an aunt to five nephews, I love these female-only interludes. They remind me of those lovely lines from Virginia Woolf's *Orlando*: "...many were the fine tales they told and many the amusing observations they made for it cannot be denied that when women get together...they are always careful to see that the doors are shut and that not a word of it gets into print." None of what we talked about will make it into print here but rest assured the conversations spanned from Chris Christie to sex toys to the perils of peri-menopause.

You would think that going away for a long weekend with your girlfriends would ensure you returned home relaxed and happy to see your teenagers. And I was, initially. I was glad to see all of my family, even though the sink was full of dirty dishes and nobody had bothered to take the garbage out.

I gave my boys kisses and T-shirts and two bags of gluten-free chocolate chip cookies that the spa sold in their cafe. While I was at the spa, I had consulted a woman who specialized in Oriental medicine. She said that one way to get rid of the chronic sinus infections I was getting was to avoid dairy and sugar. I had already given up gluten and there was no way I could sacrifice sugar, but eliminating dairy was a possibility. Since I risked becoming one of those insufferable people who talks about their food aversions, I decided not to mention it. Much.

A few minutes after I came home, my mother came to visit. Mom is also gluten-free and I offered her a bag of cookies, as a way of saying, "Thank you for returning my sanity to me." But Mom didn't want any cookies. She pointed to the waist of her jeans. "I could barely button these this morning," she said. "No thanks."

I should add that the pants my mother was wearing were a pair of Lee Jeans that I had given her – jeans I had worn in high school and outgrown during the early part of the Reagan administration. Now, she was growing out of them too. Do I need to talk about the fact that my mother and grandmother were obsessed with their weight and, ultimately, became preoccupied with mine? That my mother used to say, "When you're thin, you can wear anything" and I believed it? Do I need to talk about the fact that this is one of the reasons I need my women's weekends in the first place? I think not.

While I unpacked my bag and loaded the dishwasher, Mom sat down and chatted with my older son, who was happy to dip into the cookies. The next morning, they would return to school, I would return to teaching and writing, and the schedules that kept us sane, productive and living in close proximity to (but not on top of) each other would resume. But within two hours of my returning home, the phone rang. It was the assistant headmaster of my sons' school, announcing in a recorded message that school would be closed the next day in honor of the snow.

What the hell? It wasn't even snowing! All of my hard-won spa bliss blew away. I teach out of my house on Mondays. Where would the teenagers go when my students arrived? But more to the point, how would I get any work done, before and after class, with those large, loud, hungry young men, stomping around the house, demanding to be fed?

Despite my misgivings, our snow day commenced. With the snow coming down in heavy clumps, the Internet went down. My 13-year-old figured out how to use the hot spot on my iPhone to give us all Internet access on our computers. This was ingenious of him, but it meant we all had to work within a few feet of each other. I love my sons. They are delightful, sassy, and occasionally obedient, but that doesn't mean I want to share a hot spot with them. Tensions ran high. Cookies were eaten. By 5 p.m., both bags of spa cookies were gone.

Fortunately, the spa is generous with its recipes and I had taken the one for gluten-free chocolate chip cookies home with me. In less than half an hour, they were done. I did not make dinner that night. But I made 40 cookies.

I am betting that you, like me, do not keep three different kinds of gluten-free flour in the house. But maybe you have one kind? I used King Arthur's gluten-free flour and the cookies were heavenly — chewy, chocolate-y, and sweet. If you have all three that Canyon Ranch recommends, go ahead and use them.

These cookies are not even all that bad for you. They're gluten free, dairy-free and kind of, sort of fat-free. And if you make them yourself, you're free to polish off as many as you want.

GLUTEN-FREE CHOCOLATE CHIP COOKIES

(Yield: 40 cookies)

INGREDIENTS:

- ¼ cup canola oil
- 1 cup firmly packed brown sugar
- 2 large eggs
- 1 teaspoon pure vanilla extract
- 1½ cups sorghum flour
- ½ cup tapioca flour
- ½ cup Arrowroot flour
- ½ teaspoon sea salt
- 1 teaspoon baking soda
- 1 package semi-sweet chocolate chips, about 6 ounces

PREPARATION:

1. **Preheat oven** to 350 degrees.
2. **Lightly coat a baking sheet** with canola oil spray.
3. **With an electric mixer on high speed,** combine canola oil and brown sugar. Turn mixer to low and add eggs and vanilla and mix until just combined.
4. **In a medium bowl, combine** sorghum, tapioca and Arrowroot flours together. Stir salt, baking soda and chocolate chips into flour mixture. Add the dry ingredients mixture to the wet mixture and combine on low speed or by hand.
5. **Drop rounded heaping teaspoons** *(or use a ¾ ounce scoop)* onto baking sheet about 1½ inches apart. Bake for 10 minutes or until golden. Cool on baking sheet until cookies are set. Transfer to cooling rack until completely cooled. Store in a tightly sealed container.

17

Fried Pickles: A Love Story

Living It Up at the Beach

FEATURING

- Fried Pickles and Buttermilk Dressing

MY HUSBAND AND I recently spent one summer weekend in LBI, aka Long Beach Island, aka the Jersey shore. I wasn't always a Jersey Shore girl. One year at the end of the eighties, I summered in East Hampton. I was broke and had recently had my heart broken by a guy who did very well in finance. He had made a fortune at a young age and had given me a thick gold bangle bracelet and taken me to St. Bart's six weeks after we met. Oh, those lush French Caribbean resorts! We ate and smiled and loved at a beautiful hotel that I could never have afforded on the $19,000 a year I was making answering phones and working as an editorial assistant at *Business Week*. But this man loved me, or I thought he did, and it was all very *la di da*. Was I caught up in the rush of an intense physical attraction? Yes. Did I feel like a whore? Maybe a little. In truth, I felt like Holly Golightly with a byline.

Alas, I wasn't what or who he was looking for, so he dumped me a few months later while we were on a bike trip in France and I went back to my humble life as a journalist. I made next to nothing and what I did make, I spent on rent, dry cleaning, haircuts, aerobics classes and David's chocolate chip cookies. But I pined for the good life. So when a friend from high school found a share in a house in East Hampton with a big group of twentysomethings, I signed on, even though I didn't quite have the $1,200 to pay for it.

Neither my friend nor I had a car but my old boyfriend from St. Bart's had bought me a bike and my friend still had hers from college, so that's how we got around East Hampton. We would take step class with a guy named "Phys Ed," go to the Barefoot Contessa for croissants and iced coffee, bike along Lily Pond Lane, then make our way to Georgica Beach. My friend was also nursing a bruised heart at the time, and we were both secretly hoping our old boyfriends would show up at the beach to see us. They never did.

A couple of years later, I met my husband, my friend met her husband and eventually, we all moved back to our hometown. My husband had had a share in Fire Island, but once we settled in New Jersey, we came to our senses: commuting to New York to go to the beach was insane. So we switched to Long Beach Island.

This is not the Jersey Shore that spawned Snookie. LBI is a long, skinny, barrier island along the Jersey coast. It's 18 miles long and at the northern end, where we stay, there's almost nothing to do. Even though it's only 25 miles from Atlantic City, our end of the island has no gambling and not a single movie theater. It's even hard to find a bar. You end up telling yourself that all you really need for a good time are miniature golf, big waves, a walk on the beach after low tide, a strong wind for sailing, a light wind for paddle boarding and ice cream. (And if you don't believe yourself the first time you just tell yourself again and again until you do.)

LBI reminds me of the Midwood section of Brooklyn, where my grandparents lived for sixty-five years. The buildings are low and there are tons of kids riding around on bikes without helmets. The deli in the town of Harvey Cedars offers goodies like "nooners" (burgers) and there are lots of people of various generations, sitting around on their porches, eating lunch and talking about what they're going to grill for dinner. Parents jam their chairs, umbrellas, pails and boogie boards into grocery carts and walk their kids across the boulevard to the beach. There's no shortage of sweaty bodies on the beaches in LBI. And most of those bodies look pretty good.

The island has its charms. There's one spot in Harvey Cedars where the island is only a fifth of a mile wide and you can see the bay and the ocean simultaneously. The sunsets make the sky glow orange. There are several excellent restaurants, and the best one, Black Eyed Susan's, only takes cash. LBI is nothing fancy and somehow, despite my earlier infatuation with the lush life of the Hamptons, I've come to love it.

My husband and I spent our beach weekend eating, sailing, running and paddle boarding. Paddle boarding on a summer day is a beautiful thing. You stand on a surfboard, suck in your stomach, lower your sunglasses and use a long paddle to get yourself around. After an hour, your foot is asleep and your arms are sore. You move so slowly that people in motorboats offer to tow you in. Don't let that dissuade you; paddle boarding is delightful. There's something meditative – almost Biblical – about the experience. You're standing still, but you feel like you're walking on water.

On our way home, we stopped at a restaurant in Manahawkin called Mud City Crab House. You just know that a restaurant with a name like that is going to mess you up. One look at the menu sealed my fate. Crab claws with mustard sauce and fried pickles with Thousand Island dressing on the side. I love fried pickles. There's nothing worse for your breath or your digestive system and six hours later, you're still feeling them but they are the most delicious fried food I've ever had. Our waitress brought over six fried pickles, the vat of dressing and a small plate of crab claws. I felt sorry for the claws. They had nothing on the pickles.

A quick Wikipedia search reveals that an Arkansas man named Bernell "Fatman" Austin first invented fried pickles in 1963.

Enough said.

My husband had ordered a jerk chicken sandwich and looked at my lunch with some combination of intrigue and disgust.

"Do you want a pickle?" I asked him.

"No," he said, "I don't like pickles."

"They're good," I said out loud, but inside, I thought, *more for me.*

Oh, that initial taste of salty, crunchy pickle dipped in

buttermilk and flour and fried in oil! Some wonderful chemical shoots up into your brain and makes you feel alive like nothing else. Sort of like being in love.

When I was down to only two pickles, my husband picked one up to taste. After a bite or two he put the remaining half on his plate. Was he going to finish it? No, he was not. So I grabbed it back.

Once we got home, my husband went to the gym and I went for a run, during which I became acutely aware that I had just eaten about 3,000 calories worth of fried pickles. When I got back, I saw that our peaches, nectarines and plums had ripened nicely while we were away. I started slicing them up and making a platter for us to nibble on while we figured out what we wanted to eat for dinner. But who was I kidding? A day that starts with fried pickles has nowhere to go but chocolate.

I went to my secret stash in the freezer, the place where I keep chocolate covered espresso beans ("Mommy's Little Helpers") and two chocolate hockey pucks left over from my older son's bar mitzvah. It would be a *shanda* to eat those pucks and I didn't really feel like going on a caffeine binge at dinnertime. I poured myself a glass of wine, and started rummaging around, looking for something I might have forgotten about. There it was, a bag of white-chocolate covered Oreos from Godiva. I had bought them back in June, when I was trying to educate my older son about the pleasures of Oreos dipped in chocolate. There were three left. I ate them all in the time it took me to write this paragraph. Maybe less.

My husband came downstairs and wanted to know what we were doing for dinner. I had chocolate all over my face; I really didn't care. When you've been in a relationship a long time, you know what to do—and not to do–in order to avoid a fight. My old St. Bart's boyfriend and I were too much alike: Thin-skinned, first-born children who always had to be right. Plus, he always wanted me to be just a little thinner than I was. My husband comes from a family of restrained, disciplined German engineers and scientists. We're very different and I think that's what makes it work. So when my body demands fried pickles and chocolate covered Oreos and he wants no part of it, I just pour him a big glass of wine, and promise there will always be room for dessert.

FRIED PICKLES WITH BUTTERMILK DRESSING

(Serves 6-8 regular people. Or if you're like me, 1)

INGREDIENTS:

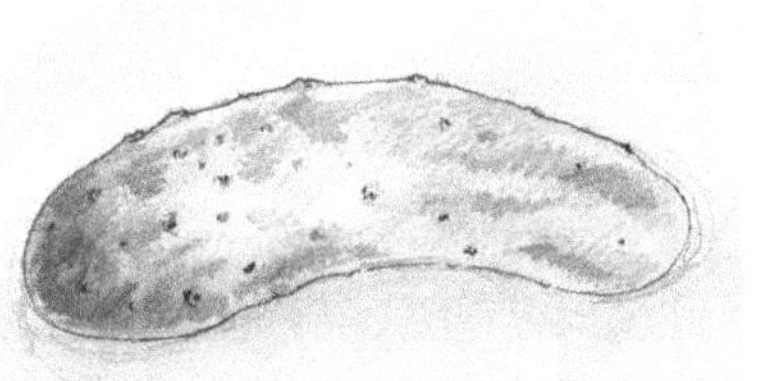

- ½ cup buttermilk
- Salt and black pepper to taste
- 1 *(16 ounce)* jar dill pickle slices
- ½ cup all-purpose flour
- 1½ cups fine cornmeal
- 1 teaspoon seafood seasoning
- ¼ teaspoon Cajun seasoning
- 1 quart oil for frying

Dressing:

- ½ teaspoon Cajun seasoning
- 1 *(12-ounce)* jar buttermilk ranch dressing

PREPARATION:

1. **Cover a plate with parchment paper** or wax paper. In a shallow dish, combine buttermilk, salt, and pepper. Place pickles in mixture and set aside.
2. **Pour the flour, cornmeal, seafood seasoning,** and ¼ teaspoon Cajun seasoning into a large, re-sealable plastic bag; shake to mix well. Add pickles, a few at a time, and tumble gently to coat evenly with the flour mixture. Remove and place on prepared plate.
3. **Heat oil to 365 degrees** in deep fryer or heavy deep skillet.
4. **Fry pickles in several batches** until golden brown and slightly crisp on the outside with a moist interior, 1-2 minutes. Drain on paper towels.
5. **In a small bowl, combine** buttermilk ranch dressing with ½ teaspoon Cajun seasoning; blend. Serve as a dipping sauce for warm pickles.

18

Bake, Broil, Grill

A Visit to Ann Patchett's Bookstore

NOT SO LONG AGO, I went to Nashville for the bar mitzvah of the youngest child of my oldest friend. Betsy and I have known each other since fourth grade. Neither of us had a sister, so we stuck to each other like glue. She was my first friend to get married, my first friend to have a baby and my first friend to lose a parent. At her wedding, I was broke, newly single and bitterly resenting the fact that I had to buy a fancy peach organza dress with white tulle netting and a sheer white gauze shawl so that I could be one of her bridesmaids. I envied her diamond solitaire and the easy life she seemed set to embark upon. She didn't complain at all when I asked her to buy a navy blue dress to be one of my bridesmaids five years later. At my wedding, Betsy's beautiful toddler daughter wore a pale pink dress, her bright blonde hair flying as she ran around the table. Betsy was beaming. I looked at them both and felt joy.

FEATURING
- Chess Pie
- Red Velvet Cake

Betsy was also my first friend to get divorced. When she called to tell me the news, I was in my kitchen, making dinner. It was late in the day, early summer. "Are you sitting down?" she said. I have no idea what I was cooking but I remember I didn't want my kids to hear the conversation so I took my apron off and walked outside to sit in a chair on the driveway.

Several years late, a bunch of us flew down for Betsy's son's blessed event. Before we arrived, she emailed us and said that the author Ann Patchett was opening a new bookstore in Nashville the day of the bar mitzvah. Did we want to go?

We sure did. I hadn't yet read Patchett's essay collection, *This Is the Story of a Happy Marriage*, or her memoir about her long friendship with the writer Lucy Grealy, *Truth & Beauty: A Friendship*, but I had read her novel *Bel Canto*. I knew Patchett's parents were divorced and knew she wrote incisively about how much work goes into the process of locating and nourishing every kind of love, and how hard and crucial it is to sustain the bonds of friendship and romance. In between the Kiddush luncheon and the Saturday night party, we drove to the bookstore where Betsy introduced us to her gentleman caller, who was originally from out West. They sure don't make men like this in the Northeast. This man grew up on a farm, flew his own plane, hunted squirrels and spent hours cooking up meals without glancing at a cookbook. He also made his own vanilla extract (split open three vanilla beans, drop into a glass cup of vodka and let marinate for two months). When my friend's mother visited from out of town, he brought over five live chickens and killed a couple for dinner. Did I mention he was tall and good-looking? By the end of our conversation, I was in a state of enchanted shock.

It was late afternoon when we got to the bookstore and Patchett had gone home, so after being thoroughly charmed by Betsy's new love, we just wandered around. *The New York Times* reported that Patchett sunk $300,000 into this store, and it is now Nashville's only independent bookstore so even without her there, the place was hopping. The store is small and part of a shopping center; the book selection was limited. Most of Patchett's books had sold out so I picked up Alisa Huntsman's *Desserts From the Loveless Cafe: Simple Southern Pies, Puddings, Cakes and Cobblers from Nashville's Landmark Restaurant.*

This was a book that was begging to be judged by its cover. The front photo was of a sinfully delicious looking Red Velvet Cake, cream cheese frosting slathered all over it. Red Velvet Cake is one of my favorites, but I'd never made it because I could never find red food coloring in the supermarket. (I eventually discovered it next to the imitation rum and peppermint extract.) Standing in that bookstore in Nashville, it suddenly seemed crucial that I rush home to New Jersey and make this cake.

Reading Huntsman's book will make you happy. By the time you're done reading it, you'll be saying, "Bring on the buttermilk and cornmeal." Many of the recipes call for ingredients you don't normally bake with: Chocolate Mashed Potato Cake is made from leftover mashed potatoes. The Tipsy Cake uses bourbon. The Guess Again Tomato Cake with Pecans and Raisins uses tomato soup, and many recipes call for cider vinegar.

The Chess Pie looked intriguing because it seemed so simple. It's made from basic ingredients — cornmeal and cider vinegar among them — and has nothing to do with the Game of Kings. I asked Betsy if she'd ever had Chess Pie. "Of course," she said. "It's just sugar and butter." That sentence alone was enough to make me want to bake it. It took about 10 minutes to make the pie dough, and five minutes to make the filling. The filling is made of sugar, butter, eggs, heavy cream, cider vinegar, vanilla and corn meal. You don't have to cut, slice, peel, mash, grate or sift anything — you just dump it all into the food processor.

The Red Velvet Cake was more of an effort but easy enough and the frosting is so dang good, it's outrageous. You will be bouncing off the walls as you eat it. The day I made the Red Velvet Cake, my younger son was off from school. While I mixed ingredients, he watched TV. At one point, he asked if we could do something together, maybe have a catch? "Okay," I said. "Soon." Once the cake layers came out of the oven, I showed him how to frost the cake and insert frosting between the layers.

My time in the kitchen with my sons is full of conversation. My boys are teenagers now, young men on the brink of forging their own lives. Sometimes they ask me about old boyfriends. They can't believe that when I was 23, shortly after Betsy got married, I met a man who took me on a blissful long weekend sunning in St. Bart's, a bitter long week biking in Burgundy and when we were done with all that, he broke up with me at my birthday party. They can't believe I then spent a couple of years dating a man who lived in Georgia or that one of my old boyfriends went to Harvard Medical School and became a psychiatrist and three others were electrical engineers.

"Who broke up with who?" they ask about my past relationships.

"Me. Him. It was mutual."

Then they ask me why and I tell them.

Because he was mean. Because he thought I was ordinary. Because I thought he was lazy. Because he wanted me to be thinner. Because I didn't want to leave New York. Because he didn't want to leave the South. Because I didn't like the way he kissed. Because he told me I looked better with my clothes on. Because he became religious. Because his father didn't think I knew enough about my own father's business. Because he liked another woman better. Because I wasn't sure he actually liked women at all. Because his father once threatened to feel me up. Because my grandfather said I had a tiger by the tail. Because in the end, we really didn't like each other all that much. Because Daddy was kinder.

These are the kinds of conversations we have while we are baking a cake.

Some of my friends have discovered their husbands had girlfriends. One discovered her husband had had a child without telling her. One realized her husband was dating a woman she knew and one cold Saturday night, that woman walked across to the train tracks and lay down in front of the train. We are tempted. We behave badly. We make poor decisions when we're tired or fed up, and especially when we think we're in love.

My sons can't believe I wanted to become a psychiatrist so I could be in med school with my boyfriend or that I thought of moving down to Atlanta because I didn't know any better. They can't believe that two of my old boyfriends married women I knew. Of course, we look back and think, *Good thing that one got away*. But that's only in retrospect. What I want to say to my sons is, *Now is the time, boys. Observe how your father treats me. Be good to the person you live with and love. Be respectful in front of your children. Wake up and say, "I love you." Go to bed and whisper, "I love you." Don't make the person you love cry. Stay put as long as it's 90% good. Do not start a second family without consulting your first one. Don't fight when you're tired. Take the long view. Bake, broil, grill.*

How much time do teenage boys spend thinking about what it will take to make their long-term relationships work? My friend Betsy says none. I spent a lot of time watching my parents make mistakes and then made my own anyway. As I stand with my kids in the kitchen, whipping up frosting, showing them how to peel shrimp and flip flank steak, screaming at them to clear the table and take the garbage out, I hope I am planting the seeds of good habits and honorable intentions. But you never really know until they start making their own love sandwiches.

My friend in Nashville ultimately broke up with Mr. Enchantment and became a filmmaker. She flew out to LA to try and sell her screenplay about a divorced woman who falls in love again and learns to fire a gun. Here's hoping that in some alternate universe somewhere, frosting a layer cake also counts as a life skill.

RED VELVET CAKE

(Serves 8-10)

INGREDIENTS:

- 2½ cups cake flour
- ⅓ cup unsweetened cocoa powder, not Dutch process*
- 1 teaspoon baking soda
- 2 tablespoons liquid red food color
- 1 cup buttermilk
- 2½ sticks *(10 ounces)* unsalted butter, softened
- 2 cups packed dark brown sugar

1 teaspoon vanilla extract

1/2 teaspoon salt

2 whole eggs plus 2 egg yolks

1 tablespoon distilled white or cider vinegar

Cream Cheese Frosting *(see recipe below)*

**Dutch process cocoa powder has been washed in a potassium solution and has had its acidity neutralized. You do not want Dutch processed cocoa powder here.*

PREPARATION:

1. **Preheat oven to 350 degrees**. Grease two 9-inch cake pans. Line bottoms with parchment paper and grease the paper.
2. **Sift flour, cocoa, and baking soda into a bowl** and whisk briefly to combine; set aside. Stir red food coloring into buttermilk and set aside.
3. **In large mixing bowl, cream butter** with brown sugar, vanilla, and salt on medium-low speed until light and fluffy, 3-5 minutes. Add eggs and egg yolks slowly, beating and scraping bowl to ensure they are completely incorporated. On low speed, add dry ingredients alternately with the colored buttermilk. To prevent streaking in cake, scrape sides of bowl as you mix batter. Finally, stir in vinegar by hand. Divide batter between cake pans.
4. **Bake for 35-40 minutes.** Let layers cool in pans for 10 minutes. Then turn them out on wire rack, peel off paper and let cool completely. Make frosting. To decorate cake, place one layer bottom side upon cake plate. Spread 3/4 cup of cream cheese frosting over cake right up to edges. Add second layer *(top side up)* and use remaining frosting to decorate sides and top by gently swirling it over cake.

CREAM CHEESE FROSTING

INGREDIENTS:

- 8 ounces cream cheese *(Don't use reduced fat or nonfat cream cheese, the consistency won't be the same.)*
- 1 stick unsalted butter
- 4 cups confectioners sugar
- 2 teaspoons vanilla extract

PREPARATION:

1. **Place cream cheese and butter** in mixing bowl and beat with electric mixer on medium speed until completely blended.
2. **Sift the confectioners sugar** into the mixture in several additions, beating thoroughly in between.
3. **Add vanilla and beat** until frosting is light and fluffy but still holds its shape, 3-5 minutes. Use immediately.

NOTE: *suggestion from Pam Riesenberg, who teaches cooking classes in Millburn, NJ: A good all-natural substitute for red food coloring is red beet powder. It is available online at Amazon, and at www.spicebarn.com.*

CHESS PIE

(Serves 6-8)

INGREDIENTS:

- 9-inch pie shell, partially baked *(recipe below)*
- 1⅓ cups sugar
- 1 stick *(4 ounces)* unsalted butter, softened
- 2½ tablespoons white cornmeal
- 1 teaspoon vanilla extract
- 4 eggs
- ½ cup heavy cream
- 2 tablespoons cider vinegar or distilled white vinegar

PREPARATION:

1. **Preheat oven to 350 degrees.** Place pie shell on sturdy baking sheet and set aside.
2. **Place sugar, butter, cornmeal and vanilla** in food processor. Run machine long enough to blend ingredients completely. Scrape down sides of bowl and while machine is on, add eggs, one at a time. Scrape bowl again and with machine running, add cream through feed tube in steady stream, then add vinegar.
3. **Scrape bowl** one last time before processing to blend well. Pour filling into pie shell.

4. **Bake until filling** has set and golden brown across the top, about 35 minutes. Let cool completely before cutting and serving.

FLAKY PIE DOUGH FOR PARTIALLY BAKED PIE SHELL

INGREDIENTS:

- ⅓ cup cold water
- 1½ teaspoons distilled white vinegar
- 2⅔ cups unbleached, all purpose flour
- 1¼ teaspoons salt
- 2 sticks *(8 ounces)* cold, unsalted butter, cut into cubes

PREPARATION:

1. **Preheat oven to 325 degrees**.
2. **Combine water and vinegar** in a cup and refrigerate while you begin dough. Place flour and salt in a mixing bowl and stir. Add butter and mix. Add in cold water and vinegar mixture and mix. Dough will form into a ball. For a double crust pan, pat one third of dough into a 4-inch ball for top crust and the remaining dough into a larger ball for bottom crust. Wrap in plastic wrap and refrigerate for at least 30 minutes before using.
3. **When ready to make pie:** Roll out one ball of dough on a lightly floured surface with a rolling pin into a round 1/16 to 1/8 inch thick. Carefully fold into quarters or wrap over rolling pin, lift and transfer to a 9-inch pie plate. Trim edges to leave an overhang of about 1/2 inch. Fold under and crimp. Refrigerate pie shell until ready to put filling in.
4. **Place pie shell** on a sturdy baking sheet to make it easier to maneuver. Line pie shell with wax paper and fill with 3 cups *(about one package)* of dried beans or pie weights. *(Make sure to dump beans out of plastic bag!)* Bake for 18-20 minutes. Remove wax paper and let shell cool before putting in filling. You can reuse these beans!

19

Existential Tuna

Dinner Courtesy of Camus and Le Bernardin

FEATURING
- Tuna Steak with Soy-Ginger and Romaine

SOMETHING IN OUR HOUSE was aggravating my sinuses. And although it was the dry-air dead of winter, I was pretty sure my husband's home office was the culprit.

The office had once been a pleasant place to work. It wasn't big; someone less charitable might call it a walk-in closet with a large window. But we tried to make it work, hiring a carpenter to make built-in bookshelves, drawers and a desk. We put up new wallpaper and my husband settled in.

Even on his best day, my husband doesn't file. Papers piled up; bank statements sat on prospectuses; the room became stuffy; the floor and counters disappeared. My husband relocated to the desk in our bedroom and the "office" became a storage room filled with dust. I announced that it was this dust that was making me sick. I had no idea if that was true, but it seemed like it could be. My husband agreed to clean the room out and he filled five garbage bags.

In the middle of the purge, he came downstairs, something waving in his hand. "Hey, look what I found!" he said. "Can you make this?" It was a greeting card from Le Bernardin, a fancy New York restaurant.

I had only been to Le Bernardin once, and it was not with my husband. An old boyfriend had taken me in the late eighties, soon after it opened. It was a summer night and we went there for his birthday. After sipping a cold glass of chardonnay, we were given a glazed ceramic ramekin, the kind that might be filled with *crème brûlée*. It was filled with teeny, tiny nails that would allow us to gently whittle out the miniscule portion of meat buried within the teeny, tiny snails the waiter had also placed on the table. You had to be very careful not to prick your tongue with the nail or bite down on your tongue as it was searching for the snail meat. It was all very sophisticated and virtually impossible to pull off, sort of like our relationship. Now twenty some-odd years later, it was clear my husband had paid the restaurant a visit without me, probably with clients. *Hopefully* with clients.

The card had a cheerful, life-is-good vibe. On the front was a picture of a handsome, middle-aged man, his gray hair closely cropped. He wore dark sunglasses and an expensive-looking watch. The sun was shining down upon him and his expression was gleeful as he lifted up the grill and peered inside. The look on his face said, "I've never even heard of a government bailout!" Inside, the card said, "Wishing You a Hot Summer!" Next to that was a recipe for Slate-Grilled Tuna Steak with Soy Ginger Vinaigrette and Romaine.

I flipped the card over to see when it had been printed; it had to be way before the stock market crashed in 2008. A quick call to Le Bernardin confirmed that in fact the card was quite old, sent out in 2002. The picture was of chef and co-owner Eric Ripert, taken from his cookbook, *A Return to Cooking*.

Let's not even discuss the fact that my husband had mail sitting in his office for more than a decade. Back to his question: Could I make this recipe? (And could I look as cool and tan as Eric Ripert while doing it?) Into my head popped a quote from Camus's *L'Etranger (The Stranger*), which, roughly translated, goes "In the midst of winter, I found within me an invincible summer." I had read *L'Etranger* in French in high school. It was the same year I read Sartre's *Huis Clos* (*No Exit*) and had recited that famous poisonous line *L'enfer, c'est les autres* (hell is other people) when our French teacher cast me as the lesbian postmistress Inès in a French language competition. Of course, the French don't do everything right but they do have a beautiful way with words and food. And it helps sometimes to remind yourself that buried beneath that enormous pile of sweaters you have a long, hot summer within you.

In the middle of January, I wanted some summer.

We had all the ingredients, except for the tuna and ripe tomatoes. Tuna was easy enough to get, but we were many months away from ripe tomatoes. The recipe also suggested you lay a piece of slate over your grill and cook on it. Maybe that worked for *les sous chefs* at Le Bernardin, but I wasn't about to attempt that in 12-degree weather. Still, a part of me thought, what the hell— if I could quote Camus and laugh at a failed romance, I could make this work. I would use canned tomatoes and broil instead of grill. (I know there are hardy souls out there who grill on their patios in winter. Go with God.)

We bought two pounds of tuna for $18.99/pound. It's not fun to pay that much for fish, but it *is* fun to start thinking about summer when it's freezing out. I used a can of tomatoes from the pantry; they ended up being fantastic with the marinade. The recipe called for two fresh tomatoes; I used four canned. The dish made enough for two meals and on the second night, my older son went searching for the tomatoes, but we'd polished them off. I suggest doubling the marinade and using the whole can.

My husband waxed rhapsodic once he dug into the tuna. "This is delicious," he said. "Great job! You should be a chef." (Oh, go on.) I think he was amazed that something he had fished out of office debris (forgive the pun) had actually turned into a meal. In the midst of winter (and *avec* cranky sinuses)...well, you know the rest.

TUNA STEAK WITH SOY-GINGER VINAIGRETTE & ROMAINE

adapted from Le Bernardin

(Serves 4)

INGREDIENTS:

- 4 6-ounce yellow fin tuna steaks
- ¼ cup virgin olive oil
- 2 tomatoes, cored and cut in half (or four canned tomatoes)
- 1 garlic clove, peeled and sliced
- 1 tablespoon minced ginger
- 2 tablespoons minced shallots
- 1 tablespoon oyster sauce
- 2 tablespoons sherry wine vinegar
- 4 tablespoons canola oil
- 1 tablespoon soy sauce
- ½ teaspoon lime juice
- Pinch cayenne pepper
- Fine sea salt and fresh ground pepper to taste
- 2 tablespoons *herbes de Provence (herbes de Provence is a combination of rosemary, fennel seeds, oregano, marjoram, thyme and savory; combine 1 teaspoon of each and save the rest)*
- 2 heads romaine lettuce, left whole, washed and dried

PREPARATION:

1. **Season tuna steaks** on both sides with salt, pepper and *herbes de Provence*. Generously rub extra virgin olive oil on the tuna, coating both sides. Season tomato halves with salt, pepper, *herbes de Provence* and sliced garlic; drizzle with oil. Allow tuna and tomatoes to marinate for 1 hour.
2. **Make soy-ginger vinaigrette** by whisking together ginger, shallots, oyster sauce and sherry wine vinegar. Whisk in canola oil, soy sauce, lime juice and cayenne pepper. Season to taste with salt and pepper; set aside.

3. **Turn broiler on** and let it heat up. Cover cookie sheet or broiler pan with tinfoil. Pour some marinade on the tinfoil and place tuna and tomatoes on top of the marinade. Broil for 5 minutes on one side. Then turn over and cover tuna steaks with more marinade. Broil for 5 minutes or more until done. Top with remaining marinade. Serve with romaine lettuce.

GRILLING TUNA

If you want to use slate and grill the tuna the way Le Bernardin suggests, follow these instructions:

1. **Start a large charcoal fire in the grill.** When coals are very hot, place slate on the grill and heat slate until it too is very hot, about 30 minutes.
2. **Pour some marinade all over the slate** and lay tuna on top of the marinade. Place tomatoes on the slate, cut-side down.
3. **Grill tuna on the slate until it is browned on the bottom**, then turn it over to grill on the other side—remove the tuna from the slate when it is browned on both sides but is still rare in the middle. When tomatoes are lightly charred, turn them over to finish cooking on the other side *(they should be soft but still hold their form).*
4. **To serve, dress romaine leaves** with some of the soy-ginger marinade and arrange on plates. Place one tomato and one tuna steak on each plate; drizzle more soy-ginger marinade around each dish.

20

An Imaginary Aunt's Meat Sauce

Bolognese Sauce, Delicious and Glorious

ROXY LOOKED AT ME with her big brown eyes. Roxy is our yellow Labrador retriever and not the sharpest knife in the drawer (she can't retrieve anything except food) but she's smart enough to know when I'm not where I should be. Although it was midday, I'd just closed the shades and lay down on my bed. Roxy must have sensed I was in distress because after one look at me she started to bark. "Woof, woof!"

FEATURING

- Bolognese Three-Meat Sauce (Ragu)

Why is that mothers can't crawl into bed and be sick?

I willed her to go away. She barked at me again. "Woof! Woof!"

I didn't need a translator. The bark went like this: "Mommy, get up! You look dead!" Silently, I barked back: *Shut the hell up.*

"Woof, woof!"

"Go downstairs, Roxy!" She stared at me hard. It was a look that said, "Move it, girl!" Coming from her, that was pretty ballsy because she herself does next to nothing. In the mornings, we run or go for a walk. Then, she spends the rest of the day napping in the family room, or waiting in the dining room for someone to ring the doorbell. She only comes to see me if she needs to go outside or wants a snack. Hours go by, and she doesn't stop by to say hello. But the minute I am prostrate, she gets hysterical.

Nobody wants to see Mom lying down. Adults are supposed to be busy. Except when they feel like crap. I got out of bed, pushed her out of the room and shut the door. She sat in the hallway and barked and barked.

Nothing is more persistent or sounds more anguished than a dog when it wants something. Expect maybe for me, when I'm sick. And I wanted someone to take care of me: An old Italian aunt, perhaps, humming in her apron on a Sunday afternoon, stirring a big pot of meat sauce. This aunt would say, "Come sit down, darling, take a load off, this is for you," and she would hand over a bowl of meat sauce and a plate of buttered noodles, and give me a kiss on my forehead. This old Italian Aunt does not exist in my real life, but still I yearn for her.

Finally, I hauled my butt out of bed. Maybe if I wandered around in a daze, I would feel better. I opened the freezer, and spotted a package of ground meat - veal, beef and pork. I did not feel like making meatballs, which I always ruin, or meatloaf, which I love but sometimes have trouble persuading my children to love too. I wanted the sauce my imaginary aunt would have cooked for me.

Who doesn't love Bolognese meat sauce? I mashed up some baby carrots, onions, celery and turkey bacon in the food processor and sautéed them in olive oil. I added ground meat, and white wine, then took a can of whole tomatoes, crushing them in my hand, and sautéed those too. I let the sauce cook and cook. At the end, I added a cup of cream. You don't need to use cream in this recipe. I have made this before with skim milk and it works just as well. You could use real bacon too, and it would be divine, but the turkey bacon makes it taste just as awesome. And at the end, you can add Parmesan cheese, making it even more delicious.

This sauce takes a long time. It involves a lot of standing and stirring. If you were feeling better than I was, you could invite people over, sip some wine while you stir the sauce and have yourself a delightful few hours. It's a great sauce to make on a holiday or a Sunday afternoon. The trick is to have friends or family around to devour it with you, or at least set aside some containers and freeze the leftovers—because this recipe makes a *lot*.

There are plenty of nights when I'm too lazy to cook, or I'm teaching and I ask my kids to boil up some macaroni and cheese, or take a box of pizza out of the freezer. But there are also plenty of days when all I do is cook—to make myself feel better, to avoid writing, to stir up my writing, or to have something tangible to share at the end of the day. Cooking takes concentrated time, and it often means you are alone in the kitchen for a long stretch – long enough to recover your composure, your sanity, your creativity, your love for the people you live with, a love that is always there but sometimes gets eroded by all the demands you feel. When you cook for someone, you are basically saying: Look! I spent time making this for you. See how much I love you? Do you love me too?

The secret ingredient here is the smoked turkey (or bacon or pancetta). But what makes it, and almost any ragu, delicious is the combination of mashed up vegetables and spices, which, when combined with milk or cream, and stirred in a heavy saucepan for a couple of hours, turns into a paste so delicious that you can no longer even identify the sweet and tart flavors, you know only that they taste like love. Which dinner should.

By the time I was done cooking, I felt better. This sauce has a strange power; it makes you feel as if you've done everything right. It's that good.

I didn't give any meat sauce to our dog. But I'm sure my imaginary aunt would have.

Meat Sauce (Ragù)

(Yields one big pot of sauce)

Note: *This sauce takes about 2 1/2-3 hours, much of it spent simmering on the stove.*

INGREDIENTS:

- 2 tablespoons olive oil
- 1 small onion, minced
- 1 carrot, peeled and minced *(I use a handful of baby carrots and mince them; the more carrots you use, the sweeter the sauce)*

- 1 celery stalk, minced
- 1/4 cup minced turkey bacon
- 1 pound lean ground beef, pork or combination
- 3/4 cup dry white wine or juice from canned tomatoes *(I used wine)*
- 1 28-ounce or 35-ounce can whole plum tomatoes, drained
- 1 cup chicken stock
- Salt and ground pepper to taste
- 1 cup cream or milk *(I use a combination of cream and skim milk)*
- Freshly grated Parmesan cheese, optional

PREPARATION:

1. **Pour olive oil into a large saucepan.** Turn heat to medium low and a minute later add onion, carrot, celery, and turkey bacon. Cook, stirring occasionally, until vegetables soften, about 10 minutes.
2. **Add ground meat** and cook thoroughly, about 5 minutes. Add wine or tomato juice, increase heat and cook until most of the liquid is absorbed, about 5 minutes.
3. **Crush tomatoes** with your hands and add them to the pot; stir, and then add stock. Turn down heat to low and cook at a slow simmer, stirring occasionally, breaking up any clumps. After an hour or so, add salt and pepper and continue to cook for another hour, until most of the liquid has evaporated and the sauce has thickened.
4. **Add cream or milk, and cook** for another 15-30 minutes, stirring on occasion, adding more salt and pepper as needed. Add Parmesan to taste. Serve immediately with pasta.

▸ *Sauce can be covered and refrigerated for a day or so, or put in a closed container and frozen for several weeks.*

21

Shark Cake

When Cake Is Simply an Excuse for Frosting

I HAVE ALWAYS ADMIRED Marie Antoinette, that vain, chic fashion plate who is known as much for bringing about the French revolution as she is for saying about the starving peasants, "Let them eat cake." Poor Marie probably did not say anything about cake, but like Anne Boleyn before her, she went down in history in part for being an aristocrat who lost her head because she liked the good life too much.

FEATURING
- White Cake with Buttercream Frosting

I am not an aristocrat, but I do like the good life and I love rich food, especially cake –a thick slice of layer cake in the summer with butter cream frosting that cleaves and covers it, a sugary primal mush dissolving slowly and languorously on the sides of your tongue. Since I have high cholesterol, as well as what my sister-in-law-the-therapist calls a "restrained eating disorder," I don't eat all that much cake. But when I do, I either bake it or buy it as rich and fattening as I can.

I created my Shark Cake for the Cake Walk at my sons' school. The Cake Walk is an event that takes place every June, at an end-of-year, here-comes-summer party that the school euphemistically calls the "Fun Fair." As we all know, anything called "fun" or "fair" involving children is rarely either.

Last year, I was the co-chair of food at the Fun Fair. Of course, it rained that day, which meant I stood inside the humid cafeteria and handed out lukewarm hotdogs for two hours. The fathers flirted with me, and the children grabbed their hotdogs and ran. I vowed that next year I would be involved with food at a much higher level. I decided I would run the Cake Walk.

I asked my friend Laurie, who had run the Cake Walk for a million years, if I could take it over. "No," she said. "But you can be my assistant." She said she was holding on to the Cake Walk crown until her youngest child went to middle school, which meant I would never wear it.

When spring came, Laurie emailed me: "We need 60 cakes. I have 40 people signed up. Find 20 more. Seaside theme."

No problem.

I got the email list for my sons' school and sent a note to anyone who had ever spoken to me, asking for cakes with a seaside theme. That meant crabs, lobsters, fish, whales, dolphins, boats, waves, mermaids, tsunamis, mercury contaminants, whatever. Offers of cake immediately poured in. In two days, we had all the cakes we needed.

The cake I was making was called "White Birthday Cake." It's a layer cake, divided by a thin sheet of raspberry jam, and smothered with a thick layer of buttercream. The recipe came from my cooking class instructor in New York who called himself "Mr. Salt and Mr. Butter." His cake recipe calls for, among other things, three-and-a-half sticks of butter, a heaping tablespoon of Crisco, and a pound of confectioner's sugar. Though I don't recommend snacking on this cake before trying on last year's bathing suit, you may get so high from eating it that you'll simply tell your suit to go to hell.

In keeping with the seaside theme, I decided to cover the frosting with Sathers Gummalo Blue Sharks – two bags for a dollar, six sharks per bag. Who can resist a shark in summer? I bought six bags.

Then, I decided to make two cakes – one for the Cake Walk and one for my then 10-year-old's fifth grade graduation lunch. I spent an hour mixing the ingredients and put the cakes in the oven. Then I started making the frosting. Before I knew what was happening, I had eaten half of it. I ate so much frosting there was not enough for the cakes. So I made more.

By the time I was done, I had blown through nine sticks of butter.

The timer went off. I was sweating. I took the cakes out of the oven, and let them cool on the racks. Once cooled and frosted, I laid out 30 sharks so that they circled the cake, ready to go in for the kill.

My shark cake was beautiful. Even my children said so. Of course, other cakes were more beautiful. Laurie placed a Beach Blanket Barbie Doll on her cake. One woman put a plastic pail and a shovel on top of hers, and covered the frosting with brown sugar so it looked like sand. Another mom filled a clear plastic bowl with blue Jell-o and placed plastic sailboats on top.

This recipe requires some preparation:

- Before you turn on the oven, set oven rack in middle of oven
- Bring butter, milk and eggs to room temperature before starting
- Buy or borrow two 9" x 1½" cake pans and 4 cooling racks

This cake really does take the cake. As complicated as it might seem, it's really not hard to make once you have all the ingredients assembled. Just make sure to use whole milk, not skim. You're already going for broke calorie wise with all that sugar and butter. Might as well let the cake be as fabulous as it can be.

During the Cake Walk, I lost track of my cake. But that night, I found out that the child who had won the Shark Cake brought it home to his mother who had been successfully battling breast cancer. We would later become friends though I didn't know that at the time. All I knew was that she, of all people, deserved to eat cake.

White Cake with Buttercream Frosting

(Serves 12)

INGREDIENTS FOR CAKE LAYERS:

- 1 cup whole milk, room temperature
- ¾ cup egg whites *(about 6 large or 5 extra large)* at room temperature
- 2 ¼ cups plain cake flour

- 2 teaspoons almond extract
- 1 teaspoon vanilla extract
- 1¾ cups sugar
- 4 teaspoons baking powder
- 1 teaspoon salt
- ¾ cup *(1 ½ sticks)* unsalted butter, softened

INGREDIENTS FOR FROSTING AND FILLING:

- 1 cup *(2 sticks)* unsalted butter, softened
- 1 pound confectioners sugar
- 1 tablespoon vanilla extract
- 1 tablespoon whole milk
- scant ¼ teaspoon salt
- ½ cup *(2 ½ ounces)* blanched silver almonds *(optional)*
- ⅓ cup seedless raspberry jam *(optional)*

PREPARATION:

1. **Preheat oven to 350 degrees.**
2. **Place a heaping tablespoon** of solid vegetable shortening in the middle of each cake pan. Use your fingertips and lightly spread the shortening all over the bottom of the pans. Sprinkle each pan with a heaping tablespoon of flour. Make sure to coat the entire inside of the pan with the flour, then flip the pan over to get rid of the excess.
3. **Pour milk into a large glass** measuring cup. Add the egg whites, vanilla and almond extracts and beat with a fork until blended.
4. **In a bowl, combine cake flour, sugar, baking powder** and salt and mix at slow speed with electric mixer until blended. Add butter and mix slowly until the mixture resembles moist crumbs, with no powdery ingredients remaining.
5. **Add all but ½ cup of the milk/egg-white mixture** to the flour mixture and beat at moderate speed for 1½ minutes. Pour in remaining ½ cup of milk/egg-white mixture and beat for 30 seconds more. Stop mixer and scrape sides of bowl. Return mixer to moderate speed and beat for 20 more seconds.
6. **Divide batter evenly** between the 2 greased cake pans. Place pans at least 3 inches from the oven walls and 3 inches from each other to allow for air circulation. Bake 23-28 minutes, until a toothpick comes out clean.

7. **Remove cakes from oven.** Let cakes rest in pans for 3 minutes, then loosen sides with a soft-edged knife. Flip cakes onto greased cake racks. Then flip them onto other greased cake racks so that they are now back to their original position. Let cakes cool for 1½ hours, before you fill and frost them.

FOR THE FROSTING:

1. **Combine the softened butter**, confectioners sugar, vanilla, milk and salt in mixer and beat at slow speed until sugar is moistened. Raise speed to moderate and beat 1 ½ minutes. Stop mixer occasionally to scrape down the bowl. Frosting will be creamy and fluffy.

   (If you want to turn this into chocolate frosting, melt a couple of squares of unsweetened chocolate and add to frosting.)

2. **If you are using almonds,** spread them over a baking sheet and bake at 350 degrees for 6 to 10 minutes. Let cool and then chop coarsely.
3. **Now you are ready to assemble your cake!** Just make sure it is completely cool before frosting.
4. **Take a pretty cake plate.** Spread small dab of frosting in center of cake plate to anchor the cake and set one cake layer on top of it. Combine ½ cup of frosting with the almonds in a small bowl and spread this over the bottom cake layer. *(If you are skipping almonds, just spread ½ cup of frosting on this bottom cake layer.)* Then spread the raspberry jam on top of the *(almond)* frosting and cover this frosted bottom layer with the second layer of cake. Take remaining frosting and cover top and sides of cake, using a spatula and a soft-edge knife to make it look beautiful and smooth.

▸ *Once frosted, the cake will stay fresh for 2-3 days in your refrigerator. Or you can wrap it up and freeze and it will stay fresh for weeks. Really.*

22

Cooking With Cream, Not Guilt

Farfalle in Vodka Sauce Is Decadent and Delicious

EVERY SO OFTEN, you need comfort food, the kind that makes you feel good the moment you bite into it. This happens to me about once a week.

During one particular week, I had been on steroids for an unrelenting sinus condition and had been yelling at my kids as a result. (I blame the steroids, not a prolonged midlife crisis, chronic sleep deprivation, and the endless juggling of low-paying, part-time jobs.) I yelled at my older son for almost missing the bus/not setting the table/taking too long to feed the dog/surfing the Internet instead of doing homework/ and not taking the garbage out quickly enough. I yelled at my younger son for bothering my older son. I yelled at my husband for not being there when I yelled at our children. By the end of the week, the only one who wasn't scared of me was the dog.

FEATURING
- Farfalle in Vodka Sauce
- Vanilla Vinaigrette

To make it up to everybody, I made a dish that I knew would make them happy: Pasta with tomato, cream sauce and vodka. I was still a little cranky and wanted to make something quickly that didn't require rushing to the grocery store or borrowing food from a neighbor. And it wouldn't hurt to use up what we had sitting around the freezer and fridge.

We had some leftover cream from some corn pudding and pots de crème I had made a few days earlier. This wasn't light whipping cream, but old-fashioned heavy cream, that staple of classic French cooking that is so often avoided in these fat-free, calorie-conscious times. I had a yet untried recipe for *farfalle* with vodka sauce that called for heavy cream and I knew it would turn out well because I had sampled it in cooking class.

Two weeks earlier, in my pressure-cooking class, Arlene Ward covered a wide range of topics and gave us basic tips for preparing and serving food that didn't go in the pressure cooker:

- Buy (or ask to be given) white serving pieces. They go with everything and food shows up best on them.
- Toss salad in a bowl but serve it on a platter. All the heavy stuff falls to the bottom of the bowl.
- Spin the salad bowl as you pour dressing onto it and then mix it with your hands.
- Put the stems of parsley into chicken stock because stems have the most flavor.
- Don't rely solely on balsamic vinegar when making salad dressing. Try pear or peach vinegar. Better yet, make your own vanilla vinegar (recipe below) and use that.
- When you rub oil into a roasting chicken, massage some of the oil into your cuticles (this has nothing to do with cooking, it's just a beauty tip).

One of the things I liked about Arlene's *farfalle* recipe was that it called for vodka. We've had two bottles of Absolut vodka in our freezer since we moved into our house. I'm pretty sure they came from my husband's 30th birthday party. We don't drink vodka but it's hard for me to throw out a full bottle of something, let alone two, and I was eager to get rid of them. (My younger son saw me take the vodka out of the freezer and asked if I was going to pour myself a shot.)

The only thing Ward's recipe called for that we didn't have was the *farfalle* (bowtie pasta). I substituted egg noodles and they worked very well. (Ward says you can use any pasta that has an interesting shape.) All of the other ingredients – canned tomatoes, parsley, sage, eggs, Parmesan cheese – you probably have on hand. I also did not have the block of fresh Parmesan cheese that Ward suggests. I used a plastic container of the cheap, already-grated stuff and it still tasted delicious.

This dish was spectacular. Here were the reactions of the people who were no longer talking to me but were still willing to eat the dinner I had made:

"Oh my God this is the best meal ever. I'm glad I didn't eat pizza at the train station." (Middle-aged husband.)

"I don't like you, but I loved dinner." (Teenage son.)

"This is great Mom. Really good." (Other teenage son.)

However, they also all asked the same thing:

"Is this healthy?"

Well, between the cream, the Parmesan cheese, and the egg, there is a lot of protein in it, and between the canned San Marzano tomatoes, the sage and parsley, there's a nice combination of fresh vegetables and herbs.

But low-cal and low fat? No.

Both my kids have become weight-conscious in the past year. My younger son plays football and both kids wrestle. They have to be weighed in before the start of games and matches. If they weigh too much, it's a problem. Once upon a time, I thought that by having boys instead of girls I would never have to worry about inadvertently giving my kids eating disorders or about them obsessing about their weight. But because they care (and because, God knows, I do), I try to make low-fat food and keep the carbohydrates to a minimum. But the wonderful thing about cooking with cream is that a little goes a long way. You don't need to eat a lot to feel satisfied. One portion is usually enough. And a little rich food in the middle of a cold, grey winter is a great treat.

This dish, though it tastes expensive, is actually pretty cheap to make. In fact, the only thing wrong with this dish is there wasn't enough of it. It made six small servings. If you have more mouths than that to feed or you want to freeze the leftovers, double the recipe.

Farfalle in Vodka Sauce

(Yield: 6 small servings)

INGREDIENTS:

- 2 tablespoons olive oil
- 4 tablespoons unsalted butter
- 2 tablespoons minced onion
- 1 teaspoon minced garlic
- ¼ cup vodka
- 5 canned plum tomatoes *(½ cup)*
- ½ cup chicken stock
- 1½ cups heavy cream
- 8 fresh sage leaves *(2 teaspoons chopped)*
- 1 teaspoon kosher salt
- ⅓ cup Parmesan cheese
- 1 extra large egg yolk
- 1 tablespoon chopped parsley
- 1 package farfalle *(12-16 ounces, I used egg noodles)*

PREPARATION:

1. **In a large shallow skillet**, heat olive oil; add butter and sauté onion and garlic until softened. Do not let it brown. Carefully add vodka and let it reduce.
2. **Add tomatoes, stock, cream, sage and salt.** Simmer sauce using a wire whisk to bring sauce together. Simmer until sauce has thickened and coats a spoon.
3. **Set sauce aside until pasta is drained** and ready to serve.

4. **In a large 8-10 quart pot, boil pasta** in salted water. When it's done, drain and set aside.
5. **Returning to the sauce, heat the cream mixture.** Add a little of the hot sauce to the egg yolk. Whisk egg into warm sauce and remove from heat quickly. Toss in cheese, sprinkle with parsley, salt and pepper to taste.

▸ *Ward suggests pouring sauce over pasta. If you want to save sauce to freeze later, serve it separately and pour sauce on individual plates.*

VANILLA VINAIGRETTE

INGREDIENTS:

- ½ cup extra virgin olive oil
- 3 tablespoons vanilla vinegar*
- 1 clove fresh garlic halved and removed before serving
- ½ teaspoon dry mustard
- Kosher salt and pepper to taste

PREPARATION:

Combine all ingredients and whisk together.

**To make homemade vanilla vinegar, select good quality white wine vinegar such as Champagne or Riesling. Add 1 split vanilla bean to a new bottle and let marry in bottle for several days or longer.*

23

Wild Mushrooms In Winter, Darling

Conjuring Grandma Through Cooking

"I still think that one of the pleasantest of all emotions is to know that I, I with my brain and my hands, have nourished my beloved few, that I have concocted a stew or a story, a rarity or plain dish, to sustain them truly against the hungers of the world."

MFK Fisher,
The Gastronomical Me

FEATURING
- Pappardelle Pasta with Wild Mushrooms

ONE OF MY FAVORITE WRITERS of all time is MFK Fisher. She wrote beautifully about food, love, France, romance and the glory and challenges of it all. She had children, husbands, dinner parties and boyfriends (sometimes simultaneously). Periodically, her life was very complicated; she cooked her way through depression, loneliness, illness and love.

My younger son and I were home sick one winter day. My husband was working from home. With the TV in the family room blaring, my son on antibiotics, my husband banging around the kitchen, wondering if there was anything for lunch other than the seafood paella left over from dinner at a Spanish restaurant two nights before, and a winter that seemed as if it never would end, I had a decision to make: Should I write my way out of this misery, or cook my way out? I wasn't up to concocting a stew but maybe I could make a plain dish that would sustain us.

Fortunately, the cupboard wasn't completely bare. There were dried shiitake and porcini mushrooms in the pantry and fresh mushrooms and heavy cream in the fridge. The week before, I had taken a cooking class with Arlene Ward, co-author of *Pressure Cooking for Everyone*, and she had shown us how to make a luscious wild mushroom pappardelle pasta dish that did not rely on the pressure cooker. Pappardelle pasta is always a big hit in our house – everyone loves the way those wide egg noodles slither around our mouths and plates. I quickly looked at the recipe and realized we had most, but not all, the ingredients. We had no shallots, just large yellow onions, and we didn't have any fresh shiitake mushrooms, only dried.

I looked at the other recipes Arlene had prepared that day: There was one that called for bone-in chicken thighs with artichokes. Naturally, we had no artichokes, and the chicken thighs we had were boneless. No, scratch that– they weren't even chicken thighs. It was a package of ground chicken, so frozen the meat had clumped to form thigh-like shapes. But the recipe could be adapted. In fact, I adapted it so aggressively that it became a simple dish of ground chicken sautéed in olive oil, capers, onions, garlic and a bay leaf.

The chicken went beautifully with Arlene's wild mushroom sauce. This is what I love about Arlene: her recipes are so adaptable. A little less cream here, a little less garlic there, farfalle pasta instead of pappardelle, it all works, darling.

The other great thing about Arlene is she always shares at least one tip that seems so obvious in retrospect: This time, she told us to butter the pasta bowl before we added the pasta, then sprinkle salt and pepper directly on the bowl, so the pasta wouldn't stick. This is such excellent advice.

We spend our lives looking for people we have lost and sometimes, if we're lucky, we find small pieces of them in other people. I found a small piece of my grandmother in Arlene. My grandmother was an elegant, frugal woman, one of nine children, raised by a single mother. She and my grandfather were married just weeks after the stock market crashed in 1929. For sixty-five years, they lived together in a two-family house in Brooklyn, renting out the first floor apartment to a widow who stole their gardening tools. They were both schoolteachers, until Grandpa retired to become a stockbroker and Grandma retired to play bridge. Grandma drank weak tea, sewed and ironed. She only drank White Russians, and that happened once in a blue moon when she went to a wedding or bar mitzvah. She lived her life in a calm, orderly way, darning socks, recycling tinfoil and shopping at Loehmann's. She answered the phone, "Good evening," and answered almost every question, "Yes, darling."

Arlene won't call you "darling" as Grandma might have (she'll call you "dear") but the feeling is the same and the advice is equally warm and firm: Make do. You can't be alone with your work today? Feed the people you love instead. And if you want, add less cream.

WILD MUSHROOMS PAPPARDELLE PASTA

(Adapted from Arlene Ward)

(Serves 6)

INGREDIENTS:

- ⅓ cup dried porcini mushrooms *(keep liquid from drained porcini)*
- 10-ounce package fresh crimini mushrooms, sliced
- 8 ounces fresh shiitake mushrooms, sliced *(I used 1 ounce dried)*
- 4 tablespoons unsalted butter
- 3 tablespoons extra virgin olive oil
- ⅓ cup minced shallotss
- 2 teaspoons garlic
- 1 cup heavy cream

- Kosher salt and ground pepper, to taste
- Grated Parmesan cheese
- 8 ounces Pappardelle pasta *(wide noodles)*

PREPARATION:

1. **Place porcini mushrooms in bowl** and add warm water to cover. Let mushrooms soak for 30 minutes. Drain and keep liquid for later. Chop softened mushrooms and set aside.

2. **In large sauté pan, sauté shallots and garlic** in olive oil and butter. When shallots start softening, add sliced mushrooms —you should have about 4 cups. Sauté mushrooms for 4-5 minutes. Add diced dried mushrooms and ½ cup of reserved mushroom liquid. Add cream and simmer with mushrooms until mixture is thick and shiny. Add salt and pepper.

3. **Pasta: Bring several quarts of water to boil.** Salt water after it comes to boil and carefully drop each nest of Pappardelle into water without stirring. Once water comes back to boil, cook pasta for 6 minutes.

4. **While pasta cooks, prepare a large serving bowl** by filling it with warm water. Drain the water, pat dry and rub bowl with softened butter, then sprinkle bowl with salt and pepper. Drain cooked pasta and drop in prepared bowl. Toss and top with mushroom sauce. Add Parmesan cheese to taste.

Ground Chicken with Capers

(Serves 4-6)

INGREDIENTS:

- 2 pounds ground chicken
- 2 tablespoons unsalted butter
- 2 tablespoons olive oil
- 2 garlic cloves, minced
- ½ onion, chopped
- 2 teaspoons capers
- 1 bay leaf
- Kosher salt and pepper to taste

PREPARATION:

1. **Heat up oil and butter in sauté pan.** Add in garlic and oil, sauté for a few minutes.

2 **Season chicken with salt and pepper**, add to pan and sauté about five minutes until chicken browns a bit.

3. **Add capers and bay leaf** and serve immediately.

24

Wrestling Up A Healthy Crash Diet

A Soup, a Smoothie, Some Chicken and Some Fish

-

I DON'T USUALLY FEEL SORRY for my teenagers. Their lives are pretty bearable. But when my older son turned 15, he started wrestling for his high school team and his life became complicated in ways I couldn't have anticipated.

I'm not a big fan of contact sports and find wrestling brutal to watch. But he had spent years playing ice hockey where the coaches were miserable and the kids weren't much better. My son loved tying up his skates and racing around the rink, ramming into the wall and barreling into other players. He loved the cold air, the weight of the equipment, the speed and power. I loved watching him fly across the ice, though I always held my breath whenever one of the other players slammed into him. The kids broke their noses, tore their lips, fractured their fingers. My son only stopped playing because he got so many concussions the pediatrician made him.

FEATURING
- "Cream" of Vegetable Soup
- Jen Meister's Flax Seed & Nut Butter Smoothie
- Garlic Lime Chicken
- Lemon Broiled Fish

Wrestling, by comparison, seemed almost civilized.

Team sports, and organized group activities in general, keep teenage boys out of mischief. All that sweating and running around–when they come home, they don't have the energy to stir up trouble or give you a hard time, they just want to eat something and go to their rooms. On a loftier note, the practices and games force them to be part of something larger than themselves and not so focused on updating their Facebook statuses. The kids on the wrestling team looked out for each other in ways I hadn't seen in hockey. Plus, I knew the high school coach was a sweetheart with twin baby girls. Surely he could keep the boys' brutality at bay.

One day, my older son came home and announced that he had to lose six pounds in a week to make weight. I told him I could help.

"This is serious, Mom," he said. "I don't think you know how to do this."

Oh, how little he knew. Of course I knew how. I hadn't been a teenage girl for nothing. I was the only girl in my family and my vain, slim mother and vain, slightly plump grandmother paid a lot of attention to my weight. In grammar school, my mother packed me a brown bag lunch. If I gained too much weight, I lost the apple and got a bag of red peppers instead. My mother and father both had sisters who were also seriously overweight, and there were a number of people on my father's side who weighed more than 200 pounds. There was no way anyone I lived with was going to let me slide in that direction. And when I did lose weight, I was rewarded with a shopping trip to Loehmann's.

My mother and grandmother had strict ideas on how girls should look and behave. Number 1 was act ladylike, so no talking back or speaking in a loud voice. Number 2 was be thin. Number 3 was pull your hair into a ponytail, tie a ribbon around it and don't wear dangly earrings. Number 4 was say please and thank you. Number 5 was write thank you notes promptly on heavy cream-colored monogrammed paper. Number 6 was get good grades, go to college, get a job, balance your checkbook, find a husband and learn to cook dinner. Number 7 was don't talk about your therapist, though you were allowed to talk about your weight *ad nauseum.*

Figuring out how to do all that without having a nervous breakdown wasn't always easy, but I tried. One summer in high school, I went to tennis camp with some very skinny girls. One was famous for having appeared in a Burger King commercial. They all had long hair, long legs, and teeny tiny waists. They looked gorgeous in their white tennis shorts. From these girls, I learned that lunch could consist of a tall glass of ice-cold Tab, a paper plate covered in raw carrots and a couple tablespoons of peanut butter. They would sit at the lunch table and slowly lick their peanut butter off their spoons. They put vinegar and lemon juice on everything.

Years later, after I had my younger son, a friend who'd had three kids in five years and looked fantastic, told me her secret: Eat yogurt for dinner, drink a small glass of wine and go to bed hungry.

I've had friends who were treated for bulimia and anorexia. Freshmen year, I met a couple of women who had transferred to Wellesley from more remote colleges like Smith and Mt. Holyoke so that they could be treated by an eating disorder specialist in Boston. They ate huge containers of yogurt and granola for breakfast and threw it up. I'll never forget the image of one girl in her graduation photo, a tiny blonde elf, her granny dress swimming around her narrow shoulders. Her face was doll-like, small and pointy, with pronounced cheekbones, taut skin, and straight hair lank against her head. She smiled bravely into the camera. She graduated Phi Beta Kappa, clearly a sharp cookie. A few years after graduation, she died.

Over the years, my weight has fluctuated. When I got married, I weighed 109. After my father tried to kill himself, I ate only jawbreakers and my weight fell to 106. I've never been that thin since. But no matter how thin I was, I felt fat. Once, when I had gained some weight (I remember the day; I was 16 and I weighed 116), my father turned to my mother and said, "She's a fat tub of lard." Whenever I became very thin, my mother would say, "What happened? You look great!"

It's no surprise I'd amassed all the tools needed for a full-blown eating disorder. But I felt like I kept them tucked away; I didn't want to dig them out and hand them off to my teenagers.

I know that being hungry can generate its own weird high. I also knew that if my son ate too little, he would be tired and irritable, and we certainly didn't need any more of that in our house. While he was dieting, he would need enough energy to go to school, do homework, and survive a daily two-hour wrestling practice, all without passing out. I told him we would come up with a high protein, low carb, low fat diet and I would join him because, naturally, I wanted to lose weight too.

The day after my son said he had to lose weight, I went to a bar mitzvah. There were a lot of skinny women there. One of the women from my old tennis camp was there and, if you can believe it, still as thin as ever. At the luncheon, I was standing with a few of them, feeling again like the fat girl. Two of them started talking about the dresses they were wearing. Apparently, they had worn the same dresses to their own sons' bar mitzvahs. The dress I wore to my older son's bar mitzvah was five pounds ago; there was no way I could fit into it. Then these women started talking about their wedding dresses. They could still zip them up. My wedding dress was eight pounds ago. Forget about trying to squeeze into that.

Fortunately, my neighbor, who is more sensible than I am, also has a teenage boy who needed to make weight for wrestling. Her son is two years older than mine and her husband wrestled in high school, so she has experience with quick and healthy weight loss. She gave me her son's menu. Breakfast: Scrambled egg whites with a little Parmesan cheese for flavor. Lunch: Tuna fish, an apple, and carrots. Dinner: Broiled salmon, steak, lamb or chicken with low-fat marinade, raw fruit and veggies. A protein bar before wrestling practice and water, water, all day long.

This was borne out by the nutritionist I called. She recommended eating five small meals a day and drinking at least 64 ounces of water. (Some nutritionists recommend up to 100 ounces of water a day. If all that water is hard to get down, she suggests adding fresh juice from a lemon or orange to it.)

She talked about removing sugar, dairy, and processed foods from your diet, and adding in lean meats, all colors of vegetables, beans, legumes, and healthy grains such as brown rice, quinoa, millet and kasha. Substitute almond butter for peanut butter; if you're missing chips and pretzels, have a few almonds, cashews or walnuts. With fruits, she advised eating what's in season: In winter, stick with apples, pears, pomegranates, bananas, and oranges. If you're in the mood for a smoothie, use frozen berries, which have the most antioxidants (see recipe below).

Here were a few more of her suggestions for losing weight and staying healthy:

- Shop the periphery of the supermarket, where the meat, fish and produce are. Eat food that will rot. Real food is alive and will eventually die.
- Eat food that you can picture in its raw state. "If it came from a plant, eat it; if it was made in a plant, don't."
- Another grim aphorism: "The whiter the bread, the sooner you'll be dead."
- Eat your color (i.e. eat your veggies)
- Cut out dairy for the first five weeks. Use almond or rice milk.
- Cut out white flour.
- Cut out high fructose corn syrup and foods that have some form of sugar in the top three ingredients.
- Cut out anything that comes in a wrapper.
- Cut out juice, soda and energy drinks. Drink water or coconut water instead. (Coconut water aids in digestion and contains more potassium than a banana.)
- Avoid food that has more than five ingredients.
- Use a 2:1 ratio for vegetables and protein. If you have a 4-ounce portion of meat, eat 8-ounces of vegetables. Cover your plate with vegetables and grains and place a "fistful" of protein on top.

What if we get the munchies? I asked. "You can have one cookie, not ten," she said. If you're really craving something sweet and crunchy, spread peanut butter or almond butter on apples and rice cakes. Substitute your craving for sugar with protein: Make a whole-wheat wrap with hummus and turkey, or dig into some cottage cheese and fruit.

And so we began. I queried my friends for tips. Janice sent a recipe for "cream" of vegetable soup. Lynne, who lost 20 pounds last year, sent recipes for lime garlic chicken and broiled fish. My friend from down South, who was studying to be a nutritionist, told me to drink buckets of water.

Over the course of the week I made flank steak, broiled chicken thighs, broiled sea bass, the soup, a ton of vegetables and garlic-lime chicken.

When my son tasted the garlic chicken he said, "Are you sure this isn't fattening? Do you promise I'll lose the weight by Saturday?"

This was a drill I knew all too well. "We'll taper off towards the end of the week. Thursday, we'll have a small dinner and Friday night, we'll basically fast. We won't even eat dinner." My son looked alarmed, although my mother and grandmother would have been proud. "Ok, we'll have a small dinner on Friday," I conceded.

Friday afternoon, I picked him up at school. When he got in the car, he said, "Coach said I really don't have to lose so much weight."

What???

"He said because it's JV, it's not as strict as varsity, they'll just line me up against someone who looks like they're in my weight class. I had a cupcake in advisory this morning."

What had happened to the fun he was having dieting with Mom?

That night, I put a frozen pizza in the oven for my younger son, left my older son to fend for himself and went out for dinner with my husband. At first, I ordered the beet salad without goat cheese. But the salad frisée with bacon lardons, blue cheese and poached egg beckoned.

"It has blue cheese," the waitress said warily.

"I want it," I said. A few minutes later, I tucked into my

husband's truffle gnocchi and meatballs.

Saturday morning, my son left for wrestling practice. He had lost two and a half pounds. I had dropped two. I wiggled into the dress I had worn to his bar mitzvah, but just barely. All I needed was a wrestling match to wear it to.

"CREAM" OF VEGETABLE SOUP

(Serves 4-6)

INGREDIENTS:

- 1 tablespoon olive oil
- ½ cup chopped onion (I used one cup, which was an entire onion)
- 4 cups vegetable broth
- 1½ pounds vegetables, chopped. Use any combo of veggies - cauliflower, broccoli, asparagus, bell peppers, spinach, etc. *(A good combination is one whole head of cauliflower and an orange pepper; I used three cups of steamed broccoli and a handful of raw carrots)*
- 16 ounces silken tofu *(I didn't use this)*
- 1 tablespoon white wine vinegar
- Salt and pepper
- Grated Parmesan on top *(I didn't use this)*

PREPARATION:

1. **Heat oil, sauté onion** for 5 minutes.
2. **Add broth, bring to simmer.** Add vegetables and cook until tender *(about 25 minutes for my combo above)*.
3. **Add tofu and vinegar.** Transfer to a blender and puree. Season with salt and pepper. If you have an immersion blender, even easier!

JEN MEISTER'S FLAX SEED & NUT BUTTER SMOOTHIE

(This was from the nutritionist. Healthy and delicious.)

(Serves 1)

INGREDIENTS:

Blend together:

- 1 cup unsweetened vanilla almond milk or coconut milk
- 1-2 tablespoons nut butter *(almond, cashew or sunflower)*
- 1 tablespoon of flax/borage oil *(if you cannot have flax, add 1 tablespoon of Chia seeds)*
- 1 tablespoon ground chia or flaxseeds
- 1 cup frozen organic cherries, bananas, blueberries, blackberries, strawberries or raspberries *(you may do a mixture)*

GARLIC LIME CHICKEN

(Serves 2-4)

MARINADE INGREDIENTS:

- 3 tablespoons lime juice
- 4-5 cloves garlic, finely minced or pressed
- 1 teaspoon salt
- 2 teaspoon pepper

PREPARATION:

1. **Mix and pour** over 1-1.5 lbs. boneless skinless chicken breasts
2. **Marinate** for at least one hour or all day.
3. **Then grill or use a grill pan** about 5 minutes per side or until done on grill. *(I broiled for 5-6 minutes on each side.)*

Lemon Broiled Fish

(Serves 4)

INGREDIENTS:

- 2 pounds fish, cleaned, scaled, fins removed
- 4 tablespoons olive oil *(divided)*
- 1 teaspoon salt
- 1 teaspoon black pepper
- 1 teaspoon soy sauce
- Juice of one lemon
- 1 large garlic clove finely minced *(press if short on time)*
- ½ teaspoon oregano

PREPARATION:

1. **Preheat broiler** *(or grill).*
2. **Lightly coat entire fish** with 1 tablespoon olive oil.
3. **Broil fish in a pan** with sides for 6-7 minutes a side. In separate bowl mix remaining oil, salt, pepper, lemon juice, soy sauce, garlic and oregano.
4. **Remove from broiler**, place in lower part of oven, pour sauce over it and cook for 1 more minute or so.

25

Rx: Comfort Food

Shrimp Risotto, Rich and Sweet

IN FEBRUARY 2012, my husband's brother Rich was diagnosed with mediastinal B-cell lymphoma. Rich's son, Dylan, had had recently turned one. A few years earlier, Rich and his wife Lorien had started a blog, which they devoted to recording their adventures in marriage, biking, eating, traveling, cat-ownership and eventually having a baby. Once Rich was diagnosed, he started writing about how he was coping with cancer and chemotherapy. And because he's an avid cook, he would also write about the meals he was cooking and the desserts he was baking. I had been blogging steadily for several years but once I learned about Rich's cancer, I felt ridiculous writing about the books I was reading and reporting my suburban mommy problems, so I decided to take a break from the Internet and find a new project that embraced life, instead of pondering it. That project was my son's bar mitzvah.

When the prospect of death knocks at your door, you reassess. We worried about Rich. He is the youngest of three boys, and my husband's baby brother. We worried about how he would respond to the treatment. We worried about the future of his wife and their beautiful son. They live across the country in Berkeley and there was a limit to how much we could do. Rich found his own oncologist but in the back of my mind I always thought that if everything went wrong, he could go see a guy I considered a fairy godfather – my old friend Kevin who became an oncologist and moved to northern California. Although we haven't seen each other since 1986, we've stayed in touch through email and I knew him to be an avid cook and reader. I thought he and my brother-in-law would get along. I also knew his practice was relatively close to Rich's home.

Periodically, when I worried about Rich, I would email Kevin and ask, "Can my brother-in-law make an appointment to see you?"

"Of course," he'd write back. "Tell him to call my office."

At some point during these exchanges, Kevin sent me a recipe for shrimp risotto. "I make this for my wife sometimes," he said. I assumed the recipe would be wonderful, but decided to save it until Rich was out of the woods.

Rich is now doing very well. He's back to work full time, back to writing about his son on his blog, back to traveling and cooking with his wife. Although his cats have unfortunately passed away, he and his wife are expecting another baby.

Rich and Kevin never did meet. By the time of his appointment he had finished chemotherapy and was in recovery. But I keep hoping they'll find some other way to meet and have happier topics to discuss than ways to treat and beat cancer.

A couple of nights ago, I saw we had a bag of shrimp in the freezer. We also had frozen peas. We always have rice so I thought, *Oh good, here's dinner* and pulled out Kevin's recipe. You can make this dish two ways: The old-fashioned way of standing and stirring, or you can do as my neighbor suggested and put it in your pressure cooker. The beauty of the pressure cooker is that you can make this dish any time of the day, go about your business and hours later, the risotto is still warm for dinnertime. But Kevin's recipe called for standing and stirring so that is what I've included here.

This dish is really good. Of course it is. Shrimp is a luxury and luxurious food almost always tastes divine. And how can you go wrong with chicken broth, warm rice and several spoonfuls of Parmesan cheese? This is good old-fashioned comfort food, amped up with wine and shrimp for adult tastes and with the extra bonus of being gluten free. I made it on a cold fall day when I didn't know what to do with myself – pay bills...obsess about table assignments for the bar mitzvah...write? – and thought that standing at the stove would at least solve the question of what to make for dinner.

My 17-year-old took two helpings. "It's really good. Though you know I don't like beans," said my younger son, the bar mitzvah boy, pushing the peas away. My husband, who had been in Paris, came home the next night, warmed up two platefuls and said, "It's very good and very rich."

Yes, it is. This risotto is rich and sweet, like life, sometimes.

Shrimp Risotto, with Peas

(Serves 4-6)

INGREDIENTS:

- 3 ½ cups canned chicken broth
- 1 cup clam juice
- ½ cup dry white wine
- 3 tablespoons butter
- 1 tablespoon olive oil
- ½ large onion *(minced)*
- 2 cloves garlic *(minced)*
- 1 ½ cups Arborio rice
- 8 ounces medium sized shrimp, shells and veins removed *(slice shrimp in half if you want to spread it around)*
- 2-4 tablespoons Parmesan cheese
- ½ cup frozen peas, defrosted
- Salt and pepper, to taste

PREPARATION:

1. **Heat chicken broth and clam juice** in saucepan until liquid is almost boiling, then turn heat to low and simmer.
2. **Put a pot large enough to hold risotto** on medium heat, add oil and 2 tablespoons butter. Melt and then add garlic and onion and cook for 1-2 minutes. Don't let onions brown.
3. **Pour the Arborio rice into the pot with the onions**, garlic, butter and oil and stir gently until all the grains are coated with the oil and butter. Add the wine and continue to stir until rice absorbs wine. Take half of simmering chicken/clam juice broth and add to rice slowly. Keep burner on medium and stir frequently as broth becomes absorbed into rice.
4. **After 10 minutes, when broth is absorbed, add** the rest of the broth and continue to cook for 12 minutes or so. Then add shrimp and peas and cook for 3 to 5 minutes, flipping shrimp over to cook fully on both sides. Add Parmesan cheese, a tablespoon of butter, and salt and pepper to taste.

26

Marriage Is Like A Marathon

Exit Husband; Enter Shrimp

I MADE THIS DISH one cold winter night when my older son and I were home alone. My younger son was out go-carting with his cousins. My husband was out too. I'd like to say that my husband was out with his clients or with his friends, having a few beers and a good old time, but the truth was quite a bit uglier: My husband had left and I didn't know where he'd gone.

FEATURING

- Shrimp with Cumin and Coriander

We'd had a big argument after taking our older son to look at colleges on Valentine's Day weekend. Married twenty years with two teenage boys, a house and a dog, our days of wine and roses were behind us. Plus, my father, now dead, had been born on Valentine's Day, so the holiday has become a strangely potent brew for me. I was supposed to be feeling romantic toward my husband, but instead I was busy thinking about my dad.

Coincidentally, my father and husband share the same name as well as a few other similarities: Both had been Eagle Scouts, lifeguards, and first born males. Both were the first in their families to pursue what they did professionally—Daddy came from a family of fur salesmen and became a doctor; my husband came from a family of scientists and became a banker.

But whereas my husband is fundamentally sweet, my father was difficult. He had a caustic wit and though he could be charming and funny, capable of bouts of outrageous generosity, he was not particularly kind or loving. In fact, on his worst days, he could be pretty vicious. He tried to kill himself at least twice. He lied to his psychiatrists and took his anti-depressants only when it suited him. When he developed cancer, his oncologist called him the least compliant patient he'd ever had. In retrospect, it was ironic that Daddy's birthday was on Valentine's Day. Still, I loved him.

So when February 14th rolls around, I usually spend more time thinking about my late father and the Valentine's Day birthday cards I used to make him out of red construction paper, handfuls of white tissues rolled up into tiny balls and glued down to make large, lopsided hearts, than I spend thinking about my husband and how much I love him. How glad I am to have married him.

My husband and I go on long bike trips in the summer and take spinning classes together during the winter. We've had our difficulties and sometimes our love reminds me of what our spinning instructor calls that "old, heavy hill." The one that is hard to climb, the one that makes you sweat and curse, the one that can be exhilarating to fly down. The one that makes you say. "Yeah, I'm glad I did that."

And yet, my father still occasionally ruins my relationship with my husband, even though he's long gone. I feel his unsettling presence out there, undermining my efforts to be kind. You may shake your head in disbelief as you read on, but as I sit writing this in a Starbucks near my kids' school, "My heart belongs to Daddy," is playing over the speaker.

But my heart no longer does belong to Daddy. Did it ever? My father broke my mother's heart when he tried to kill himself the first time. After my mother left, my father remarried and I'm sure he broke his second wife's heart when he tried to kill himself the second time. There's a good chance he broke the hearts of the two women he was engaged to after he and his second wife divorced.

He's most certainly broken mine.

That weekend of Valentine's Day, my husband, kids and I were down in Washington DC, hours from home. We'd driven eight hours through a snowstorm to spend two days looking at two colleges in two cities, with our two teenagers. Our only thought to celebrate the holiday occurred when the hotel left us a plate of chocolate covered strawberries and heart-shaped chocolates on the desk that night.

After we'd said goodnight to our kids and left them alone with their laptops, my husband went down to the hotel lobby and brought us up glasses of port and chardonnay. When he returned to the room, I was fast asleep.

The next night, as he struggled to get us out of Baltimore in the dark and the snow, he cursed that he couldn't find the right highway to take us north. All the various navigation systems were failing us. My older son, with his recently minted driver's license, told him to "relax." My husband's lips pursed. "Don't tell me to relax," he said and demanded an apology. No apology was forthcoming. My husband and son bickered as the snow fell. I told them both to shut up; it was my car and my rules. My husband made a sharp U-turn. It was too fast, and the road was too slick. We all gasped. I told my husband to hand over the keys to the car. He wouldn't. One thing led to another and we didn't speak for the rest of the ride home.

The next morning was no better. I decided a little armchair psychoanalysis was in order and told my husband that most of his problems were tied to his family of origin, not the family we'd made. I blamed everything on his parents. Imagine how happy he was to hear that from me.

He told me he was leaving and when I came home, he had gone.

Well, I guess I don't need to make dinner tonight.

In fact, I didn't have to do anything at all. I poured myself a large glass of wine and thought seriously about throwing myself on the sofa and plotting my future without a husband. I had just run over my reading glasses and the lease on my car was up. Would I be able to afford to replace them? I could teach more and write more and try to make more money. I could try to find another husband but did I really want to live with another middle-aged man?

My husband and I are very different. He grew up outside Philadelphia. In his family, voices were low and feelings were restrained. His father is German and his grandparents fled Germany in 1939 when his grandmother was nine months pregnant. Unlike my high-flying parents, who took us to the Caribbean and sent us to private school, my in-laws lived modestly. Both worked for universities. God knows what my future in-laws thought when my husband brought me home–the moody, aggressive journalist who lived in an apartment she couldn't afford but still wore Ferragamo shoes and went out to the Hamptons. Then there were the multiple divorces in my family. The infidelity. The mental illness. My father, grandfather and great grandmother had all spent time in mental hospitals. My grandmother had stuck her head in the oven and tried to kill herself when my father was two. Both my father and grandfather had received electroshock therapy. My father's first cousin had kidnapped a baby and gotten away with it. My father's sister had gotten divorced. So had my mother's. My stepfather had left his wife for my mother. My mother had left my father for another man, and left that man for my stepfather. The sad and deviant behavior was endless.

By contrast, my in-laws only knew one other couple that had been divorced and that couple still lived in the same house. They just stopped attending weddings and bar mitzvahs together.

And here I was, twenty years later, wondering if I had driven my husband away. I sipped my wine. It was cold and comforting. I checked my email. No word from my husband. I looked over at the stove. I had defrosted two pounds of shrimp that morning and they were just sitting there, cold and shriveled, almost completely defrosted, waiting to be cooked. I could ignore them, put them off until tomorrow, but two pounds of shrimp is a lot of shrimp and day old shrimp is not so delicious. Plus it was pricey shrimp— $38 worth, to be exact— and I was now possibly in no place to squander money.

I took a deep breath, knowing that cooking would put me into a better frame of mind. The pouring, the measuring, and the reading of directions: Turn the oven on, open the olive oil, smell the cumin, turmeric and coriander. Whatever you've been thinking about before disappears when you follow a recipe. Plus, my older son was poking around the kitchen. If I made something to eat, he might stay and keep me company and my future might feel a little less grim.

I removed shells. My son measured out spices.

There are foods that send your mouth singing and your heart racing, foods that make you think, *I can keep going*. This dish is one of them. Coincidentally, I had made it before for my husband, when the kids were away and we had the house to ourselves. It was a hot summer night and we had grilled the shrimp and sat outside on the patio. As the sun set, we sipped our wine and toasted our solitude. That was then, this was now. The thought of cooking outside was a joke. The grill was piled high with snow. I couldn't even see the patio furniture.

My son and I made this shrimp in 24 minutes. It took a grand total of 15 minutes to prepare and nine minutes to cook. I did not set the table. We sat on stools at the counter and ate the shrimp off of small plates. I didn't expect anything else to happen that night. My son went back upstairs and I went up to my office.

Half an hour later, my husband called. We argued, and kind of, sort of settled things. I, who rarely apologizes, said I had spoken out of turn.

"Is there anything for dinner?" my husband asked.

"Yes," I said. "There's shrimp."

Shrimp with Cumin

(Serves 4)

INGREDIENTS:

- 2 pounds large shrimp, shelled and deveined
- ½ cup olive oil
- 2 teaspoons turmeric
- 1½ teaspoons cumin
- 1 teaspoon coriander
- 2 teaspoons kosher salt
- Juice of 2 lemons

PREPARATION:

1. **Pour oil in bowl and add spices**, salt and lemon juice.
2. **Place shrimp on a sheet pan** *(or on skewers, if you are grilling)* and spread seasoned oil over them.
3. **Grill or broil** for 9 minutes.

▸ *Eat immediately.*

27

Recharging My Culinary Batteries

Chicken and Flank Steak and Pizza, Oh My!

ONE FALL, when my kids were back at school getting new lockers and tackling geometry, I decided I wanted to learn something new too. I thought about taking up knitting and bridge but I knew both activities would require hours of sitting still and using my hands, which I already did enough of as a writer. So I signed up for a cooking class with Pam Riesenberg, figuring I would *stand* and use my hands.

FEATURING

- Flank Steak with Soy Sauce and Balsamic Vinegar
- Middle Eastern Pizza
- Grandma's Old Fashioned Chicken and Rice

Pam began teaching cooking classes out of her kitchen in New Jersey several years ago, after working part time at a local cooking studio. She started the classes after hearing that what people really needed were quick and healthy recipes for their families.

The first class of the fall season was billed as a weeknight dinner series that would begin with Meatless Mondays. The idea is that on Mondays, you should cook without meat, a movement that has turned into a national phenomenon.

I'm not sure what I expected. I just knew I needed to recharge my culinary batteries, and by the end of the class, I had. Pam's kitchen isn't big and she doesn't have a large staff to assist her, which is comforting, because if she can make four different meals in two hours in her cozy, sunny space, so can you. Over the course of the class, Pam prepared the dishes and gave us these tips:

- **Costco** is great for feta cheese but don't buy the fat free version.
- **Whole Foods and Trader Joe's** sell excellent pizza dough, as do the major supermarkets. You can be super ambitious and make the pizza dough from scratch, but I did that once and it wasn't worth the effort.
- **You can also try your local pizza place.** Ours will sell you a ball of pizza dough for $4.
- **You can freeze fresh ginger**, as long as long as you mince or grate it first.
- **Sesame oil is perishable** but will last four or five months in the refrigerator.
- **Remember to get your knives sharpened** every so often.

Pam showed us how to make tomato sauce from scratch in 20 minutes (use good, canned tomatoes) but said you can also be lazy and use a high-quality tomato sauce for this dish, like Rao's.

The moment of bliss came at the end of class, when Pam served us lunch. How delightful is it to have someone prepare you a hot lunch in their cozy kitchen and give you the recipes to go with it? The Middle Eastern Pizza, with its delicious combination of eggplant, olives, sun dried tomato slivers and feta cheese was my favorite.

A few days later, I went to the supermarket on a Saturday afternoon to stock up on ingredients for the pizza. The beauty of going to the supermarket on Saturday is you can sail out your front door saying, "I'm going to the market!" and be sure no one wants to come with you. I easily found everything on Pam's ingredients list except for fresh mint and slivered, sun-dried tomatoes. I bought a basil plant to substitute for the mint and eventually discovered slivered sun-dried tomatoes at the salad bar. (The great thing about buying food from the salad bar is you can weigh it and buy exactly the amount you need.)

On Sunday afternoon, while my kids were doing their homework, I set about making the Middle Eastern Pizza. Because my younger son and my husband don't like olives or feta cheese, I poured half of the eggplant, feta and olive combination on one side of the pizza for my older son and me, and put just the tomato sauce and mozzarella cheese on the other side for them. By the end of the meal, we were all fat and happy.

I was feeling pretty good so a few days later I went back to Pam's for another class. Over the course of two hours, Pam deftly made four chicken dishes. My favorite was the Chicken & Rice with Mushrooms. Then, when one woman said her teenage son liked to eat a lot of steak and she needed a new way to cook it for him, Pam ran to find a quick recipe for flank steak marinade and read it off to us. All the chicken dishes were easy and delicious, and when I got home, I figured I would make the chicken and rice first. But when I opened up the freezer, I saw that we didn't have boneless chicken breasts. However, we did have a large package of frozen chicken parts so I defrosted them, just in time to discover that we didn't have peas, mushrooms or Carolina rice.

Oh dear. But we did have basmati rice. My grandmother used to make a chicken and rice dish that didn't rely on any vegetables and it was always good so I adapted Pam's recipe, skipping the veggies, substituting the basmati rice for Carolina and hoped for the best.

The best happened!

This dish is flexible and superb. The rice was crunchy and delicious, and if you like standing in the kitchen, and scraping spoonfuls of rice off the bottom of a pot when no one is looking, this dish is for you.

I got straight A's on this dish. My younger son, who doesn't normally like chicken-on-the-bone, called it "fantastic" and had seconds. My older son also loved it. My husband had *four* helpings, and when some chicken and rice fell off the counter and onto my foot, our dog was all over it. You will be too.

FLANK STEAK

(Serves 4)

INGREDIENTS:

- 1½-2 pounds flank steak
- 3 tablespoons balsamic vinegar
- 2 tablespoons soy sauce
- 1 tablespoon olive oil
- 1 tablespoon sugar
- 1 teaspoon garlic powder
- ½ teaspoon salt or paprika

PREPARATION:

1. **Marinate for 2 hours** to overnight.
1. **Broil or grill**, 4 minutes on each side, then 2 minutes on each side, 12 minutes total.
3. **Let sit** before carving.

MIDDLE EASTERN PIZZA

(Makes 1 large pizza)

SAUCE INGREDIENTS:

- 1 tablespoon extra-virgin olive oil
- 1 small onion, chopped
- 2 garlic cloves, chopped
- 1 28-ounce can Whole San Marzano Tomatoes *(or 2 14-ounce cans)*
- Kosher salt/pepper or hot pepper flakes, to taste

PIZZA INGREDIENTS:

- 4 tablespoons extra-virgin olive oil
- 1 pound prepared pizza dough, at room temperature
- 1 medium eggplant, peeled and cubed *(into ½-inch pieces, about 5 cups)*

- 1 large red onion, thinly sliced
- 1 teaspoon ground cumin
- 4 cloves garlic, minced or crushed
- 8 ounces fresh mozzarella cheese, diced
- 1/4 cup pitted kalamata olives, chopped
- 1/2 cup oil-packed sun dried tomato slivers
- 3/4 cup feta cheese, crumbled *(6-oz. package)*
- Fresh mint, to garnish *(optional)*

PREPARATION:

1. **Preheat oven to 450 degrees.**
2. **To make sauce: Heat olive oil** in a saucepan over medium heat. Add onion and cook until soft, about 5 minutes. Add the garlic and tomatoes and cook until thickened, about 20 minutes. *(Partially cover.)* Season with salt and pepper.
3. **To make pizza: Drizzle** a rimmed baking sheet with 1-2 tablespoons olive oil and stretch pizza dough to fill the pan. Brush the dough with olive oil and bake 10-15 minutes *(on bottom shelf)* until golden.
4. **Meanwhile, in a large skillet**, heat 1 tablespoon olive oil over medium high. Add the eggplant, red onion, cumin, garlic, and cook about 15 minutes, until eggplant is tender.
5. **Top the pizza crust** with 1 cup sauce, the mozzarella, eggplant/onion mixture, olives, sun-dried tomatoes and feta. Return pizza to oven and cook 15-20 minutes, or until cheese is melted.
6. **Remove pizza from oven;** top with fresh mint. Slice and serve with a salad of mixed greens with lemon/olive oil dressing or Tahini.

Old Fashioned Chicken and Rice

(Serves 4-6)

INGREDIENTS:

- 2 whole chicken breasts split in half *(4 pieces – about 2 1/2 pounds)*
- Salt and pepper
- 2 tablespoons olive oil
- 1 medium onion, chopped

- 2 cloves garlic, minced
- 1 package *(6-8 ounces)* whole or sliced mushrooms *(slice, if whole)*
- 1 bay leaf
- ½ cup dry white wine *(or dry white vermouth)*
- ½ cup uncooked rice *(Carolina)*
- 1½ cups chicken broth
- 1 teaspoon paprika
- ½ cup frozen peas, defrosted *(optional)*
- Chopped parsley *(for garnish)*

PREPARATION:

1. **Sprinkle chicken** with salt and pepper.
2. **Heat 2 teaspoons of oil** in a large sauté pan over medium high heat. Add chicken pieces, skin side down. Brown about 5 minutes and turn over.
3. **Scatter the onion** and garlic between the chicken pieces *(not on top)* and add the mushrooms and bay leaf. Cook 5 minutes.
4. **Add the wine and cook** until almost all evaporated, 1 minute. Add the rice and broth *(rice should not be on top of chicken pieces)* and paprika. Bring to a boil, then lower heat to a simmer, cover pan and cook about 20 minutes or until rice is tender.
5. **Remove from heat**, add peas if using and cover pan for 5 minutes.
6. **Garnish with chopped parsley**. Season with salt and pepper.

28

Ain't They Sweet

Sweet Potato Casseroles for the Jewish New Year

EVERY ROSH HASHANAH, I look at the dog-eared copies of cooking magazines piling up in our kitchen and think, "I'm going to make something new and different this year!" The stakes were really raised one year when my neighbor and I decided to join forces and celebrate the Jewish New Year together at her house. My neighbor's husband is an ambitious cook, the kind of guy who reads *The New York Times* Dining section, gets out his deep fryer on Thanksgiving and fries one turkey in the back yard while he roasts two others in the kitchen. Plus, my friend from high school was coming with her family, as were my mother and stepfather, and my neighbor's extended family. All these people had eaten my standby holiday food too many times already so I wanted to make something other than brisket, string beans and my mother-in-law Dorothy's sweet potato casserole.

FEATURING

- Amy's Sweet Potato Casserole with Triple Sec
- Dorothy's Sweet Potato Casserole with Graham Crackers

But I didn't really have time to start playing around with new recipes and making eight trips to the grocery store. I was working more than I had in years and we had just survived a hurricane. So we divvied up the food preparation. My neighbor was making roast chicken and noodle *kugel*. The most I could do to change things up a bit was to make a new kind of sweet potato casserole, the one Amy had given me.

Amy was my younger son's Spanish tutor, before he switched to French. Switching to French from Spanish was one of the stupidest things we've done as a family, not just because hardly anyone speaks French anymore but also because we lost Amy in the process. Amy and my mother-in-law Dorothy are the kind of women who make you relax as soon as they walk in the door. They smile, they say something cheerful, they offer you a compliment, they make themselves comfortable and they put you at ease all at the same time, even though it's your house and you should be putting *them* at ease. You ask them if they want something and they say maybe they'll have some water. Otherwise, they're fine, really, and they'll tell you to just do whatever you need to do. They don't need attention or handholding. They don't talk about themselves unless you ask. They don't tease or mock you; they don't mention the last impressive thing they've done or the most important person they know. They offer praise but don't appraise you. Whatever you have, you can keep; they're not vying for it. They never have to be the centers of attention. Wherever they keep their egos is their secret.

At their cores is sweetness itself.

Amy used to teach Spanish at a local public high school and she likes to cook. She retired to go to the theater with her friends and tutor kids after school. She'd come over late in the afternoons, and I always seemed to be making dinner while she was here. We've never even hugged but she had such a wonderful way with my younger son that I just wanted to kiss her. My son loved her. She may have even loved him. Every Hanukkah, she gave him a gift. One year, she even gave me a gift: Her recipe for sweet potato casserole. It was a little more challenging than my mother-in-law's in that it required buying the potatoes, boiling them and then peeling them but other than that prep, Amy's recipe was easy to make and really yummy. And her recipe steps it up a bit by calling for a bottle of apricot brandy and a jar of marmalade. My mother-in-law's recipe is more old-fashioned, relying on canned sweet potatoes, lots of melted butter, brown and white sugar and graham cracker crumbs.

Needless to say, you won't lose weight eating either casserole, but they will afford you the deep and ancient pleasure of preparing warm, soft food. Greasing an old white Corning casserole dish, pouring in the sweet, chunky mixture, adding the topping, sticking it in the oven and knowing that every hot spoonful is going to be delicious is a wonderful way to spend one hour and anticipate the next.

The afternoon I set about cooking for the holidays, I realized belatedly that I had forgotten to buy sweet potatoes and I had no idea where the apricot brandy was. This happened shortly after Hurricane Irene, when we lost power for several days and had to throw out everything in the refrigerator. The jar of orange marmalade I had bought to make Amy's sweet potato casserole was gone. Did we have what we needed to make my mother-in-law's? I looked in the pantry: There were three old cans of sweet potatoes. One can was starting to rust but the expiration date said October 16. That was my brother's birthday! To borrow an old Yiddish expression, it was *bashert* (destiny). We also had a package of graham crackers. I wasn't sure how old it was, but it didn't matter. Once you mix graham cracker crumbs with the amount of butter and brown sugar my mother-in-law's recipe calls for, it doesn't matter if you're cooking with dust. The casserole was still splendid.

When I finally did track down some marmalade and apricot brandy, I made Amy's casserole. Both casseroles were hits with the whole Rosh Hashanah party.

I don't see Amy anymore and I wish I did. Fortunately my mother-in-law is a regular presence in our home. The thing about being in the presence of such sweetness is that not only does it comfort you, it actually makes you a little sweeter too. And we could all use that.

Amy's Sweet Potato Casserole with Triple Sec

(Serves 4-6)

INGREDIENTS:

- 5 pounds sweet potatoes
- 5 teaspoons butter
- 1 teaspoon salt
- 1 cup milk
- 1 cup triple sec or apricot brandy
- 1 jar of orange marmalade
- Cinnamon

PREPARATION:

1. **Preheat oven** to 350 degrees.
2. **Boil sweet potatoes** until soft. Remove skins. Mash sweet potatoes with milk until smooth. Add all the other ingredients, except cinnamon.
3. **Put in a baking dish**, spread marmalade over the top and sprinkle with cinnamon.
4. **Bake for 30 minutes**.

Dorothy's Sweet Potato Casserole with Graham Crackers

(Serves 4-6)

FILLING:

- 2 cups *(one large can)* of sweet potatoes
- 3/4 cup sugar
- 2 eggs, beaten
- 1/2 cup milk *(I used skim)*
- 3/4 stick butter, melted
- 1/2 teaspoon nutmeg
- 1/2 teaspoon cinnamon

TOPPING:

- ½ cup brown sugar
- ¾ stick melted butter
- ¾ cups mashed graham crackers

PREPARATION:

1. **Preheat oven** to 400 degrees.
2. **Mix together sweet potatoes, butter, milk**, and sugar, nutmeg, and cinnamon. Grease a casserole dish and pour in filling. Cook for 20 minutes.
3. **While casserole is cooking, make the topping.** *(If you don't want to use graham crackers, just mix the brown sugar with the butter and pour it on top of the casserole.)* Otherwise, mix the graham crackers with butter and brown sugar, spoon onto top of sweet potatoes and cook for 10 more minutes.

29

Pray Fast, Eat

Cooking–The Ultimate Kindness

YOM KIPPUR is one of those holidays that makes me think about food. It's not supposed to do that, of course. Yom Kippur is the Day of Atonement and it's a holiday that should get you thinking about confessing, forgiving and making things right: Making peace with the people you love; reconciling your feelings for the people you used to love but don't anymore; making plans to be kinder to your family, friends, neighbors and colleagues; and eventually, forgiving yourself, even if you've made some mistakes that you shouldn't necessarily be forgiven for.

FEATURING

- Marvelous, Marinated Salmon
- Salmon with Butter, Honey and Brown Sugar
- Wendy's Challah Soufflé
- Onion-Crusted Potato Kugel

You're not supposed to eat on Yom Kippur and there are many reasons for that, but I think the main one is that when you fast, your feelings are heightened. Your stomach grumbles and you think a lot. You think about the things you said that you wished you could take back, the people you complained about or ignored, the events you skipped, the games you only half-watched, the invitations you tossed, the comments you rolled your eyes at. My neighbor's father says that the only thing that separates us from the animals is the way we mourn and celebrate. That means showing up for weddings, funerals, commencements,

Communions and bar mitzvahs. When we don't, Yom Kippur offers a chance for repentance. Alone with your thoughts and your hunger, you can think about correcting the situation. With fasting, comes forgiveness. When you're sitting for long stretches of time on a wooden pew in the same place with a prayer book in your lap, listening to the cantor sing and the rabbi speak, you end up (metaphorically) in a different place. Sometimes, if you're lucky, you end up in a place of peace.

That all sounds very high-minded so I'll just confess right here that I often end the day thinking about how famished I am and wondering how many calories I've burned fidgeting. Around 4:30, I start to wonder when I can go home, heat up the casseroles, make a pot of decaf, take the platters of lox, white fish, tuna, egg salad, herring and chopped liver out of the basement refrigerator, set them out on the dining room table and wait for company to come. Thank God, they do. Friends, relatives, and neighbors gather around the table at the end of the day, exhausted, hungry and grateful for a wide range of things, one of which is that the fast is over.

I love a good break fast. We started hosting them years ago when I realized they were a quick and easy way to have a dinner party. I'd order cold platters of bagels, fish, and cheese the day before the holiday, let the guests bring fruit and dessert, and call it a day. Then, eight years ago, my friend Wendy and I got puppies within a few weeks of each other. We started spending time in her backyard, talking about food and kids while the dogs played. One morning, she started describing her mother's challah soufflé. She said it was really easy and gave me the recipe. It was easy and my husband and kids loved it, so ever since then, I've been cooking that, along with other casseroles and kugels, for break fast. I don't make anything fancy or low-cal and I don't make anything that can't be made or frozen several days before. You won't lose weight eating any of these dishes but at the end of a fast, you're thinking about expanding your belly, not shrinking it.

The day before Yom Kippur, my neighbor and I went for a

morning run. We started talking about what we'd been talking about all week: What we were making for break fast. She said she'd bought a huge piece of salmon at Costco. Did I want half? I sure did. She offered to marinate it first. Bring it on, sister.

I spent a couple of hours making a potato-and-onion casserole that calls for fresh, chopped rosemary (a call you should answer). Then I went to pick up my younger son from school and while I was gone, my neighbor let herself in the back door and left a dish of marinated salmon in the refrigerator. I broiled it for five minutes on each side. It was one of the most delicious pieces of salmon I've ever eaten hot, but also works well cold for break fast.

I'm also including here another delicious recipe for salmon. The beauty of this fish dish is you can make it one day and serve it the next. The butter, honey and brown sugar do a marvelous job of preserving the fish. And they taste divine.

MARVELOUS, MARINATED SALMON

(Serves 4-6)

INGREDIENTS:

- Salmon (2 pounds)
- 2 tablespoons lemon juice
- 2 tablespoons soy sauce
- 2 tablespoons honey
- 2 tablespoons olive oil
- ½ teaspoon garlic powder

PREPARATION:

1. **Combine moist ingredients**, and then add garlic powder.
2. **Marinate salmon** for 2 hours.
3. **Broil for 5 minutes** on each side.

Salmon with Butter, Honey and Brown Sugar

(Serves 4-6)

INGREDIENTS:

- Salmon (2 pounds)
- 1 stick unsalted butter
- ⅓ cup honey
- ⅓ cup brown sugar
- 2 tablespoons lemon juice
- 1 teaspoon liquid smoke *(usually available in grocery stores, though you may have to ask where they keep it)*
- ¾ teaspoon crushed dried pepper flakes

PREPARATION:

1. **Combine butter, brown sugar, honey**, lemon juice, liquid smoke, and red pepper flakes in saucepan.
2. **Cook over medium heat** for 7 minutes.
3. **Cool to room temperature**.
4. **Place salmon in dish. Pour marinade** over fish. Let stand for 30 minutes, turning once.
5. **Broil or grill for 6 minutes** on each side.
6. **Serve immediately.**

▸ *This dish is also excellent the next day.*

Wendy's Challah Soufflé

(Serves 8-12)

INGREDIENTS:

- ¾ pounds cheddar cheese, sliced from the deli
- 9 eggs
- 3 cups milk
- ¼ pound melted butter
- 12 slices stale challah

PREPARATION:

1. **Beat eggs; mix with milk and melted butter.** Add salt and pepper to taste.
2. **Cube challah and lay half the cubes** in a greased baking dish. Layer some of the sliced cheese on top. Alternate layers of cheese and challah. Pour milk/egg/butter liquid over challah/cheese. Cover and let set overnight in fridge. *(If you don't have time for this, you can also cook it right away.)*
3. **Bake uncovered in a preheated 325-degree oven** for 45-60 minutes. It should be golden brown and only slightly wet.

Onion-Crusted Light Potato Kugel

(Serves 8-10)

INGREDIENTS:

- 1½ pounds onions *(6 cups)*, thinly sliced
- Salt, pepper
- 6 tablespoons oil
- 1 teaspoon minced fresh garlic
- 6 large or 8 medium russet *(baking)* potatoes *(either peeled or unpeeled)*
- 4 large eggs
- 1 teaspoon baking powder
- 1-2 tablespoons fresh, chopped rosemary

PREPARATION:

1. **Separate onions into rings.** Toss in a large bowl with 2 teaspoons salt and set aside for 20 minutes, turning onions from time to time so moisture is extracted. Dry onions between sheets of paper towels, pressing down to soak up liquid.
2. **In a large frying pan,** heat 3 tablespoons oil over medium high heat. Add onions and garlic and cook for 15-20 minutes until golden brown. Add salt and pepper.
3. **Dice 2 large or 3 small potatoes** in Cuisinart or with hand grater, and place in a saucepan of salted water. Bring to a boil, then simmer until potatoes are tender. Mash potatoes, and place in large bowl. Stir in half the fried onions, setting the other half of the onions aside for later.

4. **Preheat oven to 400 degrees.**
5. **Grate remaining potatoes**. Place potatoes in colander and rinse with cold water to remove starch. Add these potatoes to the other potatoes.
6. **Beat eggs in another bowl** until thick and light. Whisk in baking powder, combine eggs with potatoes and season with salt and pepper.
7. **Pour 1-2 tablespoons of oil** into each casserole dish *(use ceramic or metal, not glass)*. Rub oil around bottom and sides of dishes and place both dishes in oven until hot *(about a minute)*. Remove dishes from oven. Transfer potatoes to casserole dishes, spread out with spatula and top with fried onions. Sprinkle with rosemary and a few drops of olive oil.
8. **Put casserole dishes on top shelf of oven** and cook for 30 minutes at 400 degrees. After 30 minutes, turn heat down to 350 degrees and continue baking for 25-40 minutes longer until onions are crunchy and dark on top.

30

Cooking for Hanukah

What I Do, and What I Don't Do

-

IN OUR HOUSE, the winter holidays mean scrambling to find gifts my kids might actually need, cooking brisket and applesauce from scratch, and making latkes out of the box.

FEATURING

- Braised Brisket of Beef
- Grandma Sally's Apple Sauce
- Potato Latkes (Pancakes)

I know it's heresy to use potato pancake mix and many of you are probably shaking your head as you gather your potatoes and onions. Go ahead. I have spent many nights, whipping out the food processor, peeling the potatoes, slicing them up so they fit down the chute, letting the processor grate them into mushy bits and then spooning them into a pan of hot oil, exhausted but secure in the knowledge in that I have peeled the potatoes myself and my family might love me more for it. But I've found that my kids can't tell the difference between homemade latkes and the ones out of the box. (If you can tell, a decent recipe for homemade latkes is below.)

Over the eight days of Hanukkah, I'd rather spend my time making homemade applesauce and that meat dish beloved to frugal winter cooks everywhere, long-simmering brisket. (And by the way, this recipe appeals to all religions. My Irish Catholic stepfather loves it with horseradish and my friend Laurie makes it Sundays, after she teaches religious school at her church.) Brisket takes several hours to cook but then it's good for at least two or three dinners. Plus, there are always leftovers and brisket freezes beautifully so you can have it again next week.

Homemade applesauce is a delicious, old-fashioned wonder. One winter, a woman I worked with gave me her grandmother's recipe. Sandy worked as a translator in a news reporting class I taught at a local state university; she was assigned to a student who was hard of hearing. Sandy typed out everything discussed in class and put it up on a computer screen, so if the hearing-impaired student missed something, she could read it on the screen. When I first heard from Sandy she warned that I should prepare myself because having a hard-of-hearing student in the class would mean a lot of extra work. I would have to send the translator definitions, hand-outs and assignments ahead of time, so she would know how to spell what we talked about, and we would be meeting frequently during office hours. I braced myself. I was an adjunct and already overworked and underpaid.

Still, I was ecstatic to have the job. I had gone back to work after many years at home and by many years, I mean twelve. That's a big, gaping hole on your resume. I had left *Business Week* shortly after I had my first son. In the interim, I had started a blog about—what else?—being a suburban mom, because, you know, no one else was doing that. Then, *The New York Times* quoted it in a story about how the suburbs were coping post stock market crash in 2008. It was a briefly exciting time: *New York* magazine wanted to interview me! Al Jazeera wanted to send a camera crew! None of that materialized, but the *Times* story helped me get a job teaching creative writing in the city, plus an assignment for the *Times* Sunday business section. The story landed on the front page, below the fold, but still. It helped me get a second part-time teaching job, teaching news reporting to college students.

I hadn't done anything this stressful in a long time and I loved it. It was great fun to come up with writing assignments and quizzes. But I had 25 students and because I was a newbie, I let them rewrite every weekly writing assignment, which meant I was constantly sitting with a pile of papers, grading and re-grading.

The other problem was that journalism jobs were so scarce, I felt like a fraud. I was teaching my students to become news reporters, which they were likely never to become. (Some of my students were muscular young men, their taut arms covered in tattoos. They were athletes majoring in physical education and were required to take news reporting. I could never figure out why.) I could only hope the skills I imparted might help them while they were doing something else: Write everything down, type fast, don't post anything online that you don't want the whole world to read, sum up your points in ten words or less and turn it into a headline, get your facts right and make deadline.

As it turned out, the hard-of-hearing student was one of the best students in the class. She was smart, funny and punk; she dyed her hair interesting colors and pierced different parts of her face. She also turned out to be an excellent writer and outstanding reporter. She might actually start to make money from her writing.

And Sandy was fantastic. She periodically worked at our synagogue, translating for hard-of-hearing congregants on the High Holidays, so we often talked about the Jewish holidays. Her presence in class was invigorating. With a fellow adult in the room, taking notes and flashing everything I said in huge print up on a screen, I could never just wing it. She kept me on my toes. It was also comforting to have at least one other person in the room who wasn't texting.

Sandy lived with her boyfriend and was also writing a memoir. She didn't have kids, so we talked about food and writing. One day, she sent me her Grandma Sally's applesauce recipe. I printed it out and thought about making it, but also got a jar of applesauce out of the pantry just in case. Then I looked closely at Grandma Sally's recipe. I made it, and so should you.

I was given the brisket recipe in 1999, when we first moved back to town and I took a "principles of cooking" class at our local supermarket. The four women teaching the class were beyond delightful but the one I remember the best was the one who taught us this brisket recipe. Her name was Kathleen Sanderson, a cheerful, blonde chef and middle-aged mom, who took cooking seriously but didn't yell at us for making mistakes. I think I have made this recipe at least 100 times in the last fifteen years. The addition of the half bottle of chili sauce comes from my own mom.

The beauty of this brisket recipe is that this is where your old brown sugar goes to die. Keep that block of brown sugar and don't worry if it's hard as a rock. Cut off a couple of inches and throw it in the pot with the meat. It will melt quickly and smell wonderful. And don't stress about whether you have exactly the right number of tablespoons or not. Too much brown sugar is never a bad thing.

Also, Rao's marinara sauce works really well in this recipe. It may seem a little crazy to buy a cheap cut of meat and then pour an expensive jar of tomato sauce on top of it but good meals, like life, are almost always combinations of the simple and the extravagant.

Braised Brisket of Beef

(About 8 servings)

INGREDIENTS:

- 4-5 lbs beef brisket, 1st cut
- Coarse salt
- Freshly ground black pepper to taste
- Vegetable oil, as needed
- 2 large garlic cloves, minced
- 2-3 tablespoons cider vinegar
- 2-3 tablespoons dark brown sugar
- 16 ounces marinara sauce *(Rao's works well)*
- 2-3 tablespoons ketchup
- 1 tablespoon Worcestershire sauce
- Half bottle chili sauce *(about ¾ cup)*
- ¾ of a cup water, boiling

- 2 bay leaves
- ½-¾ teaspoon dried thyme, crushed
- 2-3 onions, Bermuda variety is nice and so is Spanish, cut into ½ inch slices
- Bag of baby carrots *(optional but yummy)*

PREPARATION:

1. **Preheat oven to 350 degrees.**
2. **Wipe the brisket with damp paper toweling.** Combine kosher salt and pepper and dredge the meat in it.
3. **Heat oil in large roasting pan** with a cover *(a thin blue enamel roaster is fine–just make sure it's an oven-proof pot and has a lid).* Brown the meat, starting fat side down, on both sides to seal in the juices.
4. **Spread the garlic** over the top of the meat, pour the vinegar over, letting it drip into pan, then add all the remaining ingredients except onions and carrots.
5. **Bring to a slow boil**, basting meat until the ingredients are blended.
6. **Cover pan and place in the oven** for 2-2½ hours until meat is almost tender, continuing to baste occasionally and adding small amounts of boiling water as needed. If using carrots, add to pan about halfway through cooking time.
7. **Toward the end of the braising time**, lay the onions in a single layer over the top of meat. Extra onions may be placed around meat; baste with gravy, cover pan and return to oven for about 20 more minutes or until onions are tender.
8. **Let meat stand for ½ hour** at room temperature before slicing against the grain.

Grandma Sally's Apple Sauce

(Yield: 2-3 cups of sauce)

This sauce is chunky, so get the family ready for a new taste sensation if they're used to creamy.

INGREDIENTS:

- 4-5 Rome apples, cored *(leave skins on)*
- Cinnamon and nutmeg, to taste

PREPARATION:

1. **Sit apples in a big pot.** Add water to cover the bottom third of the apples. The trick is to check water—it's better to have less than more, as apples have a lot of their own water. After 15-20 minutes, check apples with a fork as they start to soften. I help them along, breaking them down.
2. **As apples break down more and more,** continue to stir. When it reaches a consistency you like, sprinkle cinnamon, add a pinch or 2 of nutmeg and give it a final stir or two.

Potato Pancakes (Latkes)

(Serves 6-8)

INGREDIENTS:

- 2 pounds baking potatoes, Russet or Idaho *(peeled or unpeeled —I don't peel them)*
- 1 onion, chopped
- 2 eggs
- Salt and pepper *(use liberally, there are a lot of potatoes here)*
- 2 tablespoons plain breadcrumbs or matzo meal *(I used matzo meal)*
- Canola oil or vegetable oil *(I have used both)*

PREPARATION:

1. **Turn oven to 200 degrees** *(for warming).*
2. **Grate potatoes** by hand or use grating disk in food processor. Drain in colander. Grate onion. Mix together.
3. **Beat eggs in a bowl.** Add salt, pepper and matzo meal/ breadcrumbs. Stir in potatoes and onion.
4. **Heat 2 large frying pans**, add about ⅛ inch of oil to each pan *(you will be making a lot of latkes).* When oil is hot, drop potato pancake batter on it with a large spoon or a quarter cup measuring cup.
5. **Let latkes cook for 10 minutes** each side.
6. **Drain pancakes on paper towel** and keep them warm in oven until you're done cooking. Enjoy.

31

Eastover

I Had (Sort of) Arrived

FEATURING
- Chicken Marbella

SOME DAYS are just going to suck and you know it. The day I'm thinking about was almost one of them. Yes, it was a gorgeous, spring day. The sun was shining and the air was warm. It was a day of sundresses and sandals, of children laughing and people planning their pedicures, one of those days when the earth warms, the leaves are lusciously thick and green, and the daffodils bloom. Some might call this kind of day glorious. But for me, it was a day that was going to be devoted to blasting through a big pile of bills. Days like these involve no creativity, no fun. Who wants to give money away, especially when the computer lets you do it quickly?

To avoid shooting myself, I moved the pile of bills out to the patio and put up the umbrella over the table. That helped. Then, I thought about making dinner. Yes, it was 9:30 a.m. but so what? Sometimes it's better to get your dinner ready in the morning, when you're caffeinated and full of pep. There was a recipe I'd been eager to make: Chicken Marbella, otherwise known as chicken with prunes, olives, capers, brown sugar and a bunch of other delicious stuff.

I'd had this wonderful dish a few days earlier at my friend from high school's second day Seder. This friend from high school was not actually my friend *during* high school. I would have been lucky if that were the case. Imagine the parties I would have been invited to. My friend is two years older than I am and was part of the cool crowd. She played field hockey and tennis. All of her tennis racket covers were from Lily Pulitzer. Her teeth were straight, her skin was smooth and she had a great smile. She was outgoing, friendly and smart; her boyfriend, athletic, muscular and good-looking. Most of my memories involve her running outside in her tennis whites or standing outside in the "garden" where the older kids went to smoke. Yes, you read that right. This was the late seventies and kids were allowed to smoke on school property. She didn't smoke but other people did. In her down vest and topsiders, she was always leaning in to giggle with other kids in down vests.

In high school, I knew exactly who she was. She knew vaguely who I was. Enough said?

But victory goes to those who age and move back home. As adults, we both bought houses in our hometown and sent our children to the same high school we had attended. First, our husbands became friends. Then, I'd run into her in exercise classes. Eventually, we started going for long walks with our dogs until her dog started to growl and nip at my dog. So we stopped using our dogs as an excuse to talk to each other and just went for long walks and hot cups of coffee. We became close. The two years that set us apart in high school narrowed to nothing. We talked about everything: Our families, our marriages, our kids, our parents, and of course, high school, which she, God bless her, actually had fond memories of.

My friend's husband isn't Jewish and they always celebrate Easter but one year, my friend decided to have a bunch of friends from high school over for a second night Seder. She called it Eastover.

My friend is an excellent cook, as is her husband; her two other friends from high school were also great cooks. They all knew each other very well. They had played field hockey together; one of them had been the captain of the team. I remembered a picture of the captain from the yearbook. She was raising her field hockey stick, rushing for the goal, her hair flying, and a fierce expression on her face. I was afraid of her. Needless to say, she became a successful lawyer.

The night we got together, I was intimidated. I had played varsity soccer but not well. I wasn't a fast runner and I rarely started; I made one goal in four years. I also wasn't very cool in high school. A few of my friends were cooler than I was, so I tagged along to parties with them, but I had never been part of the inner circle. Now, thirty-five years later, I felt like I was. Okay, it was a Seder—there were no kegs or illicit flasks of vodka and we all had our kids in tow but so what? Belatedly and pathetically, I had arrived.

The field hockey captain made a terrific broccoli dish. The non-captain brought chicken Marbella. It was arranged beautifully on a platter and the non-captain tried to downplay it but it was one of the best chicken dishes I have ever eaten. So she could play field hockey *and* cook. Jesus.

If you haven't made Chicken Marbella, you might remember it as one of the best-selling dishes that the Silver Palate made back in the eighties, when they were still a tiny storefront on Columbus Avenue in Manhattan. You could tuck into that bite-sized place after work, spend $20 and know you were going to eat well, if alone, that night. Their food was expensive but so good; I bought two of their cookbooks and have spent the better part of fifteen years cooking from the second one, *The New Basics*.

Chicken Marbella is easy. You mix up the ingredients, marinate the chicken (the recipe says to do it all night, but marinating the chicken all day accomplishes the same thing), and then stick it in the oven for an hour before dinner. There's almost no prep involved in this recipe. And it's fabulous.

The sauce is the best part. I could not get enough of it and finally, at the end of the meal, when the kids had disappeared upstairs to do their homework or whatever they were doing, I took a spoon and lapped mine up.

If there are people in your life who look at olives, prunes and capers and scrunch up their noses, just tell them to eat around the yummy small parts (which have already done their job of marinating the chicken anyway). Now there's more for you.

Chicken Marbella

(Serves 10-12)

INGREDIENTS:

- 4 chickens, 2 ½ pounds each, quartered
  (i.e. many, many legs, breasts and wings)
- 1 head of garlic, peeled and finely pureed
- coarse salt and freshly ground black pepper to taste
- ¼ cup dried oregano
- ½ cup red wine vinegar
- ½ cup olive oil
- 1 cup pitted prunes
- ½ cup pitted Spanish green olives
- ½ cup capers with a bit of juice
- 6 bay leaves
- 1 cup brown sugar
- 1 cup white wine
- ¼ cup Italian parsley or fresh cilantro, finely chopped

PREPARATION:

1. **Preheat oven to 350 degrees.**
2. **In a large bowl, combine** chicken quarters, garlic, oregano, pepper and coarse salt to taste, vinegar, olive oil, prunes, olives, capers and juice, and bay leaves. Cover and let marinate, refrigerated, overnight or all day.
3. **Arrange chicken in a single layer** in one or two large, shallow baking pans and spoon marinade over it evenly. Sprinkle chicken pieces with brown sugar and pour white wine around them.

4. **Bake for 1 hour,** basting frequently with pan juices. Chicken is done when thigh pieces, pricked with a fork at their thickest, yield clear yellow *(rather than pink)* juice.

5. **With a slotted spoon transfer chicken, prunes, olives** and capers to a serving platter. Moisten with a few spoonfuls of pan juices and sprinkle generously with parsley or cilantro. Pass remaining pan juices in a sauceboat.

- **To serve Chicken Marbella cold**, cool to room temperature in cooking juices before transferring to a serving platter. If chicken has been covered and refrigerated, allow it to return to room temperature before serving. Spoon some of the reserved juices over chicken.

32

When Chocolate Is Your True Religion

The Best Chocolate Desserts for Passover, Easter and Just in General

FEATURING

- Persian Chocolate Bark
- Chocolate and Caramel-Covered Matzo

ONE OF MY MANY FAILINGS is that I love sugar. I can't give it up. Two of my friends have given up sugar and they look fantastic. They've each lost, like, ten or twenty pounds. They're both in their fifties and neither of them is an exercise fanatic but every time I see them, they look younger and better. The last time I saw them, one was wearing leather pants and the other was wearing a belt to hold up her jeans. The one with the belt handed me two packets of Stevia and wished me luck. I tell myself that I want to be like them and give up sugar too. I've stopped chewing bubble gum and gnawing on jawbreakers, given up gluten and milk. But it's tough to go a day without sugar.

Actually, I haven't even tried.

In addition to sugar, I love holidays. It is any coincidence that most of them call for sugar-filled desserts? Chocolate matzo, chocolate Easter bunnies, jellybeans, chocolate-covered macaroons—they're all just conduits for sugar. Why fight the urge? Especially on a religious holiday, where you're going to have to sit through some kind of ceremony before you eat, and merely the anticipation that you're going to bite into something sugar-filled at the end of that meal may stop you from sneaking into the bathroom to check your email?

In our house, we celebrate Passover, which means going to my brother and sister-in-law's for an enormous potluck, multi-generational, all-inclusive Seder. My stepfather comes and he is Irish Catholic. My Jewish friend from high school comes with her Catholic husband. The neighbors aren't Jewish and they read the Hagaddah and stay for dinner too. The way we work this holiday is it's "sort of, kind of" about the Israelites fleeing Egypt and arriving safely in the Promised Land but it's also very much about celebrating spring, drinking wine and eating a whole lot of delicious stuff.

Everyone who comes to this Seder brings something, and they're all about good food. Why is that? Because everyone who attends fits into one of the following categories. They are:

1) Writers
2) Psychologists/social workers/psycho-analysts/psychiatrists
3) Formerly married to one of the above
4) Currently married to one of the above
5) Related to one of the above
6) Seeing one of the above

Writers and therapists (and the people who love them) like to eat. Well, that may not be true in a macro sense, but in this group it seems like law. My brother (married to a psychologist) and his brother-in-law (a psychoanalyst) are both fabulous cooks. My sister-in-law's sister (once married to a psychiatrist) is an excellent cook. I'm a writer who lives two miles away from my mother, so obviously I've been in therapy, and I know my way around a kitchen. The bar is set pretty high. Everyone is allergic to one thing or avoiding another. We have celiac, peanut allergies, pine-nut allergies and a whole barrel full of gluten free people crowding around the table but fortunately, there's so much food that you can avoid whatever scares you.

For years, I have been bringing ten pounds of brisket to this Seder. I have made this brisket forever, and they still want it. But this year, I needed a challenge so I offered to bring something new in addiction (I mean addition). I had seen a recipe for Nutty Chocolate Bark with Cardamom and Coffee in Louisa Shafia's book, *The New Persian Kitchen*. This is one of the best cookbooks I have ever read. I had already tried her Turmeric Chicken with Sumac and Lime, and her Sweet Rice with Carrots and Nuts, and they were both delicious. Shafia uses ingredients that I had never used (coconut oil, turmeric, sumac) and relies heavily on ingredients that I had only used sporadically (lime juice, pistachio nuts, saffron). I spotted her Nutty Bark recipe and immediately clipped the page.

I love cardamom, cumin, coriander and cinnamon. I inhale their scents as I open the jars, exhale as I measure out their soft thick powder into teaspoons, then sniff again before I tighten their lids. It's true: just a whiff of these spices can make you briefly ecstatic. And the beauty of this nutty chocolate bark recipe is it's gluten free. Perfect for Passover!

It's easy too. It takes all of fifteen minutes to prepare, and two hours to cool in the fridge. While it cooled, I stood alone in the kitchen and started to lick the warm, nutty, fruity chocolate out of the pot. In one mouthful, you get chocolate, sea salt, dried cherries, mulberries, pistachio nuts, and almonds, followed by the powerful kick of coffee and cardamom. Your brain says, "OMG, are you kidding? Faster, faster!" The key is to use really good chocolate (I used Ghirardelli). I also doubled the amount of dried cherries, just because I like them and we had some extra.

Now, you may be wondering about the mulberries. Other than vaguely remembering the song, "Here We Go Round the Mulberry Bush," I had no idea what mulberries were. They are small, soft, shriveled fruit that look like raisins coated in granola. They have a mild, sweet taste. I ordered a package off Amazon and they arrived in two days. You can also find them at Penzey's and specialty grocery stores.

It's popular now to say that something is so good it's like crack. I've never done crack but this chocolate bark may be as close as I ever come to trying it. It was really hard not to eat the whole batch while writing this.

Happy Passover, Happy Easter, or as my Jewish friend who's married to the Catholic guy says, Happy Eastover.

Persian Chocolate Bark With Cardamom and Coffee

(adapted from Louisa Shafia's *The New Persian Kitchen*)

(Serves 8-10)

INGREDIENTS

- 2 cups semi-sweet chocolate chips *(I used Ghirardelli)*
- 1 teaspoon ground cardamom
- ¼ cup dried mulberries
- ¼ cup dried tart cherries *(I doubled this and used ½ cup)*
- ¾ cup almonds, toasted and coarsely chopped
- ½ cup pistachios, toasted and coarsely chopped
- 2 teaspoons coffee beans, coarsely chopped
- Pinch of coarse salt *(I used sea salt)*

PREPARATION:

1. **Grease a baking sheet** and line with parchment paper.
2. **Melt chocolate in saucepan** over a pot of simmering water. Add cardamom and stir to dissolve for a couple of minutes. Turn off heat, remove pot from heat and stir in half the mulberries, cherries, almonds and pistachios.
3. **Pour chocolate onto prepared baking sheet.** With an offset spatula or rubber spatula, spread chocolate in a wide rectangle about ¼ inch thick. Sprinkle with remaining nuts, dried fruit and ground coffee beans, and press gently into chocolate. Dust with salt.
4. **Cool in refrigerator for about 2 hours,** until hard. When firm, slide chocolate onto cutting board and break into pieces. The chocolate gets soft quickly so keep refrigerated until just before serving.

Chocolate-Covered Caramelized Matzo Crunch

(Serves 8-10)

Note: If you want to avoid nuts and/or just want a more traditional Passover dessert, try this chocolate covered matzo adapted from the website davidlebovitz.com and Marcy Goldman of BetterBaking.com.

This recipe is super-simple and requires no fancy thermometer, equipment, or ingredients. If you can't get matzo, use plain crackers such as saltines and omit the additional salt in the recipe.

▸ *For Passover or vegans, Marcy advises that it works well with margarine. And for our gluten-free friends, this would be superb made with any gluten-free cracker.*

INGREDIENTS:

- 4 to 6 sheets unsalted matzos
- 1 cup unsalted butter, cut into chunks
- 1 cup firmly packed light brown sugar
- Big pinch of sea salt
- ½ teaspoon vanilla extract*
- 1 cup semisweet chocolate chips *(or chopped bittersweet or semisweet chocolate)*
- 1 cup toasted sliced almonds *(optional)*

PREPARATION:

1. **Preheat oven to 375 degrees.**
2. **Line a rimmed baking sheet** *(approximately 11x17-inch)* completely with foil, making sure the foil goes up and over the edges. Cover the foil with a sheet of parchment paper.
3. **Line the bottom of the sheet** with matzo, breaking extra pieces as necessary to fill in any spaces.
4. **In a 3-4 quart heavy-duty saucepan, melt butter** and brown sugar together, and cook over medium heat, stirring, until the butter is melted and the mixture is beginning to boil. Boil for 3 minutes, stirring constantly. Remove from heat, mix in the salt

and vanilla, and pour over matzo, spreading with a heatproof spatula.

5. **Put the pan in the oven** and reduce the heat to 350 degrees. Bake for 15 minutes. As it bakes, it will bubble up but check every once in a while to make sure it's not burning. If it is in spots, remove from oven and reduce heat to 325 degrees, then replace pan. Remove from oven and immediately cover with chocolate chips. Let stand 5 minutes, then spread with an offset spatula.
6. **If you wish, sprinkle with toasted almonds** *(or another favorite nut, toasted and coarsely-chopped)*, a sprinkle of flaky sea salt, or roasted cocoa nibs.
7. **Let cool completely, then break into pieces** and store in an airtight container until ready to serve. It should keep well for about one week.

▸ *If making for Passover, omit the vanilla extract or find a kosher brand.*

33

Cooking for a Crowd

Lots to Chew On, Long After Everyone Is Gone

IF YOU COOK FOR A CROWD OFTEN ENOUGH, you learn what to bring to the party. For example, you don't offer to bring caviar or lobster Fra Diablo, swordfish or chocolate soufflé.

FEATURING

- Sweet Basmati Rice with Honey, Currants and Pistachios
- Shredded Cabbage Terra Chip Salad
- Cauliflower Frittata
- Artichoke Frittata
- Red Lentil Coconut Curry with Cauliflower
- Shakshuka
- Singapore Chicken
- Lemon Curd with Raspberries and Blueberries
- Pots of Chocolate Cream

Many years ago, when I was new in town, I joined a playgroup with my younger son. We sat around each other's basements and family rooms and talked about how long our kids napped and slept through the night, how often we got to the gym, and where we were going on vacation. The kids crawled around, kissed each other, tried to walk, fell over and amused themselves with plastic toys. We exchanged recipes and talked about what we would like to do to our kitchens. We looked for reasons to get dressed up and go out with the men who had made us mothers in the first place. One morning, we decided to organize a dinner party. I offered to marinate swordfish and tuna and grill it.

What was I thinking? I was probably in the mood for fresh fish and hadn't calculated what I'd have to spend to feed eighteen hungry people on a Saturday night. My husband and I arrived at the party late because we were busy on our patio, grilling. When we finally got there, everyone else was busy drinking margaritas and doing tequila shots. They were munching on salsa, hummus and tortilla chips. Someone had taken boneless chicken breasts, sliced them up into little pieces, slid them onto skewers with green peppers and pineapple chunks, grilled them for a few minutes, and then put them on paper plates. Everyone seemed very happy eating those; we were so late, no one was hungry anymore. I poured myself a glass of cold chardonnay, took my sandals off and pulled a piece of chicken off a skewer with my mouth. That was how I learned what not to bring.

When my father died, an enormous number of people showed up for Shiva. I'm not sure why so many people came. Dad was a polarizing figure. He was brilliant and witty, cruel and volatile. He had many employers and employees and multiple long-term romances. The guy who serviced his blue Jaguar convertible loved him. His ex-wives did not. None of his former girlfriends or fiancées came to the funeral. Neither did his sister or her kids or any of his living first cousins. It's possible that his former colleagues were there but I didn't see any of them. One of his lawyers was there and introduced himself to me. A few days later, he came looking for the money Dad owed him.

Many of my friends' fathers had already died. In my book group, we jokingly referred to ourselves as "the dead dad's club." My stepfather lost all of his four siblings in short order and then lost his oldest daughter. Shiva was nothing new. And yet, it never gets better. Everything is a blur of remorse, regret, and sadness. But some people are laughing and eating. Maybe you are too. You will want to remember the person who has passed, but you'll have time for that later. In the meantime, we have bagels, lox, vegetable crudité, cauliflower frittata and handfuls of chocolate covered almonds. We have chocolate cake and chocolate chip cookies and herring and pickles. We have cups of lemon curd, topped with raspberries.

My father loved raspberries.

At my father's shiva, we had platters and platters of food, all the food my father loved, and we ordered it from the same place where we had ordered the platters for my younger son's briss. Almost the same people, almost the same food, for vastly different reasons. Life and death often pack the same crowd. A few months after Dad passed away, his sister died. A few months later, my grandmother died. A year later, my uncle died. My kids were still young then and every time someone passed away, they asked, "Is there going to be a party afterwards, Mama?" I said yes, there will be a party afterwards and your cousins will be there and you will eat lunch with them and then play outside. Because, as it happens, most of our funerals take place in the spring and summer.

Of course, happy times call for food for a crowd too.

My friend Debbie was declared Woman of the Year by our local Hadassah chapter one spring. I'm not active in Hadassah but I am Debbie's close friend so she asked me to be on the food committee. I offered to bring a platter of sushi from the local supermarket (easy enough) and also prepare a couple of things. I forgot that the day before the event, I had an all day bar mitzvah in the city so I wouldn't be able to cook anything ahead of time. My sister-in-law, Lorien, had a great recipe for an artichoke frittata that I knew would be a hit, and my friends Terri and Helaine had given me a recipe for a cauliflower frittata that was delicious. But I also wanted to try something new. Why not ignore everything I knew about cooking for a crowd and make something that morning that I'd never made before? This is how I came to make shakshuka.

Shakshuka is a spicy Tunisian tomato stew with poached eggs on top of it. That's the best way to describe it, though some people make Shakshuka with potatoes and eggplant instead of tomatoes, so if you want to be one of those people, go ahead. I first ate shakshuka at a grape farm in Lachish, an ancient and famous biblical city near Gaza, southeast of Jerusalem, where we went to stay with relatives one summer. Feral cats everywhere, no air conditioning and hot as hell in August. But the food! I've never eaten so much delicious fresh food in my life – huge, sweet purple grapes right off the vines.

On Sunday morning, our host made shakshuka and served it in a large pan. I had never eaten such a thing: Warm, delicious, tangy and spicy, a perfect hot dish for lunch. "How did you make this?" I asked.

"It's nothing," she waved me away.

"That combination of flavors. What's in there?"

She shrugged: "Tomatoes, eggs, spices, you know."

I didn't know. But I would find out.

Shakshuka originated as an easy meal to serve Israeli soldiers – it's filling and warm, and the ingredients are cheap. You make a huge pan and everyone helps themselves. Perfect for a crowd. Perfect for Debbie's Hadassah celebration. Unfortunately, the recipe calls for fresh tomatoes and this was May.

In Israel, fresh tomatoes are easy to come by. But in May in New Jersey, the only fresh tomatoes I had were those nice little sweet grape tomatoes sitting in a bowl on the counter. I didn't have anywhere near enough grape tomatoes to feed 40 women and I didn't feel like running to the supermarket and then slicing billions of tomatoes. I did, however, have two nice cans of San Marzano tomatoes. (Use the kind with the EU DOP label on it– European Union, protected designation of origin.)

So I made shakshuka for Debbie, with a combination of canned tomatoes, fresh grape tomatoes and sliced red peppers. It was easy to assemble but the results weren't pretty. In fact, it looked like a large pan of warm tomato and egg soup. Hardly fit for company, never mind a party. And there was no way I could make it look better. I couldn't transfer it into a container without ruining the appearance of the one nice thing about it: All those lovely whole poached eggs, thick and white, sitting peacefully on top of the red tomatoes and peppers. So I put a lid on the pot and brought it as is. At Debbie's party, the sushi sat for a while. The shakshuka was gone within an hour.

* * *

My father has been dead almost ten years now. Every year, his yarzheit arrives in May, along with the azaleas and the daffodils, the forsythia and occasionally the peonies, and always the blossoming magnolia trees. Sometimes, I cut daffodils and bring them to his grave. Every year, I try to figure out what to do to remember him. Some years, I text my brother and sister and we get together for dinner and Shabbat services. Some years, I take our dog, drive to Daddy's grave, say Kaddish and leave flowers and a stone on his tomb. Some years, we do nothing.

This year, when we went to synagogue to say Kaddish, there was an older couple there—neighbors of my mother's—whose grown son had taken his own life a few years back. Thin and frail, the woman was dressed in all black and carried herself in the same elegant, erect way she always had as she walked slowly across the lobby. Her husband was dapper, with a closely cropped mustache and a fine blue suit. He held her arm; she leaned into him.

We had actually entertained this couple – the Watsons – in our home a few years back for a series of hosted Shabbat dinners for our temple. Their son, Doug, had babysat for me as a child. When I'd heard the terrible news, I'd never reached out to them. It was one of those situations where you hear something and think about writing a note but then you stop and think: *I haven't talked to them in decades, they won't even know who I am,* so you pull down the shade of shame and do nothing. And then there they were in my house.

Even though my father had tried to kill himself, at least twice, a suicidal father is not the same as a child who commits suicide. Mr. Watson had sat to my left at dinner and told me how much he had liked my father.

"He was a funny guy, your Dad," Mr. Watson said.

"Yeah, he could be." I wanted to hear more. Maybe he did too.

I told him I remembered Doug babysitting for us one Saturday night. He sat in the hallway on the floor while he thought my brother and I were sleeping. His feet were up on the door of the linen closet and he was staring at the closet door. I crept out of my bedroom and looked at him. He was a handsome guy, muscular with dark hair. I was maybe ten and too young to know what was going on inside of me but I had a few stirrings and I was curious about what we might talk about, late at night. The linen closet door had an intricate carved brass doorknob and I wondered if he was looking at that.

"What are you doing?" I asked.

"I could sit here for hours and just think," he said.

He said he didn't need to have anything in particular to think about; he could just sit there all night. "That sounds like Doug," Mr. Watson said.

I didn't ask what had happened to Doug. The death of a parent may almost slay you but it can't compare to the death of a child. I thought about my father's parents, and what they might have thought of my father plunging a knife into his heart the day after Christmas. How would my Grandma Lee have felt? My conversation with Mr. Watson wasn't intimate but I felt like we'd given each other something important.

Seeing them in temple, I wondered how often the Watsons came to say Kaddish. Whether they ever felt comfort from hearing their son's name said out loud. How they managed from day to day. After my father passed away, I used to think that I was far tougher than my friends whose parents were alive. And I felt superior to the ones who had never visited their parents in psych wards, never wondered when they were going to receive the next call that something horrendous had happened. Lowering a box holding someone you love into the ground hardens you; you take a quick leap from childhood into adulthood. But looking at the Watsons, I realized they were far tougher than I would ever be.

Inside the sanctuary, I sat on the same orange wall-to-wall carpeting I sat on for my brother's bar mitzvah, my father's second wedding, and for both my sons' bar mitzvahs. This is the synagogue I grew up in and the synagogue we belong to now. As the young woman rabbi announced the names of those who had passed away, I listened for my father's name to be called. It almost always comes last unless the occasional Zuckerman dies in May and sneaks in there. Before the rabbi arrived at Dad's name, she announced the name of another doctor, William Bernstein, who had passed away a couple of weeks earlier. I waited and waited for the rabbi to say Daddy's name. Finally, she read it out loud: Stephen Alan Zinn, MD. That was what it said on Dad's mailing labels and prescription pads and that was how he signed his checks. But Dr. Bernstein had been called "Doctor" William Bernstein. Maybe Dad should be remembered as Dr. Stephen A. Zinn, so he and Dr. Bernstein would sound like they were friends. Did Dad want to be called doctor or MD? I didn't know. This was the beauty of yahrzeit. Recite the Mourner's Kaddish, say the name out loud, and all these years later, you could still think about what might have made that person happy.

It was raining hard as we left the temple, so hard that while we were driving home, I could barely see through the windshield. The wind was howling and the raindrops fell fast and thick. To cheer myself up, I started to think about food. The next day, we'd be celebrating my father-in-law's birthday and my husband's aunt and uncle were coming for lunch. I had wanted to make chocolate pots of cream but had run out of time so we would eat a chocolate buttercream birthday cake from a bakery. I would make Singapore chicken, a delicious honey, butter, mustard dish that is prepared with curry powder, and also what I called sweet rice with honey, a Persian rice dish made with pistachios, currants, honey and coconut oil. I started to feel happy as I thought about all the steps it would take to concoct those honey-filled dishes. I would stand in the kitchen and putter around and then we would all sit down for a big noonday meal together. The honey basmati rice dish would last for days and I would still be nibbling on it long after everybody left.

In the kitchen after services, we stood around, eating purple grapes and baby carrots.

"I remember Grandpa pulling up in his Jaguar, putting me in his car and taking me swimming," my older son said.

My younger son chimed in. "What I remember about Grandpa is that one day he leaned over me and opened his wallet and said, 'Hey, how much money do you want?'"

We all laughed. That was Dad. Generous, impulsive and wildly unpredictable. My father's fury was probably rooted in the same spot as his ambition and focus. Different plants thrive in the same soil. Was his mental illness a result of nature or nurture? Am I planting the same seeds in my kids' psyches? I've tried not to echo my parents' behavior, but only the people my children make their lives with will know for sure.

Decades of therapy and meditation have quieted my nerves but I can still be volatile as hell. Some of that hard wiring can't be replaced. My children periodically refer to me as a "fun psychopath." I've thrown tantrums and stormed out of the house. It takes massive effort not to deploy the same verbal smacks my father did when I'm feeling under siege. But then I wander down into the kitchen and make something delicious to eat.

If food is love, then cooking is even lovelier. And we are all hungry.

SHREDDED CABBAGE TERRA CHIP SALAD

(Serves 6-8)

INGREDIENTS:

- 1 bag shredded white cabbage
- ½ bag terra chips crushed (not powdery)
- ½ cup craisins
- ½ cup pine nuts

DRESSING:

- ½ cup oil
- 3 tablespoons soy sauce
- 6 tablespoons red wine vinegar
- Salt and pepper

PREPARATION:

1. **Combine the cabbage, terra chips,** craisins and pine nuts.
2. **Pour dressing** on right before serving.

Artichoke Frittata

(Serves 6-8)

PREPARATION:

- 1 16-ounce jar marinated artichokes
- 1 bunch green onions (scallions), chopped
- 2 cloves garlic, minced
- 2 tablespoons fresh parsley, minced
- 2 tablespoons olive oil
- 5 eggs
- ½ cup bread crumbs (optional)
- ¼ teaspoon salt and pepper
- dash of Tabasco
- ½ pound grated cheese *(mixture of Jack and Asiago)*
- ½ cup grated Romano cheese

DRESSING:

1. **Preheat oven to 350 degrees.**
2. **Sauté green onions, garlic and parsley** in olive oil and set aside to cool.
3. **Meanwhile, pour out oil from the artichoke hearts** into a bowl. Chop up the artichoke hearts. Beat the eggs and add in the breadcrumbs, salt and pepper, Tabasco, and grated cheese. Add in artichoke hearts and greens and mix.
4. **Grease an 8-inch dish and bake for 30-40 minutes**, until lightly browned and eggs are set.

Cauliflower Frittata

ADAPTED FROM *PLENTY*

(Serves 6-8)

INGREDIENTS:

- 1 small cauliflower, cut into small florets
- 6 eggs
- 4 tablespoons crème fraiche, or heavy cream
- 2-3 tablespoons Dijon mustard

- 2 teaspoons sweet paprika
- 3 tablespoons chives, finely chopped
- 5 ounces smoked or regular shredded mozzarella
- 2 ounces strong shredded cheddar
- Salt and pepper to taste
- 2 tablespoons olive oil

PREPARATION::

1. **Preheat oven to 375 degrees.**
2. **Simmer cauliflower in large pan** of salted boiling water for 4-5 minutes, until partially cooked. Drain and dry.
3. **Add eggs to medium bowl,** along with crème fraiche, mustard and paprika. Mix until thoroughly combined and season generously with salt and pepper. Mix in chives and three quarters of the cheese.
4. **Heat a cast iron skillet over medium heat** and add olive oil. Cook cauliflower until it starts to turn golden brown, a minute or two.
5. **Pour egg mixture over cauliflower** and move cauliflower around to make sure eggs are spread around evenly. Top with remaining cheese and place pan in preheated oven. Bake until eggs are set, about 15 minutes. Then brown for one minute under broiler.

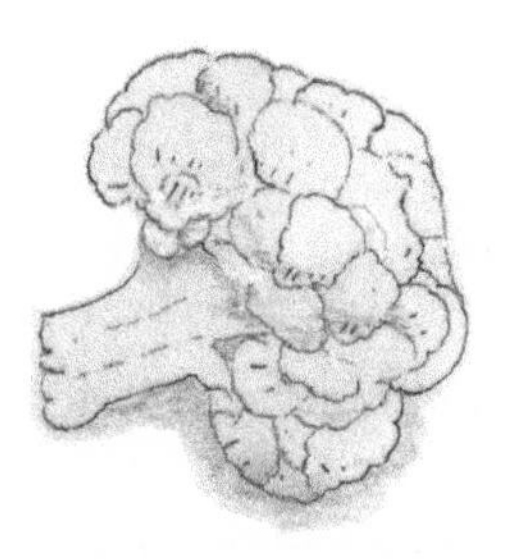

Shakshuka

(Poached egg and warm tomato/red pepper stew)

ADAPTED FROM *JERUSALEM*

(Serves 6-8)

INGREDIENTS:

- 2 tablespoons olive oil
- 1-2 tablespoons harissa *(Harissa is a spicy combination of chili peppers, Serrano peppers, roasted red peppers, garlic, paprika, sumac and coriander. The dry harissa powder is available at specialty stores and through Amazon. Mix the dry powder with equal parts olive oil and water, i.e. add one half-cup harissa powder to one half-cup water and one half-cup olive oil. If you don't have or can't get harissa, use an extra mashed garlic clove, and add a little cayenne pepper, paprika and some extra chopped red pepper to your tomato stew.)*
- 2 teaspoons tomato paste
- 2 large red peppers cut into ¼ inch pieces
- 4 cloves garlic, minced
- 1 teaspoon ground cumin
- 5 large, ripe tomatoes, chopped or 5 cups canned good tomatoes. *(I used 4 cans of good tomatoes, and then 1 cup of fresh, sliced grape tomatoes.)*
- 4 large free-range eggs, plus 4 yolks
- ½ cup plain yogurt
- Salt

PREPARATION:

1. **Heat olive oil in large frying pan** over medium heat and add harissa, tomato paste, peppers, garlic, cumin, and ¾ teaspoon salt.
2. **Stir and cook over medium heat** for about 8 minutes to allow peppers to soften.
3. **Add tomatoes, bring to simmer and cook** for 10 more minutes until you have a thick sauce. Season with salt and pepper.
4. **Take a teaspoon and make** 8 little spoon-size cavities in sauce.
5. G**ently break 4 eggs**, one at a time and carefully place each egg *(yolk and white)* into its own little cavity.

6. **Then break 4 more eggs**, this time separating the yolks from the whites, and add the 4 egg yolks into the 4 different cavities. *(Save egg whites for meringue cookies or an omelet.)* You will have 8 little cavities for eggs altogether. Use a fork to swirl the eggs whites around with the sauce.
7. **Simmer gently for 8-10 minutes,** until egg whites are set but yolks are still runny. You can cover the pan with a lid if you want to get this done in less time.
8. **Remove from heat**, let rest for a couple of minutes, then spoon onto plates and add yogurt on the side. Delicious!

Note: This delectably spicy tomato/pepper stew lasts for days! Finish off those eggs and save the leftover tomato/pepper stew for tomorrow and the next days. The spices and harissa act as a preservative. Keep a container of Shakshuka sans eggs in your fridge. When you're hungry, make two poached eggs, heat the leftover Shakshuka up and serve them together. I just ate that for lunch with 10-day old Shakshuka. Really!

Red Lentil Coconut Curry with Cauliflower

(Serves 6-8)

INGREDIENTS:

- 1 tablespoon coconut oil
- 1 yellow onion, diced
- 3 cloves garlic, minced
- 2 tablespoons garlic, minced
- 1 teaspoon cumin
- 3 carrots, cut into 1/4-inch rounds
- ½ head cauliflower, cut into small florets
- Japanese yam, sweet potato or butternut squash, cut into ¼ inch pieces *(I used sweet potato)*
- 1 cup red lentils
- 4 cups vegetable broth *(I recommend Rachael Ray)*
- 1 can coconut milk
- 1 cup chopped kale *(optional)*
- Handful chopped cilantro
- Sea salt and pepper to taste

PREPARATION:

1. **In large stockpot, heat coconut oil** over medium heat. Sauté onion and garlic in coconut oil until soft.
2. **Add curry powder and cumin** and stir to release flavors of the spices.
3. **Add carrots, cauliflower and yam/sweet potato/squash** and stir incorporating the curry into the vegetables.
4. **Add lentils and vegetable broth.**
5. **Turn heat to high and bring to a boil.** Once boiling, lower heat, cover pot and let simmer for about 30 minutes or until veggies are soft and lentils are mushy.
6. **Remove from heat and add coconut milk,** kale and cilantro. Season with salt and pepper.

Sweet Basmati Rice with Carrots & Pistachios *(Sweet Honey Rice)*

(Serves 6-8)

INGREDIENTS:

- 2 cups Quick Cook Organic Brown Basmati Rice *(I have used white and brown Texmati too– I make this in the pressure cooker)*
- 2-3 teaspoons coconut oil
- 1 large onion, finely diced
- 2 cups grated carrots *(I grate one bag of baby carrots)*
- ¾ cup pistachio nuts
- 1 teaspoon ground cinnamon
- 1 teaspoon ground cardamom
- 1 teaspoon ground turmeric
- Grated zest of one orange *(save orange and serve slices for dessert)*
- ½ cup honey
- ¼ teaspoon saffron, ground and steeped in 1 tablespoon hot water

PREPARATION:

1. **Make rice,** either in pressure cooker or traditional way. If using regular white basmati rice, soak in cold water for 1 hour, then drain and rinse under cold water until water runs clear.

2. **In a stockpot, combine 3 cups water** and pinch of salt and bring to a boil. Add the rice, return to a boil, then turn to low setting. Cover and cook for 20 minutes.
3. **For either rice, when cook time is over,** turn off heat, keep covered and let rice sit for 5 minutes.

   (If using a pressure cooker, cook rice for 7 minutes or so at high pressure.)
4. **Remove cover from rice pot and fluff rice** with a fork.
5. **While rice is cooking, heat a pan over medium heat and sauté** onion with coconut oil for 6-8 minutes, until lightly browned. Add shredded carrots, cinnamon, cardamom, turmeric and cook, stirring often, for about 7 minutes, until carrots are tender.
6. **Add ¾ cup pistachio nuts,** currants, orange zest and honey to carrot mixture and cook for 2 minutes, until heated through. Combine rice with carrot mixture, and then add saffron water and season to taste with salt.

▸ *I think this is what God meant when he said the Jews ate manna from heaven on their way to Israel.*

ARLENE WARD'S "SINGAPORE CHICKEN"

(Serves 8-10)

I love honey and mustard, separately and together, which is probably why I love this dish.

INGREDIENTS:

- 18 pieces of chicken – legs, thighs, breasts
- 1 garlic clove, mashed
- Salt and pepper
- ½ lemon
- ½ cup unsalted butter, melted
- 2½ tablespoons curry powder
- ¾ cup Dijon mustard
- 1 cup honey
- 1 teaspoon soy sauce
- 8 small green onions or 2-3 chives, chopped

PREPARATION:

1. **Wipe chicken with paper towels** and rub all over with mashed garlic. Season with salt and plenty of fresh ground pepper. Squeeze juice from half lemon over chicken.
2. **Lay pieces, skin side up and one layer deep,** in large baking dish *(or two dishes)*. In a saucepan, melt butter slowly and stir in curry powder. When heated through, blend in mustard, honey and soy sauce and pour sauce over chicken. At this point, you may cover with foil and refrigerate. In fact, this resting period flavors the chicken parts better. *(You can also cook right away if you are in a rush.)*
3. **Warm chicken to room temperature** before cooking. Cook in 350-degree oven for 1 hour, until chicken is tender and richly glazed. Do not overcook. Baste chicken occasionally with sauce.

▸ *Don't be afraid to do this early and re-warm it. It is also delicious cold. If you're feeling fancy, you can decorate the platter with green onion plumes. If you want some spice, chop up two or three chives and add to chicken after it's cooked.*

Panetica's Lemon Curd with Raspberries and Blueberries

(Serves 8)

INGREDIENTS:

- Zest and juice from 6 lemons
- 2 cups superfine sugar
- 8 eggs
- 8 yolks
- 1½ sticks butter, cold, divided

PREPARATION:

1. **Combine everything but half the butter** in heavy-bottomed saucepan.
2. **Whisking constantly, heat over low-medium heat** until mixture is completely homogenized and begins to thicken and bubbles start to pop up. Add remaining butter in 1-inch pieces and whisk to melt.
3. **Strain mixture through sieve** and press cling film directly on top of curd.
4. **Let cool, then put in fridge** and cool thoroughly, overnight if possible. Serve in individual glass cups with berries on top.

CHOCOLATE POTS OF CREAM

(Serves 4-6)

INGREDIENTS:

- 1 cup heavy cream
- 2 extra large eggs
- 1 teaspoon vanilla
- 6-7 ounces semi-sweet chocolate pieces *(I use Lindt 70% cocoa chocolate bars. Bars are 3.5 ounces each. Use 2 bars)*
- Garnish of whipped cream

PREPARATION:

1. **Bring heavy cream almost to boil.** In a small bowl, beat eggs and vanilla together.
2. **Place chocolate pieces in a food processor** or a blender.
3. **When cream starts to come to a boil**, pour eggs through the food processor tube and add the hot cream. Mix well using steel blade. Stop the machine and scrape down any little pieces of chocolate that didn't melt. Combine well.
4. P**our mixture into a 4-cup measuring cup.** This will allow you to carefully pour the chocolate cream into small cups. Cover each cup with plastic wrap and refrigerate for several hours. When firm and ready to serve, top each cup with a flourish of whipped cream (see page 241).

34

Falling Off the Bone

Roast Chicken in the Snow

I FEEL RIDICULOUS writing another story about chicken but this one is so astonishing, so easy and delicious, that when it became clear we were going to follow Martin Luther King Day weekend with a Snow Day, I had to share it.

My friend Terri, who gives me all my best ideas (in real life and in the kitchen) had been telling me for years about this website called *Stacey Snacks*. Sometimes Terri would say, "Did you see what *Stacey Snacks* wrote about this week? Did you subscribe yet?" And I would say, "No." I already subscribed to *Canal House Cooks Lunch* (lyrical prose about the pleasures of cooking and friendship), *Shockingly Delicious* (energetic posts from California), *Smitten Kitchen* (chatty, joyful posts from a tiny kitchen in Manhattan), *Joy the Baker* (hilarious, orgasmic approach to baking in New Orleans) and *Bad Home Cooking* (funny as hell and penned by my former *Business Week* colleague Julie Tilsner). Occasionally I dipped into *The Wednesday Chef* (cooking stories from Germany, written by Terri's cousin, cookbook author Luisa Weiss). I really didn't need any more electronic food advice. But Terri kept talking about *Stacey Snacks'* chicken and milk recipe. So when the three-day weekend was about to turn into four, with the kids home from school eating everything in sight and banging around the house, in New Jersey, in the middle of January, the

FEATURING

- Roast Chicken Braised in Milk

trains not running into the city and my head about to explode from the pressure of a book deadline hanging over me, I decided to click onto Stacey's website.

You know that little moment you have where you're feeling hopeless and overwhelmed with too much to do, and you're out of shape because it's cold out and no one can see your body anyway but you still wish you looked better, and your life is filled with people but you're still feeling lonely and bored out of your mind because none of those people can give you the love pep talk you're craving, the talk that goes something like, "You are fantastic! You aren't fat! You are just really funny and smart so don't listen to all those nagging negative voices in your head that 30 years of therapy can't get rid of!" and what you really want to do is sneak away in the middle of the day, pour a glassful of cold white wine into a small silver flask, tuck it into your pocket, hop on a train and disappear alone into a dark movie house in the East Village? That's how I was feeling when I opened up Stacey Snacks' post about Jamie Oliver's Roast Chicken Braised in Milk.

I wanted to go away. Get the hell out. Goodbye. Leave me alone. And then after reading that piece, I couldn't cook that chicken fast enough.

Right this minute, add lemons, garlic, a quart of whole milk or almond milk and a whole chicken to your grocery list and go shopping immediately. And if you already have this stuff on hand, open your fridge and freezer and start cooking this dish now.

I should tell an important thing about Terri and chicken: Several years ago, right around Thanksgiving, Terri persuaded me to order from Goffle Road Poultry Farm in Wyckoff, New Jersey. (Their website will tell you all about how to care for newborn chicks but that's not why I'm writing about them here.) Terri is one of those people who is willing to make field trips for food. I'm not. I get what's in the supermarket or I order off Amazon. But Terri kept going on about how we had to go to Goffle. They sell to some of the best local restaurants and only deliver to your home if your order is big enough ($150 or so); otherwise, you need to make a road trip. But Terri, bless her organized, brilliant heart, offered to pool an order for a bunch of us. She took delivery of it and let us keep our chicken in her freezer until we got around to picking it up. She told us what to order: Boneless chicken thighs, bone-in breasts, skinless chicken breasts, fresh eggs and chicken sausage.

All of it was fabulous. I started ordering from Goffle whenever Terri did. Then, a month later, I added a whole chicken to my order and put it in the freezer.

So on that miserable snow day, when we were at the tail end of a long weekend that had been filled with cold weather, carpooling to bar mitzvahs, excessive football, and grey skies before a heavy snow storm, I took that chicken out of the freezer, let it defrost and went to work.

However, therein lies the glory of this chicken. It's almost no work. You sauté for about ten minutes, cover it with milk, throw in a cinnamon stick, ten cloves of garlic (you don't even have to peel them!), some lemon rind and sage, put it all in the oven for an hour and half and that's it. And then...unbelievable. The chicken falls off the bones. The sauce is creamy and delicious. The results are just so awesome ... and you've done almost nothing.

I'm not sure what makes this chicken so good. There are so few ingredients, it's a joke.

My husband and 17-year-old couldn't believe how good this dish was. (My 13-year-old was at a friend's, betting on football.) Father and son started digging in. For a few seconds, all you could hear was the banging of fork against plate.

Then: "Mom, you should stop making everything else and just make this."

If I'd been thinking straight, I would have taken pictures so you could see how gorgeous this chicken is. Or you could just take my word for it, trust your imagination and run to the supermarket. Grab a whole chicken and some milk, turn on the oven and make yourself a feast. You won't be sorry. That's my love pep talk for you.

Roast Chicken Braised in Milk

(Serves 4-6)

Ingredients:

- 1 whole chicken, about 4 pounds
- 10 cloves garlic, unpeeled
- 1-2 tablespoons olive oil
- 2 tablespoons butter
- 2 cups whole milk *(or almond milk)*
- Zest from 2 lemons
- 1 cinnamon stick
- Handful of fresh sage
- Kosher salt and pepper

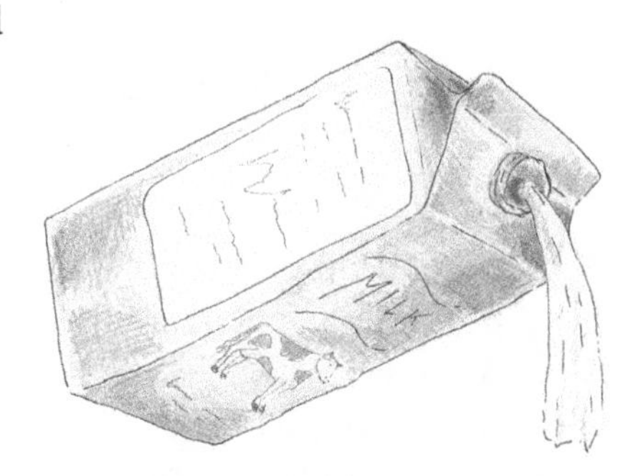

PREPARATION:

1. **Preheat oven to 375 degrees.**
2. **Rinse chicken and pat dry.** Season with kosher salt and pepper. Heat a heavy, oven-proof pot on the stove (make sure it has a tight-fitting lid; I used my mother's old yellow Dutch oven). Add butter and olive oil. Brown chicken all over, about 10 minutes, until all sides are golden brown.
3. **Sprinkle chicken with lemon zest and add** garlic cloves, cinnamon stick, milk and sage. Cover and bake in oven for 1 hour and 15 minutes. Remove lid and cook for another 15 minutes, so an hour and a half altogether.
4. **The chicken will be falling off the bone** by the end. Remove garlic from their shells. Voila. You are done, and everyone you hand this to will be deliriously happy.

▸ ***For people who are kosher and/or lactose intolerant:*** *I made this chicken and substituted almond milk for whole milk. The results were fantastic. You couldn't taste the difference. It tasted just like the original recipe. The garlic cloves and lemon zest dominate in this recipe and the milk just serves to give the chicken a nice warm bath.*

35

Potatoes Barcelona

Almost Better Than Sex

MY HUSBAND AND I decided to celebrate our 20th wedding anniversary by going on a bike trip through the Pyrénées. The trip left on a Sunday morning out of Barcelona. We arrived early on Saturday morning and made our way to the nearest beach. There we ate cold peach gazpacho and an outrageously satisfying salad of green peppers, potatoes and pesto. The sun was strong and the water was warm. When we weren't eating, we either napped or watched hordes of beautiful, tan, barely dressed Catalans flirt and frolic. Everywhere you looked there was yet another luscious, beautiful body. Many of the women went topless above their thongs and flat tummies. Bathing suits for the men were barely there or not there at all. At various moments, I sat with my eyes wide and my mouth open. *Mon dieu, regardez-la*! My husband and I had stumbled onto a hot, hot, hot beach party and I was overdressed. It wasn't an orgy but it was close.

FEATURING

- Potatoes Barcelona
- Garlic Aioli

My husband and I had travelled alone together before but we'd never journeyed this far from our kids or left for so long. We'd spent weekends alone in Maine, Vermont and the Jersey Shore and once, after I had a miscarriage, made a mad dash to Puerto Rico. But as our kids grew older, we stayed put on weekends. We wanted to be home to watch wrestling matches, squash tournaments, water polo and baseball games, supervise homework assignments and make sure the Xbox was occasionally turned off. We wanted to make sure the beer didn't get drunk and the wine wasn't watered down. Not that the two of us were together every minute on weekends. But we aimed for togetherness: We'd have drinks together on Friday nights and cook a big family dinner Sunday nights. Those nights weren't precious but they were goals. Still, on the eve of our second decade together, we decided to go the distance, literally, and leave the kids behind for ten days.

When you reach the 20-year mark as a couple, you either dig in or dig out. We decided to dig in. We'd come this far; we would try and go farther. But that decision didn't come easily. Half of our friends had gotten divorced and the idea of shit-canning a marriage was familiar to me. I was never sure I could go any further than my parents had. On the eve of their twentieth anniversary, after years of couples counseling and a trial separation, as well as a year of living with each other but dating other people, they split up for good. As I approached the 20-year mark, I panicked. When you come from chaos, it calls out to you. The tension-filled talks, the crying jags, the slammed doors, the bills from the therapists, the whispered conversations about lawyers and money—I remembered it well.

After my father died, I ran a half-marathon to raise money for leukemia and lymphoma. Along the way, there were volunteers screaming encouragement and handing out candy and water. Those shouts and the sugar that accompanied them were key; I kept making pit stops and grabbing handfuls of M&M's. But where were the cheers and M&M pit stops in a long-term marriage? Twenty years is a long time; the prospect of forty more together can seem like quadruple the time.

Fortunately, two couples close to us had excellent track records. My in-laws have been married over 50 years and my grandparents were married 65. Whenever I wondered how I was going to ease my way out of an argument, avoid it altogether or come back swinging, I thought about how my grandmother or mother-in-law would behave. They would be calm. They would be measured. They might leave the house if necessary. But they wouldn't threaten to leave forever.

My husband is calm and optimistic; he's also a realist. He never expected everything to be perfect. He just expected it to move forward. So we took a deep breath and did just that. And here we were in Spain, thousands of miles and many days from home. The grandparents were tending to the young'uns. And we were blissfully doing things we hadn't done in a long time. There's nothing like discovering that you still like spending time with the person you've been living with all these years.

After the beach, we returned to the hotel. A couple of hours later, exhausted but exhilarated, we climbed into a taxi and made our way to Cerveceria Catalana, a tapas restaurant in L'Eixample that both the concierge and our friend Howard had recommended. We made our way to the crowded tapas bar (don't try to get a table, the wait is too long), downed glasses of Rioja, and began to consume. We had plates of fois gras with Roquefort, grilled cuttlefish, and cold salmon. Then we saw the couple next to us dig into "huevos cabreados," a pile of slivered French fries, topped with fried eggs. We ordered it immediately. Oh, the ecstasy of that first, salty potato-and-protein-filled bite! There was no finish line with that dish; we ate and ate and still left half the bowl. After that we ordered more, gorging ourselves on a slice of Camembert, which had been fried in almonds. OMG. If you go to Barcelona, you must go to Cerveceria and order all this food. Dinner for two came to $42. Don't think about it, just go.

None of our subsequent culinary adventures in Barcelona were as thrilling as our first night, but for one: We went out to tour Gaudi's La Sagrada Familia and the Park Güel with a guide, asking that he take us to one of his favorite restaurants and order for us. He ordered a platter of thinly sliced, acorn-fed ham (jamón ibérico) and a heaping plate of potatoes, served with what looked like a bowl of thick sour cream. "You must eat this together," he said and smiled. "Otherwise, you will not be able to talk to each other all day." What did he mean? He pointed to the sauce and beckoned. We took our potato slices and dipped them in. Never, in my life, have I eaten anything so delicious. The bowl of sour cream was actually a bowl of garlic aioli. Our eyes widened. The potatoes were so addictive, we ordered a second bowl.

When we returned home, I thought about recreating that dish. The night before Rosh Hashanah, I found that I had spent the day cooking for the company that was coming the next day, but had nothing to give my kids for dinner. Then I realized we had had all the ingredients we needed for those Barcelona potatoes. You probably do too.

My older son took a bite of the potatoes, then dipped them in the aioli. “Wow, holy crap, Mom! How bad are these for me?” Not too, I said. They’re rich. A little goes a long way. “Really, are there more?” I had made three pounds of potatoes so yep, there were.

The next night 16 people gathered here for Rosh Hashanah dinner and were waiting for the 17th to arrive before we started to eat. While we waited, we ran out of hors d’oeuvres. I grabbed the leftover potatoes and aioli and set them out. I didn’t even bother to heat the potatoes up. “Those look like leftovers,” my brother sniffed. Yep, they were. And two minutes later, they were gone.

POTATOES BARCELONA

SERVES 6-8

INGREDIENTS:

- 4 tablespoons unsalted butter
- 2 tablespoons olive oil
- 5 cloves garlic, peeled and mashed
- 3 pounds small new potatoes, cut into slices or small chunks
- Kosher salt

PREPARATION:

1. **Preheat oven to 350 degrees**.
2. **In a Dutch oven** *(or a heavy oven-going pan)*, heat butter and oil. Add potatoes and garlic. Roll potatoes around to coat. Transfer dish to oven. Bake uncovered for 1 hour, 15 minutes.
3. **When potatoes are done**, spread cookie tray with a light layer of kosher salt. Place potatoes on tray and shake to coat. Discard garlic. Serve warm or cold, with aioli.

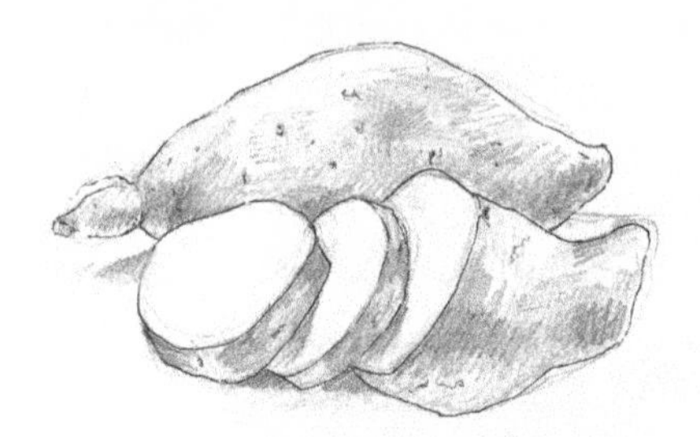

Garlic Aioli

Serves 6-8

INGREDIENTS:

- 1 cup mayonnaise
- 8 cloves roasted garlic *(peel before roasting, then mash)*
- 1 tablespoon lemon juice
- Salt and pepper to taste

PREPARATION:

Combine mayonnaise with lemon juice, roasted mashed garlic, salt and pepper. Serve.

36

Epic and Tiny, Both

Reflections on 911, Ruth Macpherson and Baked Chicken

ONE FALL, I tried to think of something to write about 9/11. I couldn't come up with anything. A boy who played on my younger son's baseball team for two years lost his father in 9/11. Whenever that sweet-looking, blonde child went up to bat, I thought of his loss and what his mother had gone through. Compared to him, I had nothing to say.

> FEATURING
>
> - Lemon and Tarragon Baked Chicken

Then I read an essay by Colum McCann in *The New Yorker*. McCann is the author of *Let the Great World Spin*, which he calls a novel but is really a book of interconnected short stories, with characters that wander in and out of each other's lives. The one event that connects them is that they all saw or heard about the tightrope walker, Philippe Petit, who rigged a wire and walked between the Twin Towers in August 1974.

In *The New Yorker* essay, entitled "Dessert," McCann describes watching a woman on the East side eat a slice of chocolate cake the day after the Twin Towers came down. The woman eats slowly and deliberately, and McCann is appalled that anyone can eat dessert the day after such a catastrophe.

> *The woman unrolled a fork from a paper napkin, held it at her mouth, tapping the tines against her*

teeth. She ran the fork, then, through the powder, addressing the cake, scribbling her intent. Our job is to be epic and tiny, both.

McCann ends the essay this way:

I still have no idea–after a decade of wondering–whether I am furious at the woman and the way she ate chocolate cake, or whether it was one of the most audacious acts of grief I've seen in a long time.

After reading that essay, I thought about how and why food takes the edge off of tragedy, as well as the grateful aversion to it. My family dodged two bullets on 9/11. My brother was near and my first cousin was in one of the Towers that morning. My cousin had a meeting on one of the top floors and stopped on the first floor to use the bathroom. He ran out of the building as soon as he heard the plane hit. My brother worked a block away. He jumped on a ferry to New Jersey and then took a train to the station near our house. His cell phone wasn't working and we were all frantically wondering where he was when he showed up at our front door. My father was still alive then and drove over. We were smiling and laughing, almost hysterical with fear and relief. My father had recently been diagnosed with the lymphoma that would kill him but I'd never seen him so happy. I started taking out cans of tuna fish and mayonnaise, heating up bagels and making everyone lunch.

My husband was out of town. Our sons were 5 and 1 then, and I remember thinking that if I just kept everyone safe and fed, crammed into one room together, everything would be okay. Of course, that's not true and it's shocking that some people can survive a disaster and go on to eat cake, but I think food and the sharing of it can provide some relief, some of the time.

I started this past September as I usually do: Writing, preparing to teach again, making dinner, walking the dog, exercising, driving my kids around, talking to my neighbors. Nothing felt particularly difficult. My classes were filled, I knew most of my students well, my kids had no pressing issues, the back to school dust was settling. But on September 11th, in the middle of the day, I had a surge of anxiety. I made a cup of hot chocolate spiked with coffee grinds, which usually serves well as Mommy's little pick-me-upper. But I still felt rattled. I decided to make dinner. It was early in the day–I had just eaten lunch–and way too early to start thinking about dinner, but I rationalized that if I made dinner now I wouldn't have to make it later. Really, I was just looking for a distraction and leafing through old cookbooks and defrosting chicken breasts provided it.

I took down Ruth Macpherson's *Food for Friends*. Macpherson used to live up the street from me, in a charming Tudor on a busy, main road. The train tracks ran behind her back yard. Shortly after I moved to town, my neighbor gave me Macpherson's cookbooks as a birthday present. Her other books are *Discover Brunch* and *That's Entertaining*. They are little spiral notebooks with soft covers, the kind of thing you see in a synagogue or church bookstore.

Macpherson doesn't break new culinary ground but her books are small blessings. The recipes always work. Her prose is charming, and she writes in an offhand, friendly way that makes you feel as if she's just dashing this great recipe off and emailing it to you. There is something simple in her approach: She doesn't expect you to have fresh herbs on hand or make breadcrumbs from scratch. There are all sorts of menus for tennis team luncheons, elegant baby showers and friend's going away lunches, which make the books feel lady-like and anachronistic, but in a lovely, old-fashioned way that works. She just knows you'll figure out a way to get the appetizers in the oven before company comes.

I used to see Macpherson walking her dogs in the reservation. She wore her hair in pigtails and she was always eager to talk about the weather, local goings on and, of course, dogs. A few years ago, I heard that one of her dogs wandered onto the train tracks and was killed. Macpherson sold her house and I don't see her anymore but I still use her recipes and am comforted by her voice.

I made her recipe for Lemon and Tarragon Baked Chicken. Then my older son called and said he'd missed the late bus. The late bus is the last bus, which meant at 6 p.m., I had to drive forty minutes round trip to retrieve him. My younger son had a test the next day and wasn't feeling well. I was not happy but I knew when I got home, I would stand at the kitchen counter where I had stood with my father and brother all those years ago, and spoon buttery crumbs of chicken and tarragon into my mouth, a moment that felt both epic and tiny.

Lemon and Tarragon Baked Chicken

(Serves 6-8)

INGREDIENTS:

- 1 stick (*½ cup*) unsalted butter, melted
- 2 garlic cloves, minced
- 2 tablespoons Dijon mustard
- 2 tablespoons lemon juice *(about 2 lemons)*
- 1 cup dry breadcrumbs, unflavored
- 1 tablespoon grated lemon peel *(takes 2 lemons)*
- 1 teaspoon dried tarragon
- 6 large chicken breasts, with bone and skin *(can also use boneless)*
- Salt and pepper

PREPARATION:

1. **Preheat oven to 375 degrees.** Line baking pan with foil.
2. **Melt butter over low heat.** Add garlic to butter and sauté 1 minute. Remove from heat and stir in mustard and lemon juice.
3. **Mix breadcrumbs,** lemon peel and tarragon in a bowl.
4. **Wash and dry chicken.** Turn chicken breasts in butter mixture to coat, then turn in crumbs, coating completely.
5. **Arrange chicken in prepared pan**, add salt and pepper.
6. **Bake about 1 hour.** Baste occasionally.

▸ *If you are using boneless chicken breasts, bake for 50 minutes.*

37

The Ugly, Beautiful Truth

You Can't Keep a Good Pie Down

ONE WINTER, we spent a week freezing in "sunny Florida," while everyone else we knew was sludging through a massive snowstorm in the Northeast. I know, boo-hoo, but before you get out the world's tiniest violin, let me say that, on average, the temperature in Islamorada hovered in the mid-50s, it was cloudy much of the time and there's nothing worse than paying for a warm tan and freezing your butt off instead.

FEATURING

- Key Lime Pie
- Whipped Cream
- Caroline's Chocolate Bread Pudding

We wandered around in sweatshirts, sandals and a daze, distracting ourselves by drinking cappuccino with cane sugar, sipping hot chocolate, and eating conch fritters, alligator tail bites, grits and a host of fish. Though we did manage a little paddle boarding and snorkeling, the highlights of the trip were reading and fishing.

I devoured *A Visit From the Goon Squad*, by Jennifer Egan. This book picks you up and drops you down into the lives of a wide range of characters connected in some way to the music industry. The book covers suicide, a drowning, suppressed homosexuality, infidelity, kleptomania, autism, dashed dreams, failed friendship, the ups and downs of the music business, suburban malaise and drug abuse, yet you finish it feeling full of hope.

Our main fishing expedition was with Captain Juan out on the

Gulf. Captain Juan spent four years in the Navy and knew his way around a boat, but it was cold and the wind was vicious as we headed out to sea. Our expectations were low, but the fish started biting right away. Because of the cold weather, they were hungry, and the minute we lowered our lines into the water, they started snapping at the bait.

We caught mangrove and lane snapper, grouper, mackerel and ladyfish. My kids were ecstatic, my husband was thrilled, and even I, who participated with little enthusiasm and mostly to be a good sport, caught so many fish that I had to put the rod down and sit down for a rest. Captain Juan estimated that we caught over 100. He kept some and packed some up for us and directed us to take it to Lazy Days restaurant in Islamorada, where he promised they would cook it up for us. It was there that we bought several slices of key lime pie, a delicious dessert I decided to replicate once we returned to New Jersey.

We arrived back home just in time for my brother and sister-in-law's annual New Year's Eve party, so I decided to make the pie and bring it. I started at 7:30 New Year's Eve morning. My neighbor wanted to go for a run but I said I was too busy baking so she came over to help. She grated the rinds off the limes and separated 16 yolks from the whites (this is why she is so lovable: she doesn't even like fruit pie). Together, we marveled at the efficiency of condensed milk–so much fat and sugar in just two tablespoons! Since my oven wasn't working properly, she took the pies home to cook in her oven.

The key lime pies looked yolky and yellow when they went into the oven and unfortunately came out looking the same way. The overall effect was Egg Yolk Pie with Parsley Bits because the green lime rind flakes had congealed on top. When I went to pick up the pie, my neighbor's son, who had just returned from wrestling practice and should have been hungry enough to eat his shirt, took one look at the pie and said, "Ew."

To entice New Year's Eve revelers to look past my pies' ugly faces, I made whipped cream and covered the pies with it. Then I took one of the remaining cans of condensed milk and the leftover graham cracker crumbs and made Magic Bars, just in case the key lime pies were a flop. When we arrived at the party, one of my nephews handed me some kind of vodka cocktail. I usually avoid vodka because the last time I drank it, it made me cry, but I didn't want to insult my nephew so I finished the drink, helped myself to some champagne and went to stand near my pies.

For what felt like forever, people crowded around the dessert table, clamoring for the chocolate bread pudding. My lime pies remained uncut and ignored. The Magic Bars (which took all of ten minutes to make) flew off the table, but even they didn't generate as much excitement as Caroline's chocolate bread pudding. It was so beautiful it made my yellow lime pies look like ugly stepsisters. But looks aside, who doesn't crave a sweet and tangy pie from the South?

Apparently everyone.

I tasted the chocolate pudding. Dang. Even in my tipsy and embittered state, I could appreciate its rich, luscious deliciousness, as it managed to combine the soft pudding texture of childhood with the sophisticated adult taste of bittersweet chocolate and vanilla bean. Adding insult to injury, my brother, who is one of the kindest men I know, felt compelled to point out that citrus flavors mostly just appeal to women. Oh, really?

I felt like I was back in a Central Park playground–there were my children, standing alone, sweet, innocent, and helpless. No one wanted to be close to them but me. I had to protect the pies and help them make new friends! Emboldened by the vodka, I started talking the pies up and handing out slices. Partygoers took them reluctantly. At the end of the night, there was still one pie left. It is now patiently waiting for us in the freezer.

That key lime pie *was* yummy; even if it didn't win Miss Popularity.

But back to Jennifer Egan: I took a writing workshop with her when I was pursuing an MFA in fiction. Egan hadn't yet won the Pulitzer Prize for *A Visit From the Goon Squad* so she wasn't yet the reigning best-selling Queen of American Fiction that she would become. In the spring of 2000, she showed up twice a week on Mondays and Wednesdays to a non-descript classroom with a long conference table in the middle of it. Though occasionally stunning, she often showed up looking exhausted, as if the night before had taken its toll. (As it turned out, she was pregnant with her first child.) She was the best writing instructor I ever had, which was ironic because she didn't even have an MFA. She was patient and encouraging and laughed easily. But she was deadly serious about the writing process. There were no secrets to writing well, she said, except this one: Sit down at your desk and write. Then rewrite. And rewrite some more.

I once turned something in she liked and she asked me how I had done it. "I always want to know how a writer makes a leap like that," she said. I didn't say, "Well, the writing went well the first day so I wore exactly the same turquoise sweater three days in a row without washing so I could harness the writing energy," which was the ridiculous truth. Instead, I said, "I just sat there for three days and wrote." Egan nodded. "It shows," she says.

Writing and cooking aren't always easy. Making something delicious and desirable can be a slow, rank business. That may sound ugly, but it's also the beautiful truth.

KEY LIME PIE

(Serves 6-8)

INGREDIENTS:

- 1 cup graham cracker crumbs
- 1 ½ tablespoons sugar
- 1 ½ tablespoons flour
- 4 tablespoons butter
- 8 egg yolks
- ½ cup sweetened condensed milk
- 1 cup key lime juice *(regular limes are fine)*
- Zest from 2 limes

PREPARATION:

1. **Preheat oven to 325 degrees.**
2. **Mix graham cracker crumbs**, sugar and flour together. Melt butter and add to graham crackers. Stir to make sure all ingredients are combined. Press mixture into a 9 or 10 inch pie plate. Set aside.
3. **Beat egg yolks until they're light**, about 3 minutes. With beater running, slowly add condensed milk. Add lime juice and lime zest. Pour into prepared pie shell. Bake for 20-25 minutes. Remove from oven and cool. Keep refrigerated until ready to eat. Can be frozen for up to a month.

Whipped Cream

(Serves 8-10)

INGREDIENTS:

- 1 cup whipping cream
- 3-5 tablespoons powdered sugar

PREPARATION:

1. **Sift sugar**.
2. **Whip cream until stiff**, about 3 minutes.
3. **Slowly add in sugar** and mix.
4. **Spread on top of key lime pie**, or serve on the side.

Caroline's Chocolate Bread Pudding

(Serves 8-10)

INGREDIENTS:

- 2 cups heavy cream
- 2 cups milk
- 1 whole vanilla bean, split in half lengthwise, seeds scraped
- 3 cinnamon sticks *(optional)*
- 1 loaf brioche—about 1 pound *(you can substitute white bread)*

- 12 ounces roughly chopped Valrhona or other bittersweet chocolate, plus ¼ cup shavings for garnish
- 8 large egg yolks
- ¾ cup sugar
- 1 package *(8 ounces)* crème fraîche

PREPARATION:

1. **Preheat oven to 325 degrees.**
2. **Place cream, milk, vanilla seeds and pod, and cinnamon sticks** (if using) in a medium saucepan and bring to a boil. Remove from heat, cover with plastic wrap and let sit for 30 minutes to infuse flavors.
3. **Cut the brioche into ¼-inch thick slices.** Cut slices into quarters, setting aside the rounded top pieces. Fill a 9 x 12-inch gratin dish or a deep oval roasting dish with the quartered pieces.
4. **Return the milk mixture to a boil**, remove from heat, and discard vanilla pod and cinnamon sticks. Add chocolate and whisk until smooth. Combine egg yolks and sugar in a large bowl and whisk together. Pour chocolate mixture very slowly into egg-yolk mixture, whisking constantly until fully combined.
5. **Slowly pour half the chocolate custard over bread,** making sure all the bread is soaked. Arrange the reserved bread on top in a decorative pattern and press firmly so bottom layer of bread absorbs chocolate mixture. Spoon remaining custard over bread until completely covered and all cracks are filled.

5 **Place a piece of plastic wrap over the dish;** press down to soak bread thoroughly. Remove plastic, wipe edges of dish with a damp towel and allow to sit for 30 minutes.

5 **Place gratin dish in a larger pan;** fill outer pan with hot water halfway up the sides of the gratin dish. Bake until set, about 35 minutes. Cool on a rack for 15 minutes.

5 **Whisk the crème fraîche until soft peaks form**. Serve pudding warm, garnished with crème fraîche and chocolate shavings.

38

Butter Yourself Some Coffee, Baby

Coffee + Butter
+ Coconut Oil = Ecstasy

FEATURING
- Buttered Coffee

IT'S YOUR BIRTHDAY. No, it's Mother's Day. Maybe it's Father's Day. Or New Year's Day or Christmas Day or Valentine's Day or Memorial Day or Graduation Day. Whatever it is, it's *your* day and you are not going to be cooking for yourself. You are not going to be making restaurant reservations either. You're going to let the people who love you take care of that.

You are, however, going to make yourself one hell of a cup of coffee, because any day that calls for celebration also calls for a little liquid pick-me-up.

Early one afternoon, at the hour that my attention typically starts to wane, I was sitting on the floor of my friend Jessica's beautiful old house. We were mapping out this book about cooking and coping, which Jessica had agreed to edit. We had printed out all the essays and lined them up on the floor of her front hall. Her teenage son was sitting in the next room with a friend, watching a movie. There were almost forty essays, so there were rows and rows of them. There were even more recipes, and we were trying to figure out how to arrange them all so that the book felt as much like a memoir as it did a cookbook. Jessica had little Post-its and was writing down the theme of each essay and trying to categorize everything. I was trying to figure out what movie the teenage boys were watching. (*Kill Bill.*)

We were only stopping for snacks every forty-five minutes or so.

The first day I arrived at Jessica's, she told me she had made a pot of red lentil curry for us for lunch. "You cooked?" I was shocked. I had brought some homemade granola bars from Panetica, a bag of baby carrots, some apples and bananas, and a big iced soy mocha with an extra shot from Starbucks. I did not expect to be fed. I knew Jessica didn't cook. I had gone into the writing of this book a confident cook and Jessica had gone into editing it an uninterested one. She was, dare I say, even slightly hostile about cooking. Still, she agreed to take on this project, perhaps out of pity, perhaps out of a latent interest in cooking, perhaps because her best friend is married to my brother. Plus, we'd worked together before. I had faith in her and she had patience with me.

The red lentil curry was outrageously good. During the course of editing the book, it appeared Jes had turned into a cook.

While we sat on the floor amid a sea of essays, she asked, "Do you want some of this coffee Scott makes?" Scott is Jessica's husband. "Sure," I said. "It's got grass-fed Irish butter in it," Jessica said. "And coconut oil. Does that sound disgusting?" No. I have been using coconut oil in everything lately and know how good it is. And a smidge of butter in your food is one of life's great pleasures. On the other hand, butter in coffee actually did sound a little gross. But the red lentil curry had given her some street cred.

"Scott says when he drinks this in the morning, he doesn't need to eat or drink anything again until 3 p.m.," Jessica said. That sounded illegal. And perfect.

Jes made some organic espresso on the stove. When it was done, she poured it into her Vitamix, telling me the Vitamix was so awesome, it would even clean itself after it was done mixing things up. "Christmas present," she said. "I don't even want to know how much it cost." She added a tablespoon of grass-fed Irish butter and a tablespoon of coconut oil to the coffee and turned the machine on. "Here you go," she said and handed me a mug of something dark and frothy.

I took a sip. Thick, rich and potent as hell. So many strong flavors, all competing for my attention and all deeply satisfying. The combination of fat and caffeine powered through my veins up to my brain. Boy, was I happy. What followed was a very productive afternoon. Then, Jessica sent me home with the essays and told me I had to revise them.

I didn't want to revise them. I wanted to write new stuff! Oh, the joy of starting something new! Hemingway once wrote about F. Scott Fitzgerald: "[He] took literature so solemnly. He never understood that it was just writing as well as you can and finishing what you start." Of course, I had to finish what we had started, but it was far more fun to think about new projects. I sent Jessica some new ideas for essays. Maybe we would write another book together! She emailed back: "Sorry, lady. I'm not reading anything new until you revise the old."

I collapsed onto the floor. Revising nearly 40 essays. Who had the strength to do that?

Buttered coffee did.

Naturally, we had no grass-fed Irish butter so I used Land O'Lakes salt-free butter from Shoprite. We didn't have the right special bag of organic espresso either so I used ground Melitta Classic Blend Coffee that was in a can in the freezer. We did have two glass containers full of coconut oil so that was good. We didn't have a Vitamix so I took out the blender. I didn't bother to fill it with hot water and warm it first as Jes had done.

I brewed two cups of coffee, poured them in the blender, added two tablespoons of butter and two tablespoons of coconut oil, and pushed "Mix." Then I carefully poured the liquid into a mug. Nothing fancy. Nothing difficult. Just delicious and restorative. Your brain will wake up and say, "Party on!" And it will thank you for this combination of caffeine and saturated fat by furnishing you with a very, very happy mood.

This coffee nailed my butt to the floor of my office and got me to work for hours at a stretch. I wasn't medicated but I was focused. Jes was a little appalled by my choice of butter so that night, I ordered some grass-fed Kerrygold Irish butter off Amazon. (You can also get it at any local supermarket.)

The next day, I went back to Jessica's. We sat back down on the floor. "Do you have any more of that coffee?" I asked innocently.

Jessica grinned. I followed her into the kitchen.

Whatever day today is, it's a Big Day for you. Buttered coffee is gonna fix you right up. Make yourself a cup. And let the people who love you generate the rest of the fun.

BUTTERED COFFEE

(Serves 1)

INGREDIENTS:

- 1 cup hot coffee
- 1 tablespoon coconut oil
- 1 tablespoon unsalted butter or more to taste
  (organic, grass-fed is the best, but regular butter will do)

PREPARATION:

Put all ingredients in the blender. Blend. Drink immediately, then have a fabulous day.

39

Tell Me More

Looking for a Few Good Men, a Nobel Prize Winner Among Them

MY MOTHER'S FATHER, Grandpa Sam, was the gentlest man I knew. He adored my mother and everyone else. "*Tateleh!*" he'd say, using the Yiddish for "father's little one." That was for his three grandsons. Me, he'd call "*mamaleh*" or "little mother." I was his first grandchild and the only granddaughter. Girls, he knew. He had two daughters and three sisters. When he walked into the first floor of the two-family row house in Brooklyn he shared with my grandmother for more than sixty years, he'd take off his hat and call up, "Buddle!" She'd call down, "Sam, up here!"

FEATURING

- Great, Simple Flourless Chocolate Cake
- Carolyn's Chocolate Chip Meringues

They adored each other. After work, he'd take a nap on the narrow couch in the "den," while Grandma heated up pasta *fagiole* (macaroni and bean soup, his favorite), set out a salad of lettuce, sliced radishes and bottled Italian dressing, and put a casserole dish of chicken and rice in the oven. Grandma wasn't a great cook but Grandpa didn't care. Afterwards they would eat diced fruit salad in little cut glass bowls and this was where Grandma excelled: She always sliced grapes in half and cut up fat, juicy figs to go along with the cantaloupe and honeydew in the fruit salad, then marinated the "salad" in its own juices, with a little orange juice thrown in. Afterwards, there were chocolate chip cookies or maybe pieces of chocolate that Grandma had snuck home from the bridge club. Grandma fixed dinner and Grandpa did the dishes. (They had a dishwasher, but rarely used it.) When I slept over Friday nights, he made us both *matzo brei* on Saturday mornings, which he served with huge pours of maple syrup. Grandma was always on a diet so I ate most of hers. Grandpa smelled like Ivory soap, which he also used for shampoo. He typed letters to my brother, cousins and me while we were away at sleep-away camp and on the backs he'd tape pieces of Trident cinnamon and Wrigley's Doublemint gum. If there were room at the bottom, he'd draw a picture of a huge tree with big branches and an apple on the ground. "The apple doesn't fall far from the tree," he'd say, trying to reassure me that I was more like him than my father. I knew this wasn't true—I wasn't gentle or sweet—but I appreciated his wish that I be so.

Grandpa Sam was the first to call me a writer. In my early twenties, when I was living in a studio on the Upper West Side, I'd go to their house for dinner on Thursday nights. The magazine closed on Wednesday nights and Thursday was a slow day, so I could leave early, hop on the Q train and have dinner with them in Brooklyn. If I wanted to go back home, Grandpa would drive me back to the city, an hour and a half round trip for him. If I slept over, I'd go in early to work with him. He worked as a stockbroker at Cowen & Company on Wall Street, which he and Grandma referred to as "the place." He'd walk around and introduce me by saying, "This is my granddaughter, the writer." I was a cub reporter at *Business Week* and barely had a byline but I was glad that he had faith.

You couldn't find a soul who didn't like Grandpa. He had various male assistants who helped him deal with clients and they played bridge or studied music at Wagner College. They were always very good at math, which was key. The one I remember best was Arnie, a former Yeshiva boy who Grandpa thought had promise as a stockbroker. (Ultimately, he went back to graduate school in music.) Grandpa would invite clients to lunch and they'd come to his office, dressed up and smiling, expecting to be taken for a posh, all-expenses paid multi-course meal in the corporate dining room. But Grandpa didn't want to leave his desk–the market might move in some unexpected direction while he was away–so he'd say, "Come, sit," and he'd hand them a tuna sandwich on an onion roll that my grandmother had made that morning. The tuna was made without mayonnaise so was tangy and acidic but the onion roll was always fresh. If you didn't want a sandwich, Grandpa would hand you a flowered blue tin of cookies from Waldbaum's—sugar cookies and chocolate chip–and offer you a cup of tea. The cookies might have been in that tin for months–he kept them in the drawer of a filing cabinet. He never seemed to run out.

Grandpa loved the women in his life. He had two older sisters, Ilma and Sophie, and one younger sister, Florence, in addition to his little brother Moey, whom he called his "kid brother." Their mother, Goldie, only spoke Yiddish, and wore her white hair in a bun; their father, Ben, owned real estate, had a full white beard and did math in his head. In pictures, he wears suits and she wears dresses that fall below her knee. They sit up straight, stare straight at the camera and look poised, serene and happy. I think they really loved each other and still had that *je ne sais quois* even towards the end of their lives. A few years before I got married, Grandma and I were sitting in her yellow and white kitchen, talking about relationships. She was wearing her old housedress and putting a pan of chicken and rice in the oven. I had broken up with someone but wasn't too broken up about it. Grandma wanted to know why. "He always made me laugh but I wasn't really attracted to him," I said, sticking a coffee candy in my mouth. Grandma nodded. She said that Goldie had once pulled her aside and confided happily about Ben: "He still bothers me," (i.e. he still wants to have sex). Grandma said Goldie didn't seem to mind. "That part is important too," Grandma said. In other words, you can cook dinner all you want but if you don't want to fall into bed afterwards, the food doesn't really matter.

Goldie and Ben must have done something right with their children because you never met a happier group of kids. Moey was the only one who moved away—he left New York for balmy southern California—the rest of them stayed in Brooklyn and Queens. You'd go to a family gathering and they'd all be laughing and smiling, hugging and kissing. They'd spot you and say, "Come here, darling!" and give you a big kiss. "How are you?" They'd look into your eyes and really want to know things: *What are you doing? Are you working? Are you dating anyone? Where are you going to school? What are you studying? Do you like it? You're taking art history? Who's your favorite 20th century painter? Do you like Matisse?*

"Tell me more," they'd say.

Grandpa's sisters Sophie and Florence were both beauties who smelled of hairspray and lipstick. They were tiny and well-dressed and wore huge hats: They were always decked out in silk blouses, wool suits and fur stoles and I never saw either of them in pants. They wore big gold pins and long dangling earrings and their fine leather bags matched their shoes. Sophie would say, "I saved so much money today!" because she'd shopped at a big sale. No matter what you looked like, they nodded their heads, kissed you and said, "Hello, darling! Look at this *shayna punim* (beautiful face!)"

Sophie looked like Zsa Zsa Gabor and Florence looked like Audrey Hepburn. Florence was the one we saw the most of; she married Grandpa's best friend from Boys High, a tall man named Karly, who was also good at numbers and became a psychiatrist. Their kids played bridge and went to Radcliffe and Harvard, and then their grandchildren went to Yale. Florence never bragged, just glowed as she reported the news: "Cindy's an architect, she married her professor at Yale. Anne's a doctor in Boston, still not married, she works so hard. And you know all about Joshua!" (Joshua worked for the city of New York, briefly dated one of my friends from college, and then went to work with his father in Connecticut. His father owned trailer parks, Laundromats, and movie theaters, among other things, and I think my mother was secretly hoping that we would start dating. We were second cousins and I guess she thought that was kosher.) Florence and Karl's apartment in Queens was full of light and modern art, furnished with low pale couches and faded rugs, with huge picture windows and wonderful views of the East River. I rarely spent time alone with them, so who knew how they were in private, but they never even remotely seemed cranky. I had Florence's dark hair and dark eyes, and I just wanted to be as happy as she was, a contented mother and a happy wife, surrounded by art and light and love.

The one we saw the least of, but suspected my grandfather loved the most, was his kid brother Moses, aka Moey. Those two beamed when they saw each other. When Moey came east to New York, he'd attend whatever family gathering was going on, and he and my grandfather would lean into each other and *kibitz*. They were short men with shiny black shoes, a smidgeon of white hair and huge smiles. They were both interested in science, numbers and higher education. One of Moey's kids grew up to be an orthopedic surgeon; the other grew up to marry a Nobel Prize winner in economics. Moey and Sammy both excelled at math; Moey received his PhD in physics, joined the Navy in 1941 as a civilian scientist and participated in tests of atomic bomb explosions in Bikini Atoll in July 1946. Two years later, he became a physics professor at UCLA, where he founded the medical physics PhD program and taught for almost fifty years. After his first wife died, he married a math professor. He always said that Sam looked after him when they were kids and taught him how to shoot marbles.

Moey and Sam loved and respected women. That seems like a strange thing to say, and perhaps out of context, but when you start to look at your family and wonder why some people died old and happy and others couldn't stay out of psych wards, you try to find the patterns. I never saw either Sam or Moey say a cross word to a woman. I suspect their mother, Goldie, loved them to pieces. In turn, my grandfather revered my grandmother and my mother. My mother looked like Grandpa's sister Florence, with the same dark hair and dark eyes, and she was prettier and more eager to please than his older daughter, Bernadette, who was overweight, easily angered and had a lopsided gait; Bertie never learned how to ride a bike but she was fantastic at math, had a wonderful memory (she knew the interest rates on all her bonds and when they were coming due) and spent decades as a music teacher in Brooklyn. I suspect that these days, Bertie would be diagnosed as having Asperger's but back then, she was just thought to be moody and difficult. She was continually upsetting my grandmother but made her sister (my mother) look great. Grandpa was always kind to her and eventually hired her husband to be his assistant.

I was always jealous of my mother for having a father who thought she hung up the sun in the morning. Women whose fathers adore them have a core of confidence that women who don't can't fabricate. My father was always trying to knock the wheels off our bus; my grandfather was always trying to screw them back on. No matter what happens to them, daughters with constant, loving fathers believe the world loves them as much as their fathers did. They truly believe that if one love fails, a new love will come along. It may not match Daddy's but it will turn up. And even if that new love doesn't materialize, they'll be fine, because they still have Daddy's love wrapped around them. Women whose fathers didn't love them, or loved them but mistreated them, are always sitting anxiously on stools, picking our fingernails, chewing our lips, drinking too much, or eating too little. We're just waiting for someone to push us off.

Before I went to work for *Business Week*, I worked for a while as an analyst at a Wall Street firm and when we took the subway home to his house in Brooklyn, Grandpa would always give me subway fare. He was a mensch; in a time when most men didn't bother, he washed the dishes every night after dinner. He played a pretty good game of duplicate bridge (Grandma was better), paid for everything in cash, carried a big pile of bills in a silver money clip, and gave all of his grandchildren Kennedy half dollars and silver dollars whenever he saw us. If we saved money in our 401K's, he matched it. I never heard him utter an unkind word or saw him drink anything stronger than weak tea. He and my grandmother both avoided doctors; he gargled with whiskey when his tooth hurt, and she stopped seeing a gynecologist after she had my mother in 1941.

All that solace and wisdom is gone now so to comfort and invariably torture myself, I often open up Grandma's box of condolence letters, the letters she received after Grandpa passed away. This grey box is large and heavy, shaped like a tombstone; I keep it in my closet, near my children's baby books and the photo album I put together when my husband and I first met.

On top of it sits a shiny, flat yellow box that contains a slender pile of ancient, beautifully pressed handkerchiefs, embroidered in different patterns and colors, gifts from Grandma's students, fifty years ago. There are pale pink hankies with scalloped edges, two delicate white pique hankies that are starting to yellow, and an almost transparent handkerchief with a white four-leaf clover woven throughout the cotton. Two striped handkerchiefs on the bottom are still tied with a ribbon, a single piece of tissue paper lies folded underneath. The handkerchiefs are as neat and tidy as the day Grandma placed them in here, just like the pile of beautiful table linens she left behind–the napkins, the tablecloths, the buffet covers—all white, thick, heavy and pristine, pressed into neat piles, folded and stacked, waiting to be used. Like Grandma, they are elegant, immaculate and helpful.

The grey box once held note cards. Initially, it held the condolence notes Grandma sent out after Grandpa died. The notes are creamy and engraved in black script: "The Family of Samuel C. Greenfield thanks you for your kind expression of sympathy." Typical of Grandma that after she sent out all her condolence notes, she would save the box they came in and reuse it to house the notes that people sent to her. Everything could be salvaged, even the sad truth. Grandma saved and recycled everything—tinfoil, rubber bands, cookie tins, safety pins, old stockings, and teabags. She held onto her husband and loved him dearly, a situation I took note of.

I spent a lot of time wandering around Grandma and Grandpa's house, pawing through their things. Of course, I did this at home too but I almost always regretted it; my search and discover missions often resulted in my finding my mother's orange vinyl diary, in which she wondered why my father had insulted her in public, or later finding her boyfriend's stash of girlie magazines, carelessly stuffed underneath the bed after my father had moved out. At Grandma and Grandpa's house in Brooklyn, I was allowed to open any drawer and try on any thing, as long as I didn't come down the steep staircase looking "wild," i.e. too much lipstick on. Grandma loved to accessorize with scarves, belts, earrings and necklaces, and encouraged me to do the same, so I was allowed to rummage through her old things and make new outfits for myself. Of course, I wanted to look slutty and unkempt, and loved nothing better than to press red lipstick against my lips and run my Grandmother's sharp silver teasing comb through my hair, pulling it up into a brown, frizzy cloud. The only time my grandfather ever chastised me was after I teased. "Go comb your hair," he said, not realizing that was exactly what I had done and then sprayed it into place.

Both my mother's and her sister's old bedrooms were available for pillaging, as was the desk in the room off the kitchen my grandparents' called "the den." Upstairs, in my mother's dresser, I would find old earrings and cufflinks, piles of suede and leather gloves in white, taupe and pink, silk scarves still smelling of perfume and hair spray, old lipsticks, and a variety of short-sleeved, scoop-neck cashmere sweaters in muted colors. Downstairs, in "the den," a small room with one window that connected the dining room to the outdoor patio and looked out onto the side of the neighbor's house, my grandfather sat at his desk, read *The New York Times* and typed letters to the editor about the state of the economy, interest rates and the questionable behavior of the Federal Reserve. The *Times* occasionally published some of Grandpa's letters, which prompted Grandpa to pick up the phone and call all his friends and relatives, the only time I ever saw Grandpa boast about his accomplishments. "Did you see my letter in the *Times* today?" he'd say gleefully. If you didn't, he would make a photo copy and mail it off to you the next day.

My grandfather believed in the power of the pen, or to put it more accurately, the typewriter. When my father, my aunt or one of us acted up—had a temper tantrum, jumped out of a car in anger, got thrown out of boarding school for doing something illicit—my grandfather took out his typewriter and wrote a little homily, trying gently to keep everyone in line. Whenever we gathered for Thanksgiving, Passover, anniversaries or birthdays, Grandpa would pass around a page of something he'd typed up and made copies of at the office. "Only people are precious," he'd write. "Money is round, and rolls hither and yon." He also loved the acronym, EED: "Enjoy every day." The subtext of his missives was always the same: "Be kind to the people you love, merciful to those you don't, and grateful for what you have."

In the den, Grandma and Grandpa sat on the couch together and listened to the opera on WQXR and watched Channel 13. They rarely watched the news; that was what *The New York Times* was for. The couch held Grandpa when he fell asleep after work and before dinner, and surrounded my grandmother while she shortened skirts, sewed on buttons and mended trousers and socks. I never saw them fight, not once, although I'd heard that they had once had a huge blow-up at a party in the Bronx, with Grandma leaving by subway and Grandpa not even realizing she'd left, prompting Grandpa to sleep on the couch that night.

Grandpa's desk was a few feet away from the couch. In his desk was a magnifying glass so that he could read the tiny stock prices in the business section of the *Times* and a pair of binoculars, that he took to the opera. The drawers were filled with balls of rubber bands, sharp yellow pencils, ball-point pens, old reading glasses, rulers, protractors, slide rules, calculators, safety pins, a metal compass that made perfect circles and with which I occasionally jabbed myself without drawing any blood. There were also stacks of yellow legal pads and scattered paper clips. You never knew what you would find in that desk, though try as I might, I could never find anything damning. There were only drawers of comfort.

Grandma is long dead now, Grandpa even longer, but this box of notes brings them rushing back to me. I open the box. Grandpa's obituary is on top. "SC Greenfield, 89, Investment Adviser," intones *The New York Times* headline. I know Wolfgang Saxon wrote the obituary but he doesn't have a byline here; of the thirteen obituaries on the page, Saxon's byline is only on top of the most important one, an obituary of the children's book writer, Jack Sendak, the less famous brother of best-selling author Maurice. I remember Wolf Saxon calling Grandma and asking about Grandpa; she was sitting on her screened-in porch in the back of the house. The sun was shining and it was a cold February day, Grandma sitting in her chair, clutching the heavy black phone in her hand while she spoke.

"Who's on the phone?" my cousins asked.

"Shhh," my mother said. "It's *The New York Times*!" We were sitting shiva, and everyone was sad, but we were also all aflutter because now Grandpa would be written up in his beloved *Times*.

The obituary tells me what I already know: Grandpa came to the U.S. from Austria as a boy, worked as a math teacher in the NY City public schools, was chairman of the teachers' union taxation committee and was a vice president concerned with pension issues. The obituary goes on to say that Grandpa taught math at Stuyvesant until 1954.

What it doesn't say is that Grandpa retired from teaching at a relatively early age—48. The reasons are unknowable or obvious, depending upon which version you believe. Grandpa had been summoned to Washington by Senator McCarthy to report on his involvement in the Socialist party. While it was true that Grandma and Grandpa had flirted with Socialism back in the 1930s, by the mid 1950s, they were die-hard capitalists who were all for shopping at Loehmann's, going to the opera and symphony, vacationing in the Poconos and investing in the stock market.

For reasons that remain mysterious, Grandpa never actually had to testify before McCarthy. Still, because accusations of Socialism had begun to be levied against him, his teaching career at Stuyvesant ended. Now this is where the truth gets murky. My mother says her father voluntarily retired from teaching, because he was writing a stock-picking letter for a Wall Street firm and making as much money doing that as he was teaching math at Stuyvesant. My father, who had been one of my grandfather's students at Stuyvesant, said the taint of the McCarthy hearings forced Grandpa's hand. We all traffic in our versions of the truth. The reality is Grandpa retired from teaching after 25 years, took his pension, gathered up his teacher friends' addresses, mailed out a weekly newsletter about investments, and started a new full-time career on Wall Street, where he invested his teacher friends' pensions and became a successful stockbroker. To hell with Socialism and teaching gifted minds in the New York City school system; actively pursuing Capitalism paid for his daughters' weddings, houses and divorces, two of his grandsons' college tuitions and ultimately, my wedding as well.

In a strange twist of fate and irony, we have Senator McCarthy to thank for my mother's abundant sense of security and confidence, and Grandpa's ability to pay for my wedding when my father refused.

The obituary concludes by noting that Sam was married to Miriam for 65 years.

I rub the yellowed obituary in my hand. Underneath is a pile of envelopes, held together by a frayed rubber band. Rubber bands abounded in my grandparents' house. They were wrapped around almost every doorknob, and then removed to hold pens and papers together. Occasionally, I wrapped one tight around my head, howling in pain when it snapped into my eyelid. I take out one of the envelopes. A stack of stamped and addressed envelopes is marked "Special." I recognize my grandmother's beautiful, bold, careful handwriting. I pick the first one up. This letter was written on February 9, 1995, more than 19 years ago. The letter is from Paul Denn of West Palm Beach. He is dead now, I'm sure. It is typed on elegant, old-fashioned stationery, the kind that is rippled at the top and has the letter writers' name written out in brown type that slants gently to the right.

> *Dear Miriam,*
>
> *I wish to tell this story, which I don't think you know. In 1931, I visited Europe. There I stayed briefly with my aunt and her family. They lived in Berlin. After I left and returned home, they became aware more than many others of Hitler's danger and wrote to my parents asking to sponsor their emigration to the U.S. My parents turned to me as the one to process it. I wrote to HIAS [Hebrew Immigration Aid Society] for the necessary papers, which I filled out and sent to the State Dept. I received a letter informing me that I was not, despite my teaching position, financially able to prove that they would not be a financial burden. I turned to my aunt's sister's husband, an insurance agent, for support. He turned me down. I then asked Sam, although he was a distant relative, for support. He instantly and without hesitation assented. As a result, they and their two sons came shortly [after] to the U.S. The sons are now grown men. I see them from time to time. If Sam had not come to my aid, you and I know where they would be in the 1940's...To Sam—Ave atque vale* (Hail and Farewell).
>
> *—Paul*

I keep digging through the "special" notes. One from Maureen called Grandpa *"an oasis in the desert of our society–the personification of the word gentleman."* Robert Dressler wrote, "*Sam was my father's boyhood friend...a man of absolute integrity. He was an advisor in whom our family placed its complete confidence.*" Pauline and Morris Pincus admitted there was little they could do 3,000 miles away in Palo Alto, but reassured Grandma in Brooklyn that they were grieving with her. "*Anyone who knew Sam, his wonderful positive outlook on life and his joie de vivre will miss him terribly, but it may be some solace to you to think about how well-loved he was by young and old alike.*"

A man named Robert Adler wrote the most eloquent letter of all:

Dear Miriam,

I was deeply saddened to learn of the death of my friend Sam. Over the course of more than 20 years, I was privileged to share with him many lunches of lox and bagels, and later of your tuna sandwiches, and to enjoy lively conversation with Sam and his many friends and clients. It was always a welcome respite from the pressures of the office, and it was a refreshing reinforcement to find someone else in Wall Street who wasn't embarrassed to identify himself as an unabashed liberal. I admired Sam's concern for the less privileged, his abiding sense of fairness, and his integrity, and I relished his genuine interest in the people who were close to him.

Of course, one of the elements that came through most prominently was his great pride in his family, which he bragged about at the drop of the faintest hint of a question (whenever his grandsons weren't present). Nearly as often as we discussed the market, or economics, or politics, we exchanged updates about our kids' progress, and it was gratifying to feel that his sincere interest in my kids was almost as great as his own.

I saw him only infrequently during the past few years, because it became increasingly difficult to take the time away from my office. Frankly, because of his infirmity, I had already begun to miss his former acuity but he never lost his warmth and his genuine pleasure at a visit from a friend. I will miss those lunches with him, but the value of his friendship will remain with me. I'm sure that, notwithstanding Sam's recent poor health, his passing was a blow to you, as well as to the other members of his family whom I never met. But many of us who were lucky enough to count him among our friends share your loss. And I hope that the knowledge that your grief is shared by so many will make the burden just a little lighter for all of you.

With deepest sympathy, Bob

Given what a sweet and gentle man my grandfather had been, I wondered how my mother had managed to fall in love with men who weren't. But really, I knew the answer to that question. Women who grow up with men who love them unconditionally don't always recognize the men coming their way who may not. This was one thing I had that my mother didn't: I could recognize a man with bad intentions a mile away.

On the back of another condolence envelope is a fortune cookie fortune, a narrow strip of paper, with words printed in pink ink. "*You will be free of the heavy burdens you have been carrying,*" it promises. Someone – Grandma, I'm sure – had attached it to the front of an envelope with a piece of tape and written above it, *February 10, 1995*. That was Grandpa's birthday. Grandma was not a superstitious person. But this is Grandma's handwriting and I know she loved Chinese food. Even she, practical, resilient, frugal, and utterly sane Grandma, occasionally needed a reassuring message from the powers above, and it made perfect sense that hers would come from a cookie.

My mother and Moey's daughter Carolyn have always been close, despite having lived three time zones away from each other for most of their lives. My theory is that because my mother didn't get along particularly well with her older sister Bertie, she reached out to the various female first cousins on her father's side,

Carolyn chief among them. And Carolyn, who had only a brother, gravitated to her sister cousins as well.

Carolyn's first husband was a doctor and they had two children. After they divorced, she married Tom Sargent, an economics professor at Stanford who won the Nobel Prize in economics in 2011.

My mother and stepfather had gone to the Nobel Prize ceremony. Not only was Tom a Nobel Prize winner, but Carolyn was a docent at the Met; here was the healthy, happy side of the family. They were smart, *haymishe* and accomplished. What could be better?

A few months ago, my younger son became a bar mitzvah. Tom and Carolyn came to the service and afterwards, Carolyn emailed my mother and told her that Tom had been impressed with David's d'var Torah and would consider hiring him to do research for him one day. You could hear my mother *kvell*. There was a Nobel Prize winner in economics in the family and he wanted to hire her grandson. My mother immediately arranged for Tom and Carolyn to meet us for dinner at a Portuguese restaurant in Newark. One cold Sunday night, we all settled into a rectangular shaped table in a private room. Tom asked to sit near the kids. You would think that a man of his stature would prefer adult company but Carolyn said he was at heart a college professor and he liked getting to know teenagers and seeing how they thought. So down he sat with my mother's five teenage grandsons.

Tom reminded me of Grandpa and Moey. Sweet, *menschy* and direct. He liked plain foods and talking to people at parties. He laughed easily and didn't need a lot of feting or hand-holding. He sat close to my younger son, leaned in and listened to what he had to say. My son is 13 and not an adventurous eater. He thinks Diet Coke goes with everything, and supermarket cookies are the bomb. We made our way through sausage and seafood paella. The food was forgettable but we were having a good time so we stayed for dessert. The waiter gave us our options: Carrot cake or chocolate cake. My younger son weighed the possibilities: "I like carrots," he said, "but I really love chocolate."

"Don't get the carrot cake, David," Tom cried. "It's a slippery slope!" He and David had been talking about their love of chocolate;

Tom didn't want him tempted by carrot. They both ordered the chocolate cake. I stole a piece of it: Light as a feather inside, fudgy chocolate frosting on top. It wasn't too rich, and in my opinion, maybe needed some coffee, but they both happily polished off what was on their plates.

It always excites me when one of my kids likes something that I might be able to make, so I looked for a recipe for a mild chocolate-y cake that we could maybe bake together. My friend Lynne sent along a recipe for a gluten-free chocolate cake that couldn't be easier to make. You only use seven ounces of chocolate (almost a cup), which doesn't sound like a lot, but there are only four other ingredients–melted butter, sugar, eggs and a tablespoon of Kahlua, so the chocolate dominates. The cake is chocolate-y without being super-rich.

The recipe called for putting the springform pan in a "bath" in the oven while cooking it, which I had never done before. David helped me make it during a prolonged homework break on a sunny Sunday afternoon right before Passover. After we put it in the oven, he disappeared upstairs with his laptop to resume his homework. When the timer went off, I called for him but he was already ensconced in his boy cave. I left it to cool on the counter. It wasn't all that impressive looking—a bit like a large, flat, round, cracked brownie. Half an hour later, he sashayed over to me.

"Mom, a crumb fell off," he said, licking his fingers.

"You mean a crumb leapt off the pan into your mouth?" I said.

He grinned. "Maybe."

"How is it?"

"Good, like a brownie."

For him, that means perfection. I took his word for it and didn't taste the cake, just wrapped it in tinfoil, put it in the basement freezer and saved it for Passover. It didn't look like much but I had made other gluten-free desserts that were good-looking so didn't worry too much about this cake's slightly pathetic presentation. Two days later, we went to my brother's for Passover. Deep into the night, after we'd finished the festive meal and we were about to start coffee and dessert, I noticed that half the cake was gone. Dessert hadn't even been served! There were various people milling around the kitchen and the cake was sitting on a low shelf, near a platter of awesome homemade macaroons, all waiting to be taken out to the dining room. I had been nibbling on the macaroons all night, which I had forgiven myself for because nobody misses a macaroon from a pile, but who had started in on the chocolate cake? Oh hell, it didn't matter—now I could too. I took a fork, stuck it in and tasted it. It was fantastic, dense and sweet. I couldn't believe we had made it with so few ingredients. The cake was delicious without being fussy, perfect for a 13-year-old and an affable Nobel Prize winner. There was no way Tom Sargent wouldn't like this cake. I forwarded the recipe to Carolyn. She returned the favor by sending me a recipe for chocolate meringues.

For years, we had big family Seders with Grandpa Sam's family on the second night of Passover at a second rate hotel in New Jersey. The hotel was in Fort Lee, right off the highway, and my husband called it the "family ancestral home." We sat around a big horseshoe table and ate charoset that was mushy, and chopped liver that didn't have enough hard-boiled egg in it. The boneless chicken breasts were bland; the Seder plate was unfamiliar and laden with too much parsley and not enough horseradish. The white wine was warm and the red wine too sweet. But these were my grandfather's brother and sisters, their kids, grandkids and great-grandkids. There were a lot of small children running around. The conversations were lively and everyone participated as we sat around the table and read from the Hagaddah. The Israelites' exodus from Egypt thousands of years earlier had brought us all together but observing this Jewish ritual and eating this festive meal was not the reason we talked into the night. We liked each other.

Those extended family Seders ended. Grandpa's kid brother Moey died two years ago at age 97. I hadn't seen him in years. And I haven't seen some of my cousins since my grandfather passed away almost twenty years ago. Eventually, our children got older and our lives became knotted with the families we had made and married into, so we splintered off and started holding our own Seders in our own houses with our friends and various in-laws.

There's always more to tell.

Great, Simple Flourless Chocolate Cake

(Serves 6-8)

INGREDIENTS:

- 7 ounces bittersweet or semisweet chocolate, chopped *(I used Ghirardelli semi-sweet chocolate chips)*
- 1½ sticks unsalted butter
- 4 large eggs
- 1⅓ cups sugar
- 1 tablespoon Kahlua

PREPARATION:

1. **Preheat oven to 325 degrees**.
2. **Butter and sugar 8-inch diameter springform pan.** Wrap tinfoil around outside of pan. Melt chocolate and butter in heavy medium pan over low heat, stirring until smooth. Whisk eggs, sugar and Kahlua in large bowl, until well blended. Whisk in chocolate mixture.
3. P**our batter into prepared pan.** Place cake in larger baking pan. Add enough hot water to larger baking pan to come halfway up side of springform pan *(the one holding the cake batter)*. Bake until knife inserted into center comes out clean, about 1½ hours (*cake will be about ½ inch high*). Remove cake from water bath. Cool.
4. **Remove foil.** Cover and refrigerate over night. *(Cake can be prepared one week ahead and kept in freezer.)*

▸ *Lynne's friend Lori, who sent her this recipe, serves this cake with Crème Anglaise or raspberry sauce or ice cream. But this cake doesn't need any friends. It is awesome on its own.*

CAROLYN'S CHOCOLATE CHIP MERINGUES

(Yield: about 20 cookies.)

INGREDIENTS:

- 2 egg whites, beaten stiff
- ½ teaspoon cream of tartar
- ¾ cup sugar
- 1 teaspoon vanilla
- ⅔ cup mini chocolate chips

PREPARATION:

1. **Preheat oven to 250 degrees** if convection, 275 degrees if standard.

1. **Beat eggs whites** until stiff but not dry.
2. **Add salt and cream of tartar.** Gradually add sugar while beating.
3. **Add in vanilla and stir** in chocolate chips.
4. **Cover a cookie sheet** with parchment paper. Drop cookies from a tablespoon.
5. **Bake about 20-25 minutes** until you can lift the cookies easily. They will feel "dry." If they begin to brown, turn oven off and let residual heat finish the baking.

40

Climbing the Family Tree

Kidnapping, Mental Illness and Me

On one side of the family we have this: A Nobel prize winner, a two-term governor, the provost at a major university, a physicist who helped develop the atom bomb, a psychiatrist, an internist, some lawyers, a few art collectors, a computer programmer, two stock brokers, a math teacher at Stuyvesant, a CPA, two architects, multiple bridge players, a trailer park developer who also owns Laundromats, a banker, and one children's book illustrator.

FEATURING

- Super Rich, Fiercely Mexican Iced Mocha
- Café de Olla

On the other side, we have this: Alleged incest, multiple suicide attempts, a couple of successful suicides, rampant obesity, several divorces, stints in mental hospitals, rehab facilities, county jails and state prisons, and what seems like ubiquitous mental illness.

I'm related to all of it, and mostly, I have stayed away.

But in the middle of my life, once my children became old enough to do homework on their own and my husband didn't need me for much except vacation-planning, sex and staying in touch with his mother, I decided to track down my cousin Trudy, who had done one of the craziest things I'd ever heard: Kidnapped a baby and got away with it.

I actually hadn't thought about her at all until one sunny morning in October 2002. I was cleaning up the kitchen; my older son had just gotten on the bus for kindergarten and my younger son was running around the family room, chewing on a Sippy cup and pulling down his diaper.

The phone rang. It was my mother. "Cookie, do you have your *New York Times* in front of you?"

In my family, it's assumed that women with small children spend a lot of time just sitting around, reading *The New York Times* after they've had their morning coffee. In fact I *was* reading *The New York Times*.

"Yes," I said. "Why?"

"Good," she said. "Go to the Metro section. See it?"

"What am I looking at?"

"That's your father's cousin, Trudy. "

I read the headline: "Woman Who Took Baby is Freed." Beneath it was a picture of my father's cousin Trudy and her husband Abe. I scanned the story quickly. Apparently, Trudy had gotten out of Rikers a few weeks earlier for kidnapping her son when he was a baby. She'd gotten away with it at the time, but now, twenty-some odd years later, the authorities had caught up with her, and she and Abe had gone to jail for the crime.

Trudy had pleaded guilty to first-degree custodial interference. She was fifty-something and diabetic and had been released after just two months, through a special program for non-violent inmates. Her husband Abe, who had pleaded guilty to second-degree kidnapping, was serving a two to six year sentence and was still in prison.

As a former reporter, I was intrigued. One of my cousins was in the news.

I looked at Trudy's picture. She certainly looked like she could be my father's cousin. The women in my father's family were, by and large, overweight. Trudy was plump and a little disheveled; she was sitting in a wheelchair, staring into the sun. She was smiling and something in her face looked kind. And happy. As if a few months in prison hadn't been such a big deal. She didn't look like a woman who had spent over 20 years as a fugitive. She looked like your mom's friend from bridge, the kind of woman who did

The New York Times crossword puzzle, shopped at Loehmann's and could probably give you a few tips on how to cook a brisket.

"Did you know Trudy?" I asked my mom.

"Of course," she said. "We knew the whole story!"

The story was that Trudy and Abe had adopted a baby boy. Why they couldn't have a baby of their own, my mother didn't know. All she knew was that the baby was tiny and delicious and that Trudy and her husband had had a wonderful time caring for him. One weekend, my parents took my brother and me to a party at their house in Queens so the family could meet the baby. The party was out on the patio and apparently I held that little baby in my arms for a very long time. But five months later, the thing that every adoptive parent worries will happen happened: the baby's birth father sent word that he wanted the baby back. Curiously, the baby's mother didn't want the baby, but the court didn't care; after almost a year of litigation, a judge awarded custody of the baby to his birth father, a young man from Long Island who was studying to be a plumber.

But Trudy and Abe had spent years trying to adopt and they weren't giving that baby back so fast. So one night they left their house and disappeared. It was like they dropped off the face of the earth, cutting off contact with everybody they knew.

They stole Social Security numbers, changed their names, created phony birth certificates, and moved across the country to raise their baby as Nicholas. They supported themselves making and selling silver jewelry in the square in Santa Fe. Eventually, they turned themselves in, but not until Nicholas was a grown man, out of college and looking for a job.

During our phone call, I could sense my mother's usual glee that she no longer had anything to do with my father or his family. But she knew that since I was a journalist, albeit semi-retired and suburban, I would be interested that someone in our family had made the front page of a section of *The New York Times*. My mother is terrified of mental illness, but she knows I am fascinated by it. I've always been drawn to the dark side of my father's family – a darkness that is frequently pitch black.

I thought about calling my father to discuss all this, but at that point, he was getting chemotherapy for lymphoma and I didn't want to bother him. Plus, I knew that even on his best day, my father didn't like to talk about his (mostly) wayward family. Maybe his family's demons reminded him of his own.

I didn't really know Trudy. My parents separated shortly after Trudy and Abe disappeared, and my mother, who had been the glue holding my father and his relatives together, stopped playing that role once she moved out of the house. Although my father supported his own father and sister financially, he barely spoke to either of them or any of his other relatives. He *never* spoke of Trudy.

Of course, I never knew that Trudy had kidnapped a baby until my mother told me the story that morning in 2002. I thought the *Times* account was the whole story.

But it wasn't.

* * *

Two-and-a-half years after Trudy got out of prison, my father died. It was May 2005.

It probably says something about my relationship with my father that, in the five years he suffered with lymphoma, I only spoke to his oncologist once, even though Dad was being treated ten minutes from our house. I often dropped him off and picked him up, but I never once sat with him while he was getting chemo. It's not that I didn't care or we weren't close. I did and we were. But my father was a fiercely independent and difficult man who didn't like asking for help.

Dad was a radiologist who for most of his career had been extremely successful, running radiology departments at various hospitals in New York and New Jersey. He made a nice life for himself, and us. We vacationed in the Caribbean, summered in Europe, went to private high school and did not need financial aid for college. At home, Dad encouraged my mother to renovate, decorate and redecorate the house, make duck *a l'orange* and chocolate mousse, and hire and fire as many housekeepers as she saw fit. Dad looked like Gene Hackman and Mom looked like a Jewish Jackie O. They played tennis, went to the theater, travelled to Asia and Europe, and gave frequent dinner parties.

On top of being a doctor, Dad was also an amateur historian and terrific debater who could win almost any argument. But he could also be nasty. He had grown up watching his grandfather Sam belittle my dad's father Nat and then saw Nat belittle Dad's mother, Lee. When my father was still a baby, his mother stuck her head in the oven. Though she had poetic impulses, she was no Sylvia Plath; she survived, living long enough to meet all five of her grandchildren, before succumbing to colon cancer. She passed away when I was in third grade, a lovely, gentle woman, quick to offer praise. I remember her in soft wool suits, with jackets and knee-length skirts; she often wore gloves and an elegant pin at her lapel. In her wedding picture, she looks shyly at the camera, her small body dwarfed by a huge train and long dress, her hands clutching what look like irises. Nat stands stoically beside her, smiling cautiously, all formal elegance in a black coat with tails. I don't think Lee had any idea what she was getting into when she married my grandfather.

Nat Zinn was one of five children born into a thriving family fur business. I visited the spot where the store once was. It was in Chinatown, on the corner of Delancey Street, a large, cluttered store that now sells restaurant supplies and housewares. The owners looked at me quizzically. When I explained that my family had once run a business there some sixty years before, they nodded nervously, as if I might make some claim on the site. What did I want? It was clear I wasn't buying anything. There were no fur coats inside, no comfortable armchairs, no mirrors. Still, I could so easily imagine my great-grandfather and his sons, roaming the store, barking orders at the clerks and making nice to the customers, their sleeves rolled up as the women tried on sable and mink, twirled around, admired the furs, and snuck peeks of themselves in the mirrors. They'd choose the satin lining for your coat and then have your initials embroidered into it. If there was extra fur, they made you a stole to wear around your shoulders on a cool Saturday night in summer. Oh, the glamour of it! To own a fur coat meant you'd arrived.

In 1954, Nat's father and brother both died and Nat took over the fur business. The remaining children fought, and in 1963, they closed the business down. My father remembers Nat periodically urging his wife to put her head back in the oven, and to remember to turn the gas on this time. It was that kind of family.

Grandpa Nat, Dad and his sister Charlotte all spent stretches in mental hospitals. Dad and Grandpa were given anti-depressants and electro-shock therapy. They became less argumentative, less irritable. But at times, the medication made my father almost unrecognizable.

I think of my father as someone who, for a long time, set the world on fire. That is, until his mood swings caught up with him and he decided instead to burn it down. By the time he was diagnosed with cancer in 2000, Dad had blown through two marriages, two engagements and too many jobs to keep track of. He'd been sued by colleagues and hospitals and wives and he sued them all right back. He lost millions of dollars in lawsuits and divorces. He'd tried to kill himself a couple of times, once when I had just turned two and he was passed over for chief resident at New York Hospital, and then again, twenty nine years later, after I'd had my first baby. My brother had also recently had his first baby. We both had boys so Dad was a new grandfather with grandsons to brag about, yet one grey winter morning right after Christmas, he took a large carving knife, tucked it under the passenger seat of his blue Jaguar convertible and drove to a quarry close to his house. He plunged the knife into his chest, just missing his aorta, and survived.

The first time I visited him in a mental hospital, he was sitting in blue pajamas. He had been transferred from the trauma center of another hospital, where he had been admitted after he had stabbed himself in the heart. Now he was in the psych ward at a local hospital. The room was small. There was a bed with a curtain that drew closed around it. He looked at me with hope in his eyes. He had always been combative. Now he was as pliant as a child. He had no books on his bed table, no papers to sign, no x-rays to read. I told him I would bring him some books. He beamed but looked surprised.

"What's wrong, Dad?" I asked.

"All this love," he said. "All this love."

My mind began to fill with the questions I couldn't ask: *Why couldn't you OD on sleeping pills like a normal person? You're a doctor, you could have written yourself a prescription! Why did you try to murder yourself, like some Shakespearean tragedy, with all this drama and bloodshed?*

Dad's pale blue eyes had always remained hidden behind thick lenses. He wasn't wearing his glasses now; they had either been taken away or he had lost them en route to the hospital. Here were his blue eyes now, large and light. He sat at the edge of the bed; his pajamas alone terrified me. He didn't own pajamas. Dad either wore custom-made suits from Hong Kong or white tennis clothes. He looked at me expectantly and then he started to cry.

"What's the matter, Daddy?"

"I don't want to be locked up."

Years later, I would see this face on my sons when something would go wrong and they would wait for me to make it right, but it was the first time I had seen this face on my father. My father had been a brute — powerful and strong, a bull ready to charge. Who was this scared little boy in pajamas, shocked that people loved him?

It took me a long time–too long– to realize that this was who he'd been all along.

At the end of his life, when his fight against lymphoma was almost over, Dad would periodically show up late in the day, unannounced, knocking on the back door of our house. My kids were small and he knew I would be home, making them dinner.

"Hi, Pup," he'd say. "How's things?"

Good, I'd tell him. Do you want to come in?

Dad would sit down with my boys and I'd make him a plate. Back then, we ate a lot of steak and lasagna, which Dad loved. He'd make jokes with the kids, offering to take them swimming and for a ride in his car, but he would also seem jittery. "You okay, Dad?" I asked.

"Yeah, but you know, your brother was supposed to FedEx me an envelope and I didn't get it yet."

An envelope was code for money. My brother was in charge of

Dad's finances and would send him what could euphemistically be called an allowance. Dad's mania had kicked in and he'd been spending like mad. He bought a nice car for my half-sister Hannah, made a four-figure donation to the Jewish Museum and kept bringing me gifts from their gift shop: A huge silver menorah, a beautiful ceramic serving platter for Shabbat, a serrated knife with an intricately painted handle. I suspected he was either dating or courting a woman who worked there. But he'd fallen behind on his car payments and to prevent him from spending all of his money, my brother was parceling it out.

"I met a nice woman, she's Irish, I'd like to take her to a bar," he'd say.

"Tonight?" He nodded. "That sounds nice."

"Could I borrow some cash?" Dad would ask. I would either empty out my wallet for him or I would offer to go to the ATM. But going to the ATM presented a problem because it meant that Dad would offer to watch the kids, and I never knew what I would find when I got back. Best case: They'd be peacefully watching TV while he slept. But he could also be sleeping while they jumped on the trampoline he had given them. I started keeping extra cash on hand.

When my father finally did die it was a shock, even though we'd all expected it and, in my case, occasionally longed for it. Still, I was devastated when we lowered him into the ground.

My father had left no instructions about how or where he wanted to be buried, so my brother and I bought him a plot in New Jersey, not realizing that Dad had been maintaining a family plot in Brooklyn that his grandfather had bought some seventy ago.

Oddly, it was Trudy who told me about that plot, after we'd paid the funeral bill.

* * *

"Hi, I'm your cousin Trudy, your Dad's first cousin," she wrote in an email in June 2005. Dad had been dead two weeks.

After Dad died, Trudy had sent a condolence email to my mother who, as Dad's ex-wife of 23 years, didn't really need much consoling. "He was a difficult person," Mom wrote back to Trudy, "but he was the children's father and you only get one per customer."

With that, she turned Trudy over to me.

When a parent dies, that's one less person in the world who loves you. You're not likely to find that kind of love again. And even if that parent has taken you on a ride that was chaotic and occasionally terrifying, that ride is over now, for good.

But it's hard to stop missing your parents once they're gone, as loony and unpredictable as they might have been. My desire to go on a ride with my father again, this time with a seatbelt and 20/20 hindsight, is what led me into an email relationship with Trudy, and ultimately, a friendship with her husband Abe, the brains behind the whole kidnapping operation.

I was pretty thrilled to hear from Trudy. For years, I had wondered about my father's family. Why was there so much depression? Why were there so many suicide attempts? In addition to my father and my grandmother, two of my father's first cousins had thrown themselves off the Golden Gate Bridge in San Francisco. Another of his cousins died of a drug overdose in Florida. One great aunt was a paranoid schizophrenic. Then there was the family business. Why had it once thrived, supporting my grandfather and his four siblings, turning my great-grandfather into a millionaire, and then ended up in bankruptcy proceedings? Why did my great-grandfather die without a will, leaving his children to squabble over the business and ultimately, shut it down? The former business reporter in me was particularly interested in this tale of corporate mismanagement and woe.

"*WOW!*" Trudy wrote me, after I'd sent her a list of questions about her side of the family tree. "*Families are complicated things*."

Yeah, they are. And now here she was, the infamous cousin Trudy, a woman who had been on the FBI's most wanted list, the one link to my father's past that I knew of, a woman who'd had the gumption to disappear with little more than a baby and a stroller, a woman who had defiantly lived her life as a fugitive under an assumed name, a middle-aged mom who'd dyed her hair and worked for cash so she could send her son to college, a woman with a college degree and an affable manner who had eluded the authorities for more than twenty years so she could raise her baby in safety and peace. Here she was, crazy Cousin Trudy – criminal Cousin Trudy—lighting up my computer screen with both soothing words and good sense.

The news of her kidnapped baby was all good: He had grown into a handsome young man, with a wife, a young daughter and his own baby boy on the way. This kidnapped baby had—I kid you not–worked as a policeman, a prison guard and an EMS worker. He had gone to college and graduate school and now worked full-time as a fireman. And he had done this all with a fake birth certificate. He knew all about his birth family and had spent some real time with them, but he didn't speak to them much. According to Trudy, he was just fine about being kidnapped. Abe and Trudy, despite being ex-cons, were great parents. They may have committed a federal crime and dodged the law for decades, but their intentions had been honorable.

Trudy's first email was cheerful and chatty, and she sounded intelligent. More to the point, she sounded *sane*. "*The last time I saw all of you was 26 years ago at my house in Queens, New York,*" she wrote. "*We were celebrating the birth and pending adoption of my son, Nick. You spent the entire afternoon holding and playing with him; he was about two months old at the time. Unfortunately, the adoption was challenged and after fighting in court for 10 months we fled New York, lost contact with everyone...*"

Trudy concluded by saying she was willing to tell me anything I wanted to know about the family.

I wanted to know it all. And I especially wanted to know about *her*.

So she told me. Nick's birth father wanted him back. At first, that seemed impossible, ludicrous, because the birth mother wasn't interested. Nick had been born to a couple who wasn't even sure they wanted a baby. They were young, they weren't married. They both smoked and drank. Trudy and Abe, who had been looking to adopt a baby, stepped up and paid for all the doctor visits during the mother's pregnancy. When the baby was born, they went to the hospital and took him home. Everything was perfect. Until the father decided he wanted him back. Trudy kept her early emails brief:

> *If you want detail, you can Google us and get press info. When we turned ourselves in in 2001 we were in all the papers and on all the morning shows. We eventually returned to our lives here in New Mexico and resumed contact with friends and family. Your dad and aunt didn't make contact and we chose not to force the issue. After all that time and all the publicity, not everyone wanted to keep in touch.*

I decided to start by asking her about the extended Zinn family. She was eight years younger than my Dad, and an only child. My father had lived with her family one summer when he was in medical school so she had gotten to know him even better. And unlike my Dad, who was hell-bent on getting good grades and spent most of his time holed up in his bedroom, studying, Trudy was a social teenage girl who spent a lot of time chatting with her mother and aunts. She was also close to her cousin Eric who had secretly helped her and Abe make their way from New York to New Mexico and sent them money over the years from Trudy's father.

> *There is a big problem with depression throughout the family. Of course, years ago, it wasn't called depression. One was said to have had a "nervous breakdown." At least three of the five Zinn siblings suffered from serious depression. Among their children, most if not all of us have had to deal with it. No bipolar diagnosis that I know of, [but] Grandma Esther has a sister who was a paranoid schizophrenic.*

Her observations validated what I already knew: Far too many people in my father's family were mentally ill. But Trudy was not.

And maybe I wasn't as bad as I thought either.

Occasionally, Trudy would take her time answering my emails. Weeks would go by. Her health wasn't good. She was extremely overweight and though I didn't realize it at the time, she spent a lot of time in a wheelchair or in bed, and had trouble walking.

Every time I found an email from her in my inbox, my spirits soared. I knew within them I would find a helpful insight, some comfort and maternal wisdom. She was the only person from my father's side of the family that I actually spoke to. My father's sister Charlotte died shortly after he did, and though Charlotte had three children, I wasn't in touch with any of them. My father had other first cousins but not one of them showed up at his funeral or reached out to us after he died. But Trudy did. Not only that, she was a woman who had survived growing up in a Zinn household. She understood the rough way they treated each other. She knew the drill. But she had emerged thoughtful, kind, helpful and intelligent, and even though she had done one of the craziest things imaginable, you could understand her motive: She had adopted that baby in good faith. She loved him. She wasn't planning to be a mother temporarily; she had adopted for life. Just because the baby's birth father had had a change of heart, she hadn't.

I tried to imagine the love Trudy had for that baby: she loved him more than she loved her job, her friends, her financial security, her extended family. After the courts ruled in the birth father's favor, she and Abe gave up their savings, their earning potential, and all contact with almost everyone they knew so that they could keep that baby safe and raise him to manhood. Now that Nick was an adult having his own babies, Trudy was elated, free to kick back and relax. She and Abe had done their time in prison. They had paid their debt to society. Her carefree vibes made their way across the Internet and landed with a joyful thud in my inbox.

Then we lost touch. I was gearing up for my older son's bar mitzvah and had taken a more time-consuming job, teaching news reporting at a local state university. I was also teaching creative writing at Columbia. I was busy. I guess Trudy was too.

Then in September 2008, I received an email from her.

Sorry to have been out of touch for so long. My father died 9/18/08 here in New Mexico after a brief illness. He was the last of his generation on both his and my mother's side of the family. I'll be in touch again as soon as I can.

Love, Trudy

I sent Trudy an email telling her how sorry I was. And how lucky she was to have had her father for so long. That was it. We had my son's bar mitzvah and I kept working. Trudy and I stopped emailing.

In the fall of 2011, I decided to reach out to her. It had been three years since we'd communicated, and two years since my older son's bar mitzvah. I had become acclimated to teaching and had written a piece for *The New York Times*. I was feeling more confident and thinking of other things I could write. Trudy had an interesting story, maybe I could write about her. So, early one afternoon, nine years after I'd first read about her in the news, I wrote Trudy an email, quickly scribbling that I was thinking about writing about our family and wondering if we could talk by phone. An hour later, I received an email back:

Hi Laura,

I'm sorry to let you know that Trudy passed away the December before last. We all miss her terribly. I recall Trudy mentioning that she had been in touch with you and enjoyed trying to help you fill in the information about the Zinn family. I wish I knew more so I could help you. If you think I might be of any help, I'd be glad to try.

Abe

Trudy was dead. She had died of complications from diabetes. I went in search of her last email. There it was. Her daughter-in-law was expecting another baby and she was busy buying baby presents. "*What fun!*" Trudy had written.

I regretted that our emails had petered out and I tried to figure out why they had. Part of it was that once I had gone back to work, I had less time to wonder about my father. Not that we are ever really done trying to reconcile the confusing behavior of the people we once loved, but my longing to remember him and understand him was no longer so acute. He was dead, the mystery of his mental illness only partially solved, though Trudy had definitely helped answer some questions about it. As for why Trudy hadn't bothered to continue to email me, the answer seemed clear: She was happy. She had a husband, a son, a daughter-in-law and a grandchild on the way. What did she need from me? We had once served a purpose for each other, and that purpose had been fulfilled. She had wanted to rebuild a piece of the life she had abandoned decades before and perhaps do a kindness for her late cousin's child. I was trying to rebuild memories of my father.

Still, how could I not know that Trudy had died? How could I let so much time go by, when she had been so kind to me? What an idiot I was, thinking she would live forever, endlessly available to answer my questions about my father and their family whenever it occurred to me to pose them! Trudy was in her sixties. I had blithely assumed she would be right there waiting for me, staring at her computer screen, whenever I got around to writing her back. *If* I got around to writing her back.

Embarrassed, I screwed up my courage and emailed Abe, expressing my regret that I hadn't realized Trudy was ill. "*How are you? How is Nicholas? Your grandchildren?*

Abe emailed back right away.

> *We have two grandchildren, Tammy, who is now six, and Alec, who is four. Trudy lived for them and despite severe pain, she was always ready to do whatever they needed. Alec has no memory of her, but Tammy really got to know her well.*
>
> *Love, Abe*

He again offered to help me out in any way.

I knew all about Abe, but didn't remember ever meeting him. Now, I started to wonder about him. He had been in prison and now he was out. How did he support himself? Now that Trudy was gone, what did he do? I decided to look for him on Facebook. There he was. Someone had done a lovely pencil drawing of him: He looked like a Talmudic scholar – bearded, glasses, a middle-aged man with a kindly expression. He looked neither menacing nor capable of any great crime. The artist had captured him in the midst of thought, as if someone had asked him a question and he was about to answer. I sent him a friend request. We started trading emails and then almost immediately, we started playing Words with Friends.

When my family finished dinner, I would disappear into the powder room on the first floor to play games with Abe on my iPhone.

"What are you doing in there?" my husband once asked.

"Playing online Scrabble with Abe!" I hollered.

"Isn't he a convicted felon?"

"He's really good at this game," I said.

My husband appreciates word games. His grandmother had been a champion Scrabble player and his mother was always playing Words with Friends on her Nook. "Maybe you should go into the kitchen and do that on the computer," my husband said. "You'll be able to see better."

But I didn't want to. I liked to play with Abe alone, on my phone, on the toilet, away from everyone, the loud hum of the bathroom's fan drowning out all household noises. Abe was my link to my father, even though he was nothing like my father, was not related to him and could barely remember him. Abe called Trudy, "the family encyclopedia," but Abe hadn't read the parts about my father. They had spent most of the last thirty years in hiding, barely talking to any of us. Why should Abe care about his late wife's late cousin?

Months went by. Our online game playing accelerated. Even though I'm a word person, Abe beat the pants off of me in Words with Friends. Shockingly so.

We started playing Scramble, which I was better at. Abe was

great at long-term strategy, at seeing the possibilities of unusual, complicated words that might bud unexpectedly out of other words. Perhaps it was this gift that made him so successful at the kidnapping.

At some point I realized I loved Abe. Here was a man in my family who didn't seem to have designs on me or care what I looked like. My father was always preoccupied with my weight, and couldn't seem to decide if he wanted me to be thin and pretty like my mother, or fat and familiar like his sister. My mother's boyfriend, who lived in our house for ten years before my mother left him for my stepfather, was as obsessed with being thin as my mother. He'd always notice when I'd lost a few pounds and made a game out of guessing my weight. My stepfather, a gentle man who was otherwise kind and generous to me, once stood in our dining room on Rosh Hashanah, admired my dress and told me he was in love with me. Not the kind of attention you want from the men in your family.

Abe didn't want anything from me. He didn't care if we never met at all. All he wanted to do was play games. Our relationship was completely benign. We kept each other company online. He was kind. He wasn't particularly interested in my husband or kids, never asked me a thing about them, and that was fine; I wasn't in this relationship for them. I was in it for me. Indeed, I was dining out on it. I'd tell people I was playing word games with my cousin the kidnapper and they'd imagine a lecherous pedophile, all evil and wrongdoing, but in fact, Abe was a benevolent guy with a graduate degree in psychology who had been a long-term employee in the human resources department of a government agency before he and Trudy took their baby and disappeared. In prison, he had taught summer school and learned to cook. Now, he spent most of his time with his grandkids or, because his kidneys were failing him, on dialysis. He didn't seem to be living large but he didn't seem to need money either.

The only thing Abe was looking for in me was a friend. He was lonely. Trudy was gone and Nicholas was busy with his young family. Perhaps I was lonely too. My kids were in school all day. And though

I was teaching and writing, I had plenty of time alone. Too much, sometimes. I started to think we could write a book together. In June 2012, when my kids went off to sleep-away camp, I told Abe I was coming out to Albuquerque to see him, and then leaving for Santa Fe and to a writer's retreat in Taos. The truth is, I was going there with the express purpose of seeing if he wanted to work together, though I was not explicit about that in my emails to him. The fact that he was the kindly, courtly father figure I had always craved didn't hurt either.

I couldn't wait to meet him. Of course, Trudy had insisted that we had already met, those thirty some-odd years ago, but I had no memory of it. He wrote that he'd love to see me and that I could stay in the big house that he and Nicholas just bought. *We have an indoor swimming pool*, he wrote.

An indoor swimming pool? How could he afford a house with an indoor pool? Was he selling drugs? He had, after all, spent decades on the lam, and then in prison. He had defied the law, kidnapped a child, and stayed in hiding for more than twenty years. This was all very intriguing. I was a tiny bit scared of him, but too excited to give my fear a chance to flower. Plus, he was 66, the same age my father was when he died. I felt like I was flying out to visit the benevolent living ghost of my father.

I booked a flight to New Mexico, making a reservation at the Mabel Dodge Luhan writers' retreat in Taos. My husband questioned my motives: Why was I going? How was I justifying the expense? I told him a book might come of it and then the plane tickets would be tax deductible. *What book are you going to write exactly?* A memoir, I said, about Abe and Trudy and my father and the whole family. My husband, whose family endured horrors in World War II and goes out of its way not to talk about feelings and memories, never mind publish them, told me to save all my receipts.

My mother had known all along that I'd been emailing with Abe but was surprised I was going to see him. Still, she understood my curiosity. She had fond memories of him and even fonder memories of Trudy. "Abe was seriously obese," Mom said. "I wonder if he lost weight in prison."

I called him the minute I got off the plane. Two hours later, Abe and I met in the lobby of Little Anita's. He was shorter than I'd expected and much slimmer. He wasn't thin but he wasn't fat either. The food was terrible but we had a wonderful time. We ended up spending four hours together. I picked up the bill and broached the subject of a book. He said he was interested and, in fact, had been wanting to write down what had happened so his grandchildren would understand once they were old enough to read about the kidnapping. At the end of the meal, he hugged me and said, "I love you."

"I love you too," I said. I really did. I adored him. I didn't know anyone like him. He was funny, reflective, intelligent, and patient. Perhaps he had once been ambitious, but now he seemed to have nowhere to go and nothing he'd rather do than eat mediocre Mexican food with me. He suggested we get together again the next day so that I could start to take notes. It was Monday. We'd see what we could accomplish during the day because I was driving up to Santa Fe that night.

The next day, I met him at the Flying Star Café. I ordered an iced Mexican Mocha, a delicious spicy chocolate and espresso drink. Abe had a hamburger, French fries and a milk shake. He made sure we sat near an outlet, so I could keep my laptop plugged in, and I interviewed him for four hours about the kidnapping, his life with Trudy, and his efforts to keep Nicholas from spending all the money Trudy's father had left him when he died. Abe told me that Nicholas's birth parents had actually gone on to get married and have two more children together. But the mother had left the family and moved down South. Of the two remaining children, one had died of carbon monoxide poisoning in his car and the other was in prison.

Abe was a fabulous storyteller. He remembered all the details of the kidnapping: The time of night they left, how they had thrown everything in the back of a Volvo and driven down South, how they had gotten rid of their car, the weather when they arrived, the clothes Nicholas had been wearing, how much money they had taken with them, how Trudy had dyed her hair to match Nick's, what they used for documentation (Abe was artistic and spent months making them fake birth certificates with raised seals). He talked about what he ate in Sing Sing ("kosher meals because there were always fresh vegetables, cold cuts, cheese and an occasional hard boiled egg, and we would have Shabbos dinner"), who he hung out with in prison ("the murderers – they were the more regular people; the car thieves had no morals, they thought nothing about stealing from you"), and why he and Trudy eventually turned themselves in (when Nick turned 21, they didn't want him to get in trouble using a forged birth certificate). He explained how they outwitted the FBI by cutting off contact with almost everyone the FBI thought they would reach out to. Abe didn't speak to his mother for almost three years after the kidnapping and was estranged from his brother. "Every year, the FBI paid a visit to my brother on his birthday, thinking I would call him," Abe said laughing. "They didn't know we didn't talk to each other."

He talked about how committing a crime had actually made him a better father. "Before we had Nick, I used to spend 70 hours a week at the job," he said. Selling jewelry at the square in Santa Fe was less time-consuming than human relations work, "so I was at every single Little League game and every single practice. I did not miss one." Then he told me what I had already suspected: That it was Trudy who had wanted to keep the baby, no matter what. "Trudy was the primary force behind everything," Abe said. "As much as I was committed to keeping him, her resolve was tenfold."

Abe had no regrets. "I've had a good life," he said. "Not in spite of everything, because of it."

I left for Santa Fe and then Taos, and two days later, I returned to Albuquerque. Again, Abe and I met at the Flying Star Café and again, I drank two Mexican Iced Mochas. The sun spilled in on us from outside. I typed furiously as we talked, caffeine teeming through my bloodstream. We were having so much fun. We sat there for hours. My brain was racing. There was a book here, a good book, maybe even a great book that no one else had written, a book that involved my father and his cousins, kidnapping and identity theft and prison time, and all sorts of crimes that no one would expect from a New York City-based, middle-class, Jewish family.

I emailed my agent, who said that given what I'd told her, the book might work better as a novel, if only because Abe did not want me writing about Nicholas's birth parents, or even speaking to them at all. A friend who was a lawyer sent me the court documents and I started reading through them, underlining and highlighting like mad:

FINDINGS OF FACT

In November 1978, a young, unmarried couple conceived a child. The birth father and his family offered to support this child. The parents of the birth mother sought to have this child surrendered for adoption. A private placement adoption was arranged through his birth mother's family and the defendants. Through somewhat deceitful practices, the birth mother's consent to surrender the child for adoption was obtained. Shortly after the child's birth, the defendants took custody of the child. When learning of this, the birth parents commenced an action in Family Court to void the adoption based on a lack of consent to the adoption by the birth-father…

On June 2, 1980, a second order was issued by the Family Court ordering the defendants to return the child to the birth parents. On June 5, 1980, the birth – parents, accompanied by the police, sought to enforce this order only to learn that the defendants had fled the jurisdiction with the child. The defendants were indicted for Kidnapping in the Second Degree and arrest warrants were issued. Private searches by the Giordano family, the family of the birth-father, and a search by the FBI failed to locate the missing child.

The defendants ultimately established residence in New Mexico under assumed identities. For over 20 years they cared for and raised the person now known as Nicholas Frame as their son. There is no indication that this relationship was anything other than a loving, caring one. It is clear to me that the person known as Nicholas loves the defendants and fears that they will be incarcerated as a result of these charges–an event he wishes will not occur. It was a serendipitous event that led the defendants to tell Nicholas the circumstances surrounding his birth and the defendants' ultimate surrender on this charge to the authorities.

I loved reading about how much Trudy and Abe had sacrificed for their child. They had given up everything so they could raise this baby with love in poverty. I was enthralled by their story. They had fought so hard to keep this baby and raise him to manhood and they had won! But the reporter in me knew that this was not just a love story. I had to assemble all the facts and interview as many people as I could who had been involved in the case. That meant lawyers, judges, birth parents. Even though I'd received an MFA in fiction-writing, I didn't consider myself a novelist, especially not when I had so many mind-boggling facts at hand. The reporter in me was pushing the fiction writer in me aside.

A friend introduced me to an editor at a major publishing house who said she was interested in my story. "It sounds very intriguing," she wrote in an email. "Lots of room for plot twists, tender family relationships, moral dilemmas. I would be happy to take a look at whatever you have to share."

This was all very exciting. What should I do? My agent said one thing and the publisher was interested in another. Truth was stranger than fiction, but the truth also had to incorporate more than one person's version of the story.

I wrote to Abe, saying if he did not want me to interview the various parties, we would have to call this story a novel.

Abe did not like that suggestion.

Hi Laura,

I'm happy to hear that you spoke to your agent and that there appears to be some interest, however, I'm somewhat concerned about fictionalizing parts of the book. I'm not quite sure what you mean. My motivation for telling my story is to leave a legacy for my family, so saying that part of the story is fiction would not make sense in my case. I know that you're busy and there's no need to get back to me in any rush. We can discuss this matter when your kids go back to school in September. Meanwhile, I'm getting ready to move and feel both excited and scared to death. It will be the first time in my life that I've lived alone.

Love,
Abe

Things disintegrated from there. There was no Trudy to appeal to. I was in New Jersey, Abe was in New Mexico. We continued to play Scramble and Words With Friends. He was still beating me but I was improving. Then, his game started to deteriorate too. He texted me and said he was in the hospital. He'd broken his pelvis and was going to rehab. "*Do you need help*?" I texted back.

Abe and I exchanged a few emails about the possibility of talking to Nicholas about his birth parents – something no one seemed especially interested in besides me.

I sent Abe a long email, explaining to him what we would try to do in the book, and that I would do my best to protect Nick. When I didn't hear from him, I sent another email, in April 2013, a few weeks after Passover. He wrote back, almost immediately:

Hi Laura,

Sorry I didn't get back to you sooner. I've been spending time trying to figure out how best to respond. Nick is dead set against the idea of any book. I told him that I wanted to write it so that my side could be heard by my grandchildren and he was annoyed that I didn't expect him to be a good enough advocate for [Trudy] and me. I would be very upset if you tried to get in touch with Nick's biological parents. I've never had any form of hatred for them, but the same is not true of them. They are still very bitter and any attempt to contact them would be like throwing salt into a wound. Nick's relationship with them is strained at best, if there is even any relationship left. In 2010 when Nick's biological mother got in touch with me on Facebook, I noticed she was holding an infant and told Nick he might have a niece or nephew; he had no interest and was adamant about not wanting any contact with her. Last, before going ahead with the project, I'd like a clearer picture of what your intentions are and how you described the project to your publisher. I really don't think I ever was clear on what the book was supposed to be about. I thought I knew but when you mentioned fictionalizing some of it, it totally threw me.

Abe

You might think that at that point, I would have given up, but I was undaunted. When I was at *Business Week*, companies often said they didn't want to cooperate with stories we were writing about them. Our editors would tell us to write the story anyway, send the company a list of questions, give the company a chance to comment and hope they eventually came around. The majority of the time, they did. My clever, loving, games-playing cousin was behaving a lot like an uncooperative public company. I could deal with that. I would just keep reporting and writing.

I made plans to fly to Asheville, North Carolina. My father's cousin Eric was there for the summer. We met in Asheville the third week of July. I was excited to see Eric, who I'd been emailing, and talking to on the phone. He had become a successful lawyer, who had stayed close to both Abe and my father. Like my father, he also had a caustic wit.

I met Eric for dinner at a wonderful tapas place in downtown Asheville. Though I hadn't seen him since my brother's bar mitzvah thirty-three years earlier, he looked much as I remembered him – lively blue eyes, thick white hair and my father's chin. In fact, from the nose down, he looked eerily like my father, with many of the same speech patterns. He had homes in various places, two children, two grandchildren and one on the way. He had been president of his synagogue and enjoyed teaching religious school.

Eric was chatty and seemed happy to see me. He asked how Abe was doing; he hadn't talked to him since Trudy had died. When I told him what was going on ("at first Abe said yes to the book, now he's saying, no..."), Eric said he wasn't surprised. "You'll never be able to pull together all the facts to this story," he said. And then, after having spent five hours with me on the phone and knowing that I had come to Asheville expressly for this project, he said that he didn't want to have his name associated with the story either.

I returned home, considering this just another small setback.

But two weeks later, I woke up in a cold sweat. Without Abe or Eric's cooperation, I wasn't going to write a book about them. How could I? It was August and I had been busy working on this book for more than a year. I fell into a deep depression; how could I have let it come to this? Abe and Eric had each embraced me like the long lost cousin I was, eager to talk about their lives and catch up, but the reality was, that was all they wanted. They didn't want their words recorded, their stories told. There was too much at risk, for both for them. Abe could lose the love of the son he had fought so hard to raise and protect, and Eric could lose his right to practice law. If I pursued this book, I would hurt the people I had come to love and would be acting even crazier than some of the people I was related to.

I went back to writing about food.

* * *

I found out that Abe had died the same way I found out what he looked like: On Facebook. In December 2013, there was a posting from Nicholas. I had friended him, too, and had sent him several messages that he had never responded to. He posted that after a long illness, his Dad had died.

I hadn't seen Abe since that afternoon at the Flying Star Café in July 2012 and, aside from the one afternoon when I had held baby Nicholas in my arms, had never actually met Nick. Trudy was long gone. I had loved her and been grateful to her but Nicholas didn't know about that. He'd only known about my relationship with Abe and he hadn't liked what he knew. There was nothing tying me to Nicholas. I had no business being on his Facebook wall. Since he had been adopted, he was not even a blood relative; I was technically a stranger. Still, I sent him a condolence note, telling him how sorry I was for his loss, praising his father for being such a kind and wise man.

I did not hear back.

* * *

Looking back, I don't know what I was hoping to learn from hunting down my long lost relations. At the time, I chalked it up to my journalistic curiosity, but deep down I knew I was looking for some biological clue as to whether I was capable of such madness. Perhaps I had been crazy to think I could write about my cousin the kidnapper, even though my cousin only wanted to tell his side of the story. But more to the point, if I wasn't crazy now, was I capable of going off the deep end? My father tried to end his life in the most violent way possible when he was 57. I was only a few years away from that. Would I end up getting shock treatments in the middle of my life, as he and his father had? Could I stay married, as neither of my parents had been able to do? Would I be cruel to the people I loved most in the world, as my father, grandfather and great grandfather had been? Would I be able to raise my kids without the constant fear that something terrifying might happen?

When your parents have cycled through romances, and countless relatives have landed in the loony bin, jumped off bridges, stabbed themselves in cars, stuck their heads in ovens, or landed in prison, you start to think that insanity, deviance and viciousness might be your birthright. I've worried, and still worry, that mental illness, like Dad, will one day knock on my back door.

And so, I cook. When all hell breaks loose in my head, I pull down some recipes, set the table, sharpen the knives, chop up some onions, and turn the burners on. I find ways not to give in to lunacy. The chopping and measuring and sautéing soothes the nerves and distracts the demons. It might be dark in some corners of this house of mine, but I've stockpiled light bulbs. And I'm roasting a chicken in that oven.

MEXICAN ICED MOCHA

(Serves 1)

INGREDIENTS:

- 1 tablespoon chocolate syrup *(I used Hershey's)*
- ½ cup cold café de olla *(Spiced, sweet coffee, easy to make. See recipe below. Make this first and let it cool.)*
- 1 tablespoon heavy cream or half-and-half *(I used almond milk)*
- Pinch cinnamon
- Pinch cayenne pepper
- Several ice cubes

PREPARATION:

1. **Drizzle chocolate syrup** on the bottom of a glass.
2. **Add the café de olla** and milk/heavy cream/half and half. Sprinkle with cinnamon, cayenne pepper and ice cubes.

▸ *Makes one drink, which is over way, way too fast. But you still have several cups of café de olla left so fear not. You can make another one!*

Café de Olla

(Yield: 8 servings)

INGREDIENTS:

- 4 cups water
- ¼ cup packed light brown sugar
- ½ tablespoon molasses
- 1 cinnamon stick
- ⅔ cup ground coffee beans *(I used ground Melitta Premium Blend Classic Coffee)*

PREPARATION:

1. **Bring water, brown sugar, molasses, and cinnamon sticks** to a boil in a large saucepan or pot over moderate heat, stirring occasionally until sugar is dissolved.
2. **Stir in coffee and boil 5 minutes.** Pour through a fine-mesh sieve into a clean pot or jar, discarding coffee beans and cinnamon stick
3. **Serve hot or chill** to make iced coffee recipe above. Makes about 4 cups.

Sweet Survival
Acknowledgments

WITH LOVE AND GRATITUDE to Carole Balin, Julie Fingersh, Cynthia Price Gaylord and Steve Fromm, who patiently read various drafts of this book and gave invaluable feedback and support at the beginning, middle and end; Ruthi Byrne, who showed me how to cook and live; Debbie Laiks Goodman, for leading the way into the kitchen in New Jersey; Dorothy Fromm, for sharing recipes and her oldest son; Mike Zinn, for following Mom's lead into the kitchen and showing me I should too; Terri Friedman, loving friend and generous, scientific cook; Laura Kessler, awesome friend and neighbor, who always has cilantro and lemon extract to spare; Carolyn Hough, Lolly Raphael, Pam Riesenberg, Kathleen Sanderson, Scott Savokinas and Arlene Ward, for knowing far more about cooking than I do and sharing their recipes and vast knowledge of cooking; Jessica Wolf, editor extraordinaire, who originally didn't like to cook but shepherded this book with humor and insight into print and turned herself into a great cook along the way; Bob Lascaro, a fantastic book designer as well as one of the most decent and patient men I know; Charles Salzberg at Greenpoint Press, for publishing a book he wasn't all that interested in reading but embraced anyway; Kathy Karp Cohen and Jonathan Karp, for giving me invaluable advice when I needed it most, and their mom Margie Karp, who wrote my first fan email; my writing students in New York and New Jersey for showing up every week with their own work in hand; Maria Pereira, for filling our house with food and love while I was busy writing about food and love; Bette Blank and Sophie Friedman-Pappas for creating beautiful art; Christopher Power at

Bloomberg Business Week, who taught me early on how to find, report and write a story and make deadline; Lynne Shore Abbott, Wendy Beckerman, Janice Beckmen, Marian Brown, Julia Burns, Brendan Byrne, Angie Comiteau, Elizabeth Conn, Jennifer Egan, Amy Schulman Eskind, Katherine Fausset, Lorien Fono, Nancy Friedman, Sally Friedman, Eli Fromm, Larry Fromm, Richard Fromm, Caroline Gentile, Galit Gertsenzon, Mike Gertzman, Denise Glassman, Rebecca Brody Gold, Liz Brous Guevara, Kevin Knopf, Allison Feman Haltmaier, Kate Levin, Shivaun Mahony, Jen Meister, Amy Saffer, Carolyn Sargent, Jodi Skriloff, Elaine Strum, Bill Troffer, Linda Schechter Warshavsky, Madeleine Weiner, Renee Welner, Laurie Wilkens, Helaine Winer, Suzanne Woolley and Rachel Zinn, for advice, recipes and encouragement; the various members of my father's extended family who, over the course of multiple meals, phone conversations, photographs and emails, helped to make this book a reality; my father, Steve Zinn, a wonderful writer and the first person to say, "Write it down, pup, write it down." Finally, hugs and endless kisses to my husband Steve and our sons, Matt and David. Thank you for tasting everything, giving me everything and keeping me loved and honest. I love you.

Some of these essays first appeared in *Patch*, *New Jersey Life & Leisure* and *Huffington Post.* Many thanks to Shelley Emling, Laura Griffin and Jessica Wolf, wonderful editors who weren't as interested in food as I was but were willing to give me the space to write about it anyway.

Thank you to Colum McCann, Mary Oliver and the estates of Laurie Colwin and MFK Fisher, whose books have sustained and inspired me. We are nothing without food, books and the people we share them with.

Sweet Survival Recipe Guide

POULTRY

BEEF

FISH

MEATLESS MEALS

PASTA, RICE AND GRAINS

POTATOES

VEGETABLES

SOUPS

DESSERTS

DESSERTS *continued from page 297*

OTHER TASTY TREATS

Resources

BOOKS

How to Cook Everything, Mark Bittman

From Julia Child's Kitchen, Julia Child

Mastering the Art of French Cooking, Julia Child

My Life in France, Julia Child

The New York Times Cookbook, Craig Claiborne

Home Cooking: A Writer in the Kitchen, Laurie Colwin

The Homesick Texan Cookbook, Lisa Fain

The Gastronomical Me, MFK Fisher

Desserts from the Famous Loveless Café, Alisa Huntsman

The New Basics Cookbook, Sheila Lukins and Julee Rosso

Food for Friends, Ruth Macpherson

Jerusalem: A Cookbook, Yotam Ottolenghi and Sami Tamimi

Plenty: Vibrant Recipes from London's Ottolenghi, Yotam Ottolenghi and Jonathan Lovekin

Pressure Cooking for Everyone, Rick Rogers and Arlene Ward

The New Persian Kitchen, Louisa Shafia

Food in History, Reay Tannahill

WEBSITES

Cuisine-inspirations.com

Davidlebovitz.com

Homeappetit.net

Jamieoliver.com

Panetica.com

Simplecleanandwhole.com

StaceySnacksonline.com

Cover Art: Bette Blank is a New Jersey-based painter, sculptor and print-maker. She has a PhD in engineering from U.C. Berkeley. For more of her work, please go to Betteblank.com.

Book Illustrations: Sophie Friedman-Pappas is a student at Maryland Institute College of Art, where she studies painting.

About The Author

LAURA ZINN FROMM graduated from Wellesley College and received an MFA from Columbia University. She teaches fiction and creative non-fiction through New York Writers Workshop and has taught at Columbia and Montclair State University. A former editor at *Business Week* magazine, she is the winner of the Clarion Award and the Newspaper Guild's Page One Award for Labor Reporting. Her work has been published in *The New York Times, Business Week, Huffington Post, Ducts.org, Wellesley* magazine and elsewhere. She lives in New Jersey with her husband, two sons and their dog, Roxy.

- Laurazinnfromm.com
- Twitter@Laurazinnfromm

Author Photo: Jamie Karlin